10 25
K3
6)

D0580338

TRADING POST GUIDEBOOK

Susan Makov and Patrick Eddington

TRADING POST GUIDEBOOK

WHERE TO FIND THE TRADING POSTS, GALLERIES, AUCTIONS, ARTISTS, AND MUSEUMS OF THE FOUR CORNERS REGION

SECOND EDITION *Revised & Updated*

Northland Publishing

Text type is set in Stempel Garamond
Display type is set in Friz Quadrata
Designed by Trina Stahl
Edited by Rose Houk, Erin Murphy, and
   Stephanie Bucholz
Production supervised by Lisa Brownfield

Manufactured in Hong Kong by
ColorCorp, Inc.

Copyright © 1995 by Patrick Eddington and
Susan Makov
All rights reserved.

This book may not be reproduced in whole
or in part, by any means (with the exception
of short quotes for the purpose of review),
without the permission of the publisher.
For information, address Northland Publishing
Company, P.O. Box 1389, Flagstaff, Arizona
86002-1389.

All art represented in this book is also copy-
righted individually by the artist, and it is an
infringement of that copyright to reproduce any
such material in any medium without the
permission of the copyright owner.

All photographs by Susan Makov and
Patrick Eddington, as follows, unless otherwise indicated:

SUSAN MAKOV: cover (Morning Talk, vessel,
and concha belt), half-title page, fontispiece, title
page, back cover; pages x, xi–xiii, xv, 1, 7, 10–17,
19, 21–26, 28, 29, 34, 36–38, 40–43, 45, 47,
49–51, 52 (Mistena Hathale), 55, 57, 58, 59
(Verkamp's), 62–65, 67, 68, 70, 71, 73, 75, 76–83,
86, 87 (rug), 88–94, 97–101, 103–110, 112–119,
121, 123, 125–129, 131–134, 136, 137 (Mexican
Springs), 139, 140, 141 (Jim Turpen), 142, 144,
145, 148, 149, 150 (necklace), 151–153, 155, 157,
158, 161–163, 165–167, 169, 172, 174, 175, 178,
179 (pendant and pin), 180, 182–184, 186 (Ray
Tracey), 187–189, 191–193, 195, 196, 197, 199,
200, 203–205, 208, 209–211, 212, and 213.

PATRICK EDDINGTON: cover (Santo
Domingo); pages 33, 46, 52 (Zonie Barlow), 53,
56, 59 (Watchtower), 61, 85, 87 (Rug Room),
111, 124, 137 (Hannah Smith), 138, 150 (Edna
Leki), 177, 179 (Robert Tenorio), 186 (Old
Original Curio Store), 190, and 198.

Artwork dimensions in photo captions refer to
height or length unless otherwise specified.
When two dimensions are given they refer to
height x width.

Hand-tinting of photographs by Susan Makov.

COVER: Cow skull greets visitors at Morning
Talk Indian Shop in Taos Pueblo, New Mexico;
vessel by Randy Nahohai, courtesy of Pueblo
Zuni Arts and Crafts, Zuni, New Mexico; Santo
Domingo Trading Post, Santo Domingo, New
Mexico; and concha belt from Dewey Galleries
Ltd., Santa Fe.

HALF-TITLE PAGE: Big-Horned Sheep
Basket, by Peggy Rock Black, Navajo, courtesy
of Blue Mountain Trading Post, Blanding, Utah

FRONTISPIECE: Cow Canyon Trading Post,
Bluff, Utah

BACK COVER: Enormous arrows stop
visitors at Mud Creek Hogan in Mancos,
Colorado; Navajo man and woman listening
to juke box, photograph by J.H. McGibbeny,
Special Collections, University of Utah
Library; Navajo wedding basket, artist
unknown, courtesy of Sacred Mountain
Trading Post, north of Flagstaff, Arizona

Page xxi constitutes an extension of this copyright page.

SECOND EDITION
ISBN 0-87358-612-3

Library of Congress Catalog Card Number
pending

0653/7.5M/5-97

To the memory of our parents,

Vernon and Kate Eddington, and

Boris and Ruth Makov.

CONTENTS

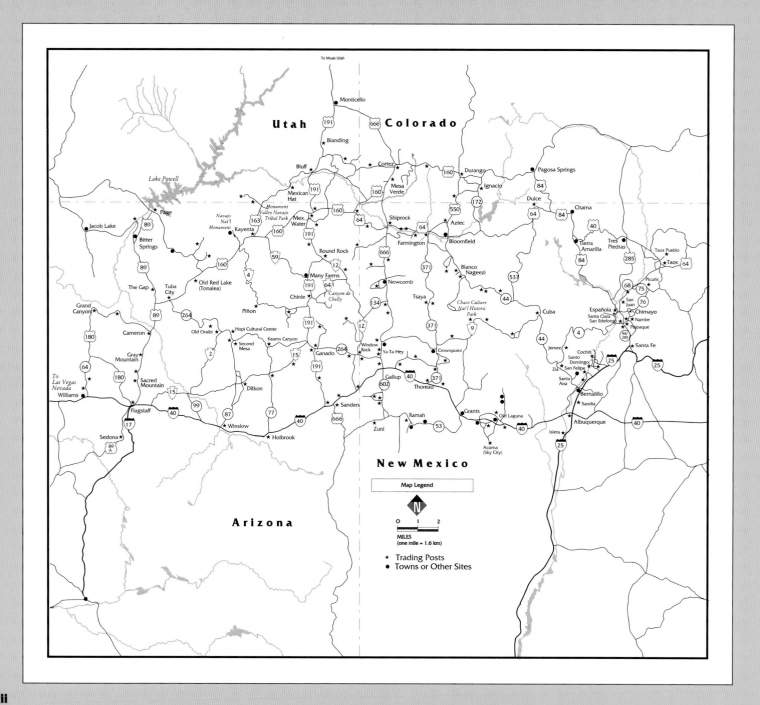

Preface

◆ ◆ ◆

Interest in the arts and crafts of the native Southwest is at an all-time high level. Books and museums are showcasing traditional, innovative, beautiful, and timeless creations of Native America's brightest and talented artists. Collecting these arts and crafts has become complicated, challenging, and fraught with possibilities. We have written this book to help with this pleasant dilemma.

Although interest in the Southwest and its talented artists has grown to grand proportions, a clear guide to the region's rich artistic resources has been lacking. We searched in vain for such a guide as we drove the lonely expanses of the Four Corners country, looking through back rooms of trading posts for finely crafted work, and tracking down artists in canyons or on solitary mesa tops. Misinformation or no information led us down impossible backroads to trading posts no longer open or to homes where the artist no longer lived.

To help others avoid our problems, we decided to create this book. Waist deep in this project, we realized why no one else had attempted such a book. It took four years of interviews with more than five hundred traders, artists, and merchants, and hundreds of visits to trading posts and galleries, to complete this task.

The result is a guidebook that is as comprehensive as we could make it. Our goal is to put you in touch with traders, galleries, auctions, and many of the talented artists. Included are addresses, telephone numbers, directions, and descriptions of some five hundred trading posts, galleries, museums, artists, and other arts and crafts outlets throughout the Navajo, Hopi, Ute, Paiute, and Apache reservations, the Rio Grande Pueblos, and major border towns and cities.

To make it easy for travelers to follow, we have arranged the sites geographically, with each site number in the text corresponding with a number on one of the sectional maps. Information is also included about means of payment, shipping services, handicapped accessibility, and the arts and crafts in which each site specializes.

SAMPLE LISTING

7. Santo Domingo Indian Trading Post
401 San Felipe NW,
Albuquerque, NM 87104
505-764-0129
Daily 8:00–7:00
Owner: Lita Wagner
♦ M, V, AE, C, S, HA
(one step)
    Indian-owned and operated, this business offers a wide selection of jewelry. All nineteen pueblos are represented. Navajo work is also available.
J, P, P

♦ The number of each entry corresponds with a number on the map on the first page of the section.

♦ Hours of operation can sometimes vary.

♦ Payment options and services available from each business are listed with abbreviations *after a diamond bullet:*

M—Mastercard

V—Visa

D—Discover Card

AE—American Express

C—Checks

T—Traveler's checks

S—Shipping

HA—Handicapped accessible

I—Indian Arts and Crafts Association member

♦ Types of merchandise carried by each business are also listed with abbreviations *at the end of the entry* (items in **bold type** are the business's specialty):

B—Baskets

Bk—Books

C—Cassettes and musical recordings

D—Navajo dolls

F—Zuni fetishes

I—Musical instruments (drums, rasps, flutes)

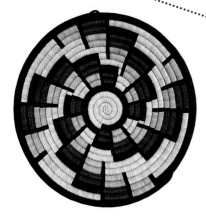

Chasing star plaque (Hopi coil), 10" diameter, by Jewel Wauneka, Second Mesa, Arizona. Courtesy of Garland's Navajo Rugs, Sedona, Arizona

J—Jewelry

K—Hopi kachina dolls

M—Moccasins

P—Pottery

Pt—Paintings (oil, acrylic, watercolors)

R—Rugs, weavings

S—Sculpture (typically alabaster, but possibly other materials)

Sp—Sandpaintings

Sv—Souvenirs (cards, posters, t-shirts)

We also offer some tips to help you make informed choices about buying art. Education is your best ally, and we urge you to learn more about art forms in which you are interested. The suggested readings at the end of the book are included to aid you in this goal.

We hope this book will be useful to beginning and experienced collectors. We also hope it will be useful to those who may not be able to travel here, but who may wish to purchase artwork by mail, phone, or fax. We highly recommend that you make purchases from established businesses, especially ones that are members of the Indian Arts and Crafts Association.

The people of the Southwest, like the magical landscape in which they live, are unique. We encourage you to interact with them. Ask questions, get to know the traders, artists, and everyday people who make this one of the most captivating places on earth.

PLANNING YOUR TRIP

If possible, plan your trip to coincide with fairs, ceremonials, feast days, arts and crafts markets, and other special events. Including these in your itinerary also necessitates hotel or motel reservations in advance, especially if you

Self-Portrait, *cardboard cutout, 36", by Mamie Deschillie, Fruitland, New Mexico*

are traveling on the Navajo or Hopi reservations where accommodations are limited.

Because of the great distances, we recommend that you keep your radiator and gas tank full. We have encountered stations that were out of gas or closed unexpectedly. If your tank is low, fill it up.

Roads are often dirt or gravel tracks across what appears to be wilderness. These can offer true adventure and reveal wonderful surprises, but be aware of your vehicle's limitations. If the road is marked "four wheel drive," believe it. Also be aware of weather. It can change rapidly, making dirt roads impassable when wet. We also recommend avoiding long drives after dark. Roads are dark, livestock can wander onto them, and drivers can become fatigued.

In the summer months carry a cooler for your film, snacks, and drinks.

Counselor Trading Post, Counselors, New Mexico

Pack a hat, sunscreen, first aid kit, and anything you deem a necessity. Don't plan on finding these items on the trip.

Don't try to see the entire Southwest in one trip. You could never do so anyway. The Southwest changes with the seasons and with the time of day. Don't schedule your time too tightly. Stop and explore a canyon, look closely at the plants, the horned toads, and the distant mesas. The Southwest is famous for its rich, brilliant light and colors. Dusk and dawn are the most dramatic times. Getting up early also means you may have major tourist sites to yourselves.

The Southwest that Maynard Dixon painted and Willa Cather wrote so lovingly about is still here, and it lives up to its reputation. The Four Sacred Mountains of the Navajos, the slickrock mesas, and the wild geography continue to inspire the best of artists and writers. Allow yourself to be immersed in its expansive beauty, and charmed by its small wonders.

TIME ZONES

Be aware that Arizona does *not* go on daylight savings time. The one exception is the Navajo Reservation, so during this period it is one hour ahead of Arizona or Hopi time. This can make for many changes on your watch and missed appointments if you fail to take time changes into account.

INDIAN COUNTRY ETIQUETTE

We asked trader and author Ernie Bulow to comment on visitors' behavior in Indian country. He offers the following essay, *Walking in Beauty:*

Badges, 2 1/2", Trader Jack's Flea Market, Santa Fe

ABOVE: (Top) *Old Red Lake Trading Post, Tonalea, Arizona, and trader Johnny O'Farrell, 1915.* Photograph by Emry Kopta, courtesy of James E. Babbitt. (Bottom) *Oljato Trading Post, Kayenta, Arizona; Hollywood Movie producer John Ford behind counter, circa 1945.* Photograph courtesy of Fred Alan Carson

In 1966 I saw the last Snake Dance ever held at the Hopi village of Walpi from the vantage point of a rooftop behind the Snake Plaza, surrounded by Hopis and a scattering of Navajos in cowboy hats and Pendleton blankets. When the crowd started to gather in the early afternoon there had been a fair number of white faces in sight, but as the day wore on most of those white faces turned red and then disappeared from sight and there were few Anglos still on the plaza when the dance finally started. I had the feeling they weren't missed. I have seen hundreds of ceremonies in the thirty years since, but none that was more impressive or powerful. The drumming eventually began to resonate in my chest cavity, a thing more felt than heard, the Heartbeat of Mother Earth Herself. The short, stocky, brown dancers in their earth colored kilts seemed to literally grow in front of my eyes and there was something undeniably primal about the deadly snakes they held in their mouths as they paced in the cramped space of the mesa top. It was nearly sundown when the dance finally climaxed and the Snake Priests, serpents in hand, charged down steep, rocky paths to the desert floor far below. The sky had been cloudless all afternoon with the sun boring down through the thin air of the high plateau. Suddenly a charging wind tore at the spectators, stealing a few parasols and tossing cowboy hats off the steep cliff. A black cloud, roiling and twisting, formed overhead with the speed of time-lapse weather film, and fat, stinging drops of rain pummeled the laughing crowd for a few minutes; hardly enough water to settle the dust around us, but a magical rain all the same. By then there were almost no white faces in sight, and nobody at all in tourist garb.

Common sense and ordinary courtesy are almost all that are needed to have a good experience among the diverse cultures of the Four Corners region, plus a lot of patience. In the Southwest patience is not only its own reward, it is a necessity for anyone who cares to interact with the local

people in any significant way. Most of the dances at the Hopi mesas have
been closed to outsiders, and there is talk every year of closing the great
Zuni ceremony of Shalako. Some pueblos are completely closed to outsiders, and it is getting more difficult all the time to find Navajo ceremonials in progress. Native Americans have gotten simply fed up with Anglo
rudeness and insensitivity. For some reason Anglo Americans can't seem to
get the idea that these aren't performances put on for their entertainment,
but ancient, living religions in action. One of the ironies is that, unbe-
knownst to most observers, anyone attending a traditional ceremony is
automatically considered a participant in the event and a recipient of the
blessings and resultant good luck and well being.

The three villages atop First Mesa are tightly policed these days, but
only a few years ago I was visiting some friends there when a small group
of tourists, invited into the house to look at some pottery, demanded that
the Hopis price some personal belongings on the wall. They were so rudely
insistent that I finally spoke up on my friends' behalf and the visitors left.
Probably the only thing I accomplished was ruining a pottery sale. The
family told me that not long before some visitors had simply walked into
their house about dinner time, without knocking, and poked about the
place, ignoring the family at the table. My friends didn't articulate the
incident as I would have, but the truth is, they were treated as if they
weren't people at all, with a right to privacy in their own homes.

Many Indians in the Southwest depend on sales of arts and crafts to
tourists for their livelihood and will consequently put up with a lot of
rudeness. What I find difficult to understand is why the visitors have to be
so insensitive in the first place. Much has been made of the Native American
"phobia" of being photographed, but I don't care much for having my picture taken by strangers myself. In most cases a little friendly talk and a
modest gift of some sort will smooth the way if you really feel compelled to

Kachina doll, 14", by Randolf David. Courtesy
of Raette Mullen, Southwest Indian Traders,
Park City, Utah

Unknown location, 1926. Photograph copyright © Dudley Scott Archive #6784, Grand Canyon National Park

take a photograph of a weaver or kachina doll carver at work. Pictures of ceremonials are simply out.

Bargaining is not really part of the Southwestern business world. There is an established value on most craft items and spending a little time pricing things in a curio store or trading post will give you an idea of the prevailing retail prices so you know what kind of deal the craftsman is offering you. There are plenty of good books on the arts and crafts of the area and a little homework will pay big dividends. In some circumstances, a little polite negotiation is acceptable.

Native Americans are used to dealing with visitors for the most part, but they are still uncomfortable with a few things that are polite behavior elsewhere. Most Indians are very modest and rather shy and dislike being touched. Hearty handshakes, steady eye contact, and in-your-face proximity can make them uncomfortable. Confrontational behavior of any kind is bad form. Shyness around strangers is probably the root of the silly

stereotype of the "stoic" Indian. In my experience, Indians have a wonderful sense of humor and are great kidders and practical jokers, love puns and wordplay, and mockery is even part of their religious observance. Act like a jerk and you can count on providing some laughs once you're out of sight.

On the other hand, Native American hospitality is legendary. Ceremonies and feast days provide occasions to feed all visitors; and giveaways are an integral part of most dances. If you are invited to observe or take part in a ceremony, a gift of groceries is always good form—especially nonperishable staples such as flour and sugar.

Pueblos, Navajos, and other tribes of the area are usually assumed by outsiders to have some sort of generic "Indianness," but in reality, there is a tremendous diversity of language and culture. A little advance reading about the groups you are visiting will be very useful. On the other hand, differences among people are often more apparent than real—superficial matters of dress and hairstyle. Deep down we all care about the same things, and good manners are pretty universal. The Golden Rule, simplistic as it is, is still the final measure of proper behavior.

This book is as accurate as possible at press time. Things invariably change; places close, change hands, or change hours. If you are planning a trip, we suggest verifying information before you visit. We cannot be responsible for changes or errors that may occur. If you do encounter errors, changes, new locations, or items that should be included in future editions of this guide, please write the authors in care of Northland Publishing, P.O. Box 1389, Flagstaff, AZ 86002-1389.

Acknowledgments

◆ ◆ ◆

To the following members of Weber State University, Ogden, Utah, thanks are given for their support, encouragement, and assistance: Dr. Paul H. Thompson, President; Dr. Robert Smith, Provost; Dr. June Phillips, Dean of Arts and Humanities; Brooke Arkush, Chair of Research and Professional Growth; James McBeth, Chair, Department of Visual Arts; Laura McBeth; and Elaine Luhn, Secretary.

We are grateful to those who graciously and enthusiastically responded to our request for visitors' and buyers' guidelines for the introduction to this book. The expertise of Ernie Bulow, Barton Wright, Mark Bahti, Leslie Muth, Dan Garland, Robert F. Nichols, Buzz Trevathan, Greg Hofmann, Bruce McGee, Steve Simpson, and Joe E. Tanner, Jr., is most appreciated.

This book could not have been written without the cooperation and assistance of the following people whose knowledge and expertise were generously offered: Bill Beaver; Barry Simpson; William Garland; Ferron McGee; Anne Hedlund; Gordon Moore; Nina Meyers; Milford Nahohai; Bruce Burnham; the Smouse family; Jack Beasley; Don Bachelor; Bill Malone; James Blair; Brian Dowty; Clarence Wheeler; Gregg Leighton; Fred Carson; Bruce Burns; Lorraine and Bob Garlinghouse; Joe Babbitt; Chuck and Jan Rosenak; John Kennedy; Indian Arts and Crafts Association; Don Owen; Cheryl Hartley, Southwestern Association for Indian Arts; Governor Henry Shije of Zia; Governor Robert E. Lewis of Zuni; Chairman Ferrell Secakuku of Hopi; Joe L. Garcia, Development Office, Nambe; Frank Chaves, Business Development Office, Sandia; Rebecca Martinez Grandbois, Director of Tourism, Jemez; Frank and Barbara Waters; James E. Babbitt; Ross Ashcroft; Mickey Vanderwagen; Joe Atkinson; the Adobe Gallery; Joe and Janice Day; Leo Polo-Trujillo; Beryl Stuart; and Martin Link.

OPPOSITE: Trading Post Pictorial Rug. *19" x 18", by Laurenthena M. White, Red Mesa.* Photograph courtesy of Scott Peterson.

Acknowledgments

Special thanks to the artists, especially Ernie Franklin; Louis and Virginia Naranjo; Virgil, Seferina, and Guadalupe Ortiz; Alex Seowtewa; Alfred Aguliar; Toni Roller and Margaret Tafoya; Lonnie Vigil; Mary and Robert Tenorio; Ida and Andrew Sahmie; Joseph and Barbara Cerno; Anthony Durand; Rick Honyouti; Lawrence Jacquez; Clarence Lee; Lydia Peseta; Evelyn Cheromiah; Gladys Yellowman; Sharon Burch; the Cellicion family; Mary Holiday Black, Sally Black, and Lorraine Black; Leo Coriz; Dennis Pioche; Johnson and Lorena Antonio; Manuel Dinet Chavarria; Lowell Talashoma; Randy Nahohai and Rowena Him; Lena Leki Boone; Ignacio Duran; Lorraine Williams; Alice Cling; Rose Williams; Faye and Emmett Tso; the Manygoats family; Mamie Deschillie and daughter, Jane Jones; Juanita Fragua; Sofia Medina; Stella Teller; Andrew Tsihnahjinnie; and Silas and Bertha Claw.

Additional thanks to Sam Wilson and Kristie Krumbach; Michelle Belon; Kent Maxwell; Ken Sanders; Neal Whitman and Elaine Weiss; Judith Wolbach and Bob Edminster, supportive good friends; Lois Bingham, Mail Boxes Etc.; Borge B. Andersen, for special care with film processing; David Anderson for patient color printing; Joe Marotta, University of Utah Photography Department; Dr. Nathan B. Winters; Scott Petersen, photographer; Mark Biddle, Jim Jacobs, Ernest Farr, and Jayne Stringfellow for computer assistance; Michelle Marthia, typist; Pat Berrett, photographer; Michael Quinn, Grand Canyon National Park archivist; Carol Edison, Utah Arts Council; Arthur Olivas, Museum of New Mexico archivist; and The King's English Bookstore for their enthusiasm and encouragement.

This book would not have happened without the unanimous support of the staff at Northland Publishing. A debt of gratitude is due to editor Erin Murphy and art director Trina Stahl for their supervision and direction, and to editor Rose Houk and Assistant Editor Stephanie Bucholz for their attention to detail.

We are grateful to the following writers and publishers for permission to use excerpts from their books:

Cather, Willa. *The Professor's House.* New York: Alfred A. Knopf, 1925.

Harjo, Joy and Steven Strom. *Secrets from the Center of the World.* Tucson: University of Arizona Press, 1989.

Hegemann, Elizabeth Compton. *Navajo Trading Days.* Albuquerque: University of New Mexico Press, 1963.

Lawrence, D.H. "New Mexico," from *Phoenix: The Posthumous Papers of D.H. Lawrence,* edited by Edward D. McDonald. Used by permission of Viking Penguin Press, New York; Laurence Pollinger Ltd., London; and The Estate of Frieda Lawrence Ravagli. Copyright 1936 by Frieda Lawrence, copyright renewed 1964 by The Estate of the late Frieda Lawrence Ravagli.

Lummis, Charles F. *Mesa, Cañon, and Pueblo.* New York: The Century Company, 1925.

McNitt, Frank. *The Indian Traders.* Norman: University of Oklahoma Press, 1962.

Momaday, N. Scott. *The Names.* New York: Harper & Row, 1976.

Schmedding, Joseph. *Cowboy and Indian Trader.* Caldwell, Idaho: The Caxton Printers, Ltd. , 1951.

Waters, Frank. *Masked Gods.* Athens: Swallow Press/Ohio University Press, 1984.

Wright, Barton. *Hopi Kachinas: The Complete Guide to Collecting Kachina Dolls.* Flagstaff: Northland Press, 1977.

Williams, Terry Tempest. *Pieces of White Shell: A Journey to Navajoland.* New York: Charles Scribner's Sons, an imprint of Simon & Schuster, 1983, 1984.

Acknowledgments

We appreciate the use of the archives of the following individuals and institutions:

Dudley H. Scott and David Humphrey Scott
Michael and Peggy Verkamp
Grand Canyon National Park
National Park Service
Leo Polo-Trujillo
Fred A. Carson
Joe Cline
James E. Babbitt
Nina Meyer and Rowena Martinez
Randy Nahohai
John W. Kennedy
Guy Berger
Rex Arrowsmith
Joe Atkinson
Museum of Northern Arizona
Cline Library—Northern Arizona University
Museum of Fine Arts—University of Utah
Photo Archives—Museum of New Mexico
Photo Archives—University of Utah
Utah Museum of Fine Arts

Introduction

◆ ◆ ◆

The only Indians left as integral groups today exist within the immemorial boundaries

of their ancient homeland. The village Pueblos and semi-nomadic Navahos, fringed by the mountain

Utes and desert Apaches—these today are the last homogeneous remnants of what we call the Vanishing American.

And they all live within the one last wilderness of what they may well call Vanishing America.

—FRANK WATERS, *Masked Gods*

Trading posts have always been portals between two worlds—a place where Indians and Anglos meet to exchange merchandise, ideas, jokes, news, and some of the finest arts and crafts of the day. The breathtaking Navajo rugs, now showcased in prestigious museums, once changed hands across the humble wooden counters of these isolated outposts. Today, arts and crafts of equal and at times superior quality continue to be exchanged in such modest, and unlikely, places.

TRADING POST HISTORY

While traveling through the Southwest desert and redrock, we often come across a sign: "Trading Post." For those of us who live here, the trading post and the Native Americans themselves represent some of the last authentic contacts with the Old West. Within its wood- or adobe-covered walls, the trading post presents an opportunity not only to

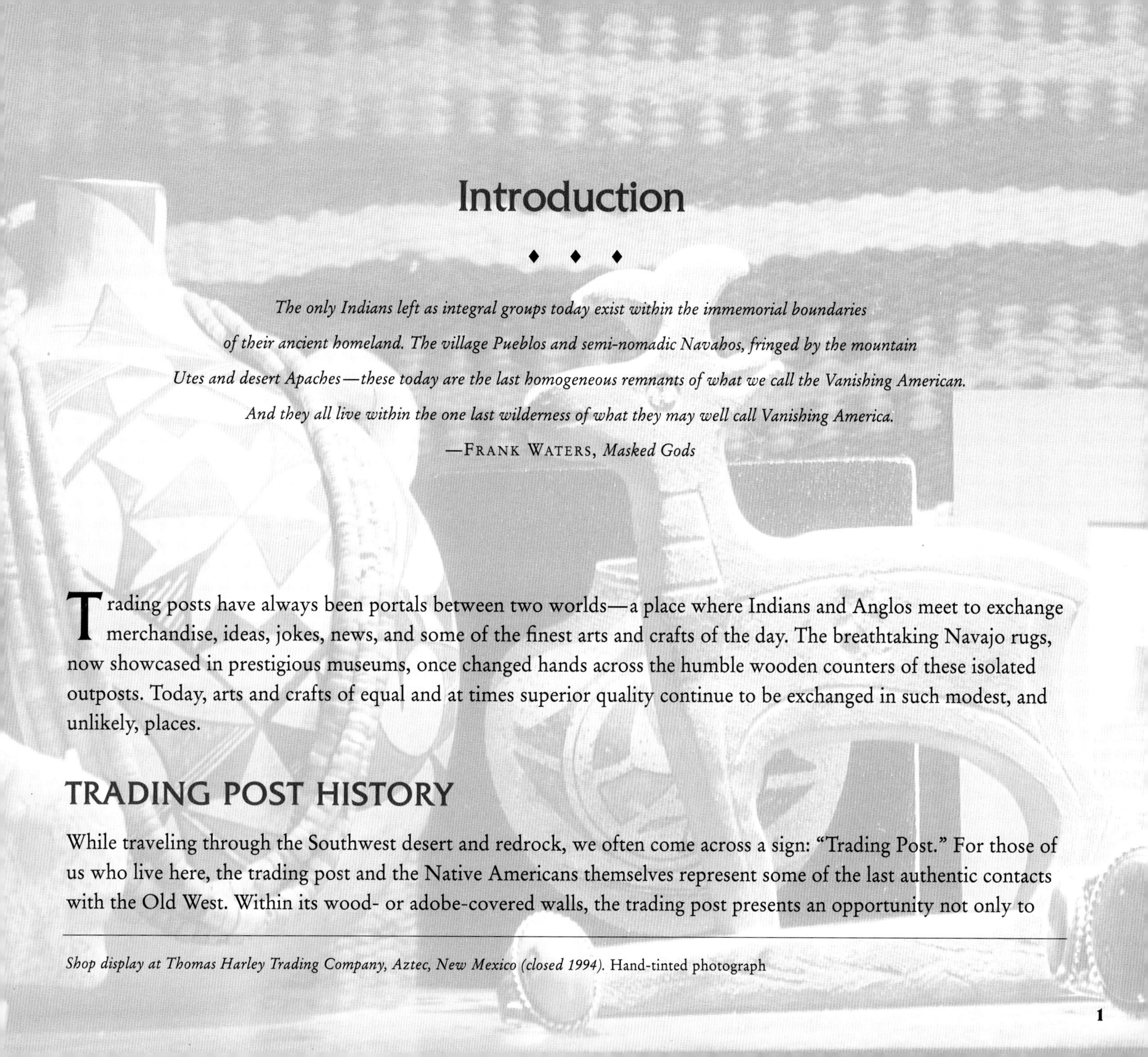

Shop display at Thomas Harley Trading Company, Aztec, New Mexico (closed 1994). Hand-tinted photograph

John Verkamp in front of his tent store, Grand Canyon, 1898. Photograph courtesy of Peggy and Michael Verkamp

see a multitude of finely crafted items, but also to see history, especially Navajo history.

The Southwest of the mid-1800s was home to a number of different groups—Pueblo people, Utes, Hopis, Zunis, Southern Paiutes, Spaniards, Navajos, and Anglos. The Navajos were sheepherders, dependent upon migration of their herds and raiding of other groups for their wealth. With an interest in Southwestern land, the United States government signed treaties to limit the Navajos to land in western New Mexico and eastern Arizona, causing antagonism between the two groups. The United States responded to continuing raids by the Navajos with a "scorched earth" policy, decimating Navajo homes, livestock, and crops. On March 4, 1864, government troops under Kit Carson initiated the roundup of Navajos to confine them to Fort Sumner in eastern New Mexico. Referred to as the "Long Walk," some 8,000 Navajos were forced to walk 350 tortuous miles to this desolate area. In 1868, after four years of dire living conditions, government neglect, and disease, a new treaty was signed with the U.S. government and the survivors were allowed to return to their homeland to live within reservation boundaries.

Traders followed the Navajos, setting up businesses on or near the reservation. These merchants were Santa Fe and Taos traders, Mormons sent by the church, and immigrants. The Navajo lifestyle changed due to the interaction with these traders and with the promised livestock from the government. Navajos were extended credit for necessary goods, particularly sugar, flour, coffee, canned peaches, and blankets and paid with wool, sheep, hides, piñon nuts, and textiles. The reservation's isolation made the Navajo and trader dependent upon one another. Traders became more than mere merchants. As Frank Waters stated in *Masked Gods:*

> *Their posts were oases in the desert, landmarks in an unmarked wilderness. They were bankers, doctors, interpreters, school teachers, art agents, repre-*

sentatives of an encroaching White civilization to the Indians, and champions of Indian tribes against an inimical government. Scarcely 150 men in an area of over 25,000 square miles for a period of fifty years, the Indian traders were the media through which were exchanged the values of two ways of life.

Usually located along a wagon road or by a crossroads, trading posts supplied essential commodities to the local community. Since the traders were not allowed to own the land their posts stood on, the buildings were small, simply built, and upgraded only when absolutely necessary. Trading posts developed a distinctive though utilitarian look, especially their interiors. Joseph Schmedding, in *Cowboy and Indian Trader,* describes them:

Upon entering, one saw counters running the full length of the store at both right and left sides, and also at the rear, forming a large U. Back of the counters, shelves ranged upward about eight feet from the floor, while

Keams Trading Post, Keams Canyon, New Mexico, circa 1890. Photograph by Ben Wittick, courtesy of Museum of New Mexico. Neg #16473

ABOVE: *Trader Carl George Ashcroft, Sr., with Navajo man and woman at Bisti Trading Post circa 1950.* Photograph by J.H. McGibbeny, Special Collections, University of Utah Library

BELOW RIGHT: Memories of Powell's Trading Post, Toh-La-Kai, New Mexico, *11" x 14", watercolor and ink drawing, by Ernie Franklin, Tohatchi, New Mexico.* Photograph courtesy of Scott Peterson

the space above the shelves was used for suspending various articles of merchandise. From nails and pegs driven into the walls, and also into the exposed roof beams, dangled pots and pans, pails, galvanized tubs, slickers, assorted saddlery and harness items.

The key to success for a trader was integrity, humor, patience, courage, and good business savvy. The traders acted as interpreters, advised on day-to-day problems, and assisted in developing a market for native crafts. This is not to say that traders were saints. They were there foremost as business-men who would stay in business only as long as they maintained sound judgment. Traders developed many strategies to guarantee their neighbors' loyalty, such as issuing tokens that could be redeemed only at one post, instead of paying cash for rugs and other items. However, isolation and lack of transportation were usually enough to insure loyalty.

Often when the Navajos had no money or goods to barter, they pawned many of their belongings, including jewelry, guns, and horse tack in exchange for goods from the trader. The items would be tagged and held for six to twelve months. After that time, if the belongings were not redeemed, the trader sold the goods as "dead pawn." Though there were many incidents of exploitation, ideally, this system made just enough money for the trader while helping the locals. The pawn system existed until 1973 when the Federal Trade Commission enacted so many new rules that pawn was discontinued on the reservation. Pawn is received only off the reservation today, but many traders buy off-reservation pawn and resell it from their own businesses.

The trader was very influential in the growth of the Southwestern arts and crafts market. With the coming of the railroad in 1881, traders sent tons

Navajo man and woman buying supplies from Marion Noel (behind the counter) at Bisti Trading Post, circa 1950. Photograph by J.H. McGibbeny, Special Collections, University of Utah Library

Early post card of Chimayo Trading Post, Española, New Mexico. Photograph courtesy of Leo Polo-Trujillo

of wool and thousands of blankets and rugs back East. The expanded market meant more motivation for weavers to continue their craft. Traders Lorenzo Hubbell of Ganado and J.B. Moore of Crystal produced nationwide mail-order rug catalogs. Hubbell influenced the growth of weaving by having his artist friends like E.A. Burbank, H.G. Maratta, and Bertha Little paint rug designs for weavers to copy or interpret. The famous Ganado Red style became an adaptation of period blankets. J.B. Moore had rugs designed with an Oriental flavor because these were popular with his eastern customers. Navajo rugs soon captivated a worldwide market.

The influx of tourists brought by the railroad greatly expanded the market for Native American arts and crafts. By 1900, the Fred Harvey Company, whose business was to provide good food and accommodations for tourists along the route of the Santa Fe Railroad, recognized the business possibilities for Native American arts and crafts. The company bought rugs in great quantities from traders. In the interest of making Navajo jewelry more marketable to eastern tourists, Harvey's Herman Schweizer provided materials for Navajo craftsmen, who made jewelry to appeal to the sensibilities of tourists. Both Navajo and Pueblo crafts were bought in large quantities and sold at Fred Harvey shops along the railroad line and places such as the Grand Canyon.

Navajos depended on the local trading post until cars and trucks replaced horses as the preferred mode of travel. James E. Babbitt of Babbitt Brothers Trading Company states:

What killed off the old trading posts as economic entities was when they started paving roads and improving highways in the 1950s. Navajos got cars and trucks and became mobile. American enterprise was hard at work all around the reservation with K-Marts and yellow Wal-Marts. By the late 1970s, early 1980s, trading posts were not economically viable. Old trading posts couldn't make it. This change allowed the Navajo, Hopi, and Zuni peoples to fully participate in the American economic system.

Squash blossom necklace, artist unknown.
Courtesy of Judith Wolbach, Salt Lake City

Many trading posts began to modernize, offering gasoline and tourist amenities. The function of many posts changed to provide a direct market for Native American arts and crafts. Today, artists go where they get the most money for their work. In many cases, it is still a trading post close to home, an auction, or anywhere within a day's drive of the reservation. The smart trader is highly aware of what the market offers elsewhere. Today's trading post is sometimes a gallery and an excellent source for arts and crafts in addition to its other functions. It still provides a meeting place for Anglos and Native Americans. Trade continues, with arts and crafts, piñon nuts, piles of wool, sheep, and everyday necessities supplied to the locals. Modern conveniences such as video rentals and car repair exist alongside the finest quality arts and crafts.

Dr. and Mrs. Albert Einstein meet the Hopi, 1931, the Hopi House, Grand Canyon, Arizona. Photograph collection of Museum of Northern Arizona, Neg. # 78.001

While places such as Hubbell Trading Post National Historic Site in Ganado closely resemble the trading post of the past, nothing exists today that duplicates an old working trading post. James E. Babbitt reminds us to "Strongly make the point that people aren't seeing what used to be. What they do see is a unique setting very different from what the old traders knew and experienced."

So what is the future? Many posts today still are maintained by the original trading families, some going back five generations. As you drive the Southwest and visit the traders, artists, and galleries, you will still find the pungent flavor of the wild West, but it is not the same experience as visiting J.B. Moore, Lorenzo Hubbell, or other early traders. Yet artists today create work that is equal to and many times superior to that which came before. And the posts are still full of unique and personable characters who will crack a joke, spin a tale, and make your trip memorable.

BUYING ART

Visitors to the Southwest can purchase arts and crafts from galleries, trading posts, auctions, and artists. Each source is an experience, and we suggest that you acquaint yourself with each. Galleries and trading posts allow you to view and compare the work of a number of artists. You can compare prices, ask questions, and educate yourself about the various art forms. Most galleries and trading post owners are honest and will guarantee the work they offer.

In visiting a trading post, you can call a trader ahead of time and ask for particular types of work. Most are more than happy to photograph or even send a piece on approval. Telephone numbers and addresses are included here. We go to trading posts for great artwork, atmosphere, adventure, and a taste of history that you can't find in the cities. We have found all of these abundantly available, and have also made lifetime friendships.

Galleries are the most accessible sources of Native American art. They are found in major towns and cities, carry top-quality work, and offer a much larger choice than an individual artist. In addition, gallery personnel take great pride in assisting and educating visitors to the subtleties of an artist's work.

When dealing with trading posts or galleries we suggest:

♦ Do not be taken in by offers of enormous discounts or claims of "wholesale-to-the-public." Only consider the price you must ultimately pay.

♦ Don't feel rushed. If something feels wrong, put off the purchase, shop around, and compare quality and prices. Take the gallery's card, write down the title of the piece, price, and the salesperson's name. If you change your mind, you can always purchase it over the phone.

♦ Have a clear description of the item, any guarantees, and if possible, the artist's name written on your sales receipt, along with the name of the individual who assisted you, in case you have future questions. Keep your receipt in a safe place.

♦ Try to deal with established businesses. A guarantee from someone who is no longer in business is as good as no guarantee at all.

♦ Love whatever you purchase. No matter how lucrative an investment it seems, don't buy what you don't like. Trust your intuition.

♦ Ask questions. Be sure you understand exactly what it is you're purchasing and how to care for it. Don't be concerned that the question might sound foolish. It is important that you feel good about your purchase. Businesses with integrity welcome such enthusiasm.

Many people buy art directly from the artists because they want to meet the people and learn something about them or their craft. When buying or commissioning work, do not assume that the artist will have an inventory of work available, or that you will pay less than you would at a trading post or gallery. Artists are usually well aware of the retail price for their work.

It can be an inspiring experience to visit with an artist, but do remember that the artist needs to make a living. Do not expect lengthy demonstrations or explanations without some sort of remuneration. If you are simply curious, seek out the person at artists' markets where demonstrations are expected. When purchasing work from an artist, we suggest the following:

♦ Be sure you know an artist's work before commissioning something. If an artist has a reputation for integrity and finely crafted work, then you will probably purchase a work of equal quality. Most of the artists we know, we trust implicitly.

♦ Obtain a receipt for the item. Make sure the receipt has a clear description of the item, price paid, name of the artist, and any guarantee that was given verbally.

♦ Inquire about packing and shipping if you are ordering work through the mail or by phone. Don't assume the artist has materials or packing expertise. We suggest you use a professional packer or shipping agent. Most larger towns have Mail Boxes Etc. franchises. If the artist is not aware of this service locally, suggest one. Insure the package at full value.

Mud toys, figures 4", by Mamie Deschillie, Fruitland, New Mexico.

♦ Be absolutely clear about what you are ordering. Miscommunication is frustrating for both parties.

♦ Uphold your end of the bargain. Unless agreed upon ahead of time, if you order a work, the artist expects you to purchase what he sends you.

♦ Expect to make at least a partial payment in advance for commissions. This pays for materials and assures the artist that you will not change your mind. Get a receipt for the amount paid, and be sure the receipt is clear about your agreement. If you do change your mind, you will probably forfeit this money unless your agreement states otherwise.

♦ Be sure to stress in advance and in writing if you need the work by a specific date. Be aware of the seasonal availability of work. Many artists prepare all year for the Santa Fe Indian Market and save some of their best pieces for this event. At the market, their work may be sold out, making it

Detail of silver box, approximately 5" x 9" x 7", by Clarence Lee, Gallup, New Mexico

A B O V E : (Top) *Silver and gold overlay bolo, 2", by Vidal Aragon, Santo Domingo Pueblo, New Mexico.* (Bottom) *Silver appliqué bolo with turquoise, 2 1/2", artist unknown.* Courtesy of Ya-Ta-Hey Trading Company, Ya-Ta-Hey, New Mexico

difficult to buy something immediately after. Some potters do not work during the winter months or during wet weather, while many weavers find more time to work during the winter.

♦ Visit artists in person. Go for the atmosphere. Locating them, however, may require a little detective work. Often no phone or street address is available, and a visit can take time. Be prepared for this possibility. When asking for directions, be sure to say you wish to purchase work. Otherwise neighbors are reluctant to tell outsiders how to locate individuals.

♦ Be careful getting out of your car in remote areas. Rural houses are often accompanied by dogs. If there are dogs present, wait for someone to come out of the house to greet you before you get out.

♦ Be prepared for problems. We had pots sent to us in fruit crates and scratched by nails protruding from the box, and we had artists take up to a year to fill an order. If you are an impatient or cautious person, we recommend sticking to businesses that provide a no-questions-asked, money-back guarantee. Galleries and trading posts often offer the best choice of artwork and can save much worry, frustration, time, and disappointment. But if you are fascinated with an artist's work, we encourage you to seek out that person.

We asked experts in various arts and crafts to give advice to help you avoid problems and mistakes. Your opinions and selections are only as good as the information they are based upon. Education is an important component of every collection.

NAVAJO RUGS

Nothing evokes the romance of the Southwest more than Navajo rugs. Their rich colors and intricate designs can fill a room with rich warmth. Each rug retains the artist's personality while it reflects the proud tradition whence it came. We have included many examples of the most common rug styles throughout this book. Within each style there can be wide variation. Some rugs resist categorization by synthesizing different styles or simply fitting no traditional style. The creativity of Navajo weavers never slumbers. The greatest difficulty in purchasing a Navajo rug is making a choice. Dan Garland of Garland's Navajo Rugs in Sedona suggests the following:

- ◆ Place the rug on the floor; the best rugs lie flat with no puckering.
- ◆ The designs should be symmetrical and the lines straight.

BELOW: (Left) *Chinle rug, 51" x 34", by Daisy Cody, Leupp, Arizona.* Courtesy of Garland's Navajo Rugs, Sedona, Arizona. (Right) *Twill rug (diamond), 60" x 31", by Esther Tsosie, Keams Canyon, Arizona.* Courtesy of Garland's Navajo Rugs, Sedona, Arizona

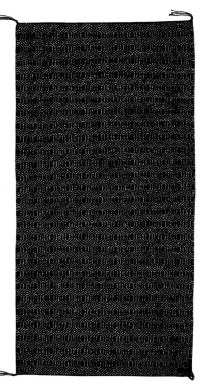

TWILL RUGS

In Twill rugs the weaver allows the weft to glide over more than the usual two warp strands. This creates the diamond, diagonal, or herringbone pattern that typifies the rug. Bill Malone of Hubbell Trading Post says, "Twills are becoming endangered because weavers are reluctant to weave them. They are difficult to weave, but are considered horse blankets and weavers prefer more difficult designs, which they hold in higher regard. After they weave a Ganado or Two Grey Hill, they will rarely create a Twill."

CHINLE RUGS

"Chinle rugs are banded rugs, borderless with bands of repeated geometric designs. They ususally have nice vegetal-dyed colors. Chinle rugs are usually simpler than the other two banded rugs, Crystal andWide Ruins."
—GREG LEIGHTON,
Notah Dineh Trading Post, Cortez, Colorado

CRYSTAL RUGS

Crystal rugs are banded like Chinle rugs but they have a line that is wavy because the weavers use varied colors of weft. They have solid or wavy bands in rows of two or three, then complicated bands of geometric patterns. With a few exceptions they are soft, warm, vegetal-dyed colors.
—GLENDA PILGRIM,
Old Crystal Trading Post, Crystal, Arizona

BELOW: *Crystal rug, 52" x 38", by Mary H. Wilson, Crystal, New Mexico.* Courtesy of Garland's Navajo Rugs, Sedona, Arizona

♦ Slight imperfections are acceptable; Navajo rugs are handmade.
♦ Buy the rug that appeals to you most; it is the right one. You will like it even more the longer it is with you.

Dan also suggests that you consider dealing with a dependable dealer. Establish your requirements of style, size, color, quality, and budget. Select a number of rugs that meet these requirements, then eliminate until the right rug remains.

Some of the best rugs ever made are being created today. Navajo

BELOW: *Pictorial rug, 34" x 40", by Betty Patterson, Many Farms, Arizona.* Courtesy of Garland's Navajo Rugs

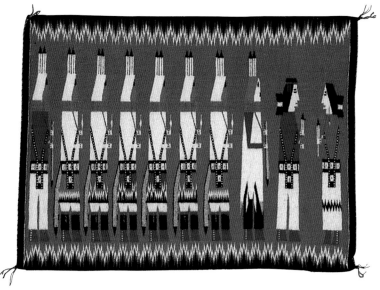

ABOVE: Yei'ii bichai *rug, 17" x 24", by Ella Yazzie, Sawmill, Arizona.*
Courtesy of Garland's Navajo Rugs, Sedona, Arizona

BELOW: *Revival rug, 26" x 44", by Irene Chase, Hard Rock, Arizona.*
Courtesy of Garland's Navajo Rugs

YEI'II BICHAI RUGS

The distinction between the *Yei'ii* and *Yei'ii bichai* rugs is the *Yei'ii bichai* are usually shown in profile and represent ceremonial dancers, where the *Yei'ii* rugs represent actual supernatural beings. They are a fairly common rugs are popular with weavers, and are becoming increasingly complex and detailed in design.
—JED FOUTZ, Shiprock Trading Company, Shiprock, New Mexico

REVIVAL RUGS

There is something magical about blankets from the classic period. They are universally appealing. Revival pieces were encouraged by Hubbell and continue to be popular with weavers and collectors alike.
—DAN GARLAND, Garland's Navajo Rugs

*Pottery, Pueblo Pottery, San Fidel,
New Mexico*

weavers are expressing themselves as their ancestors have for the past three hundred years.

POTTERY

Robert F. Nichols on Canyon Road in Santa Fe is a highly regarded expert on contemporary Pueblo and Navajo pottery. He offers the following advice:

> One of the most striking characteristics of Pueblo Indian pottery is its variety. Variations of color, form, and style of decoration seem to be almost endless. This variety is one of the qualities of the pottery that tends to appeal to collectors. By selecting only the work of one group of families or of one family or individual even a small collection can have amazing diversity.
>
> The same variety that attracts more seasoned collectors can simply

overwhelm anyone looking at Indian pottery for the first time. The result is that many who are drawn to pottery tend to seek the guidance of others before making their first purchases. But by understanding the reasons for the variety I think a person will be better able to understand that there is no easy formula to selecting one piece over another and it is perfectly all right to buy what you like rather than what someone else likes.

There are several factors that contribute to the variety of Pueblo Indian pottery. These can be lumped into three basic categories: materials, traditions, and innovations. My discussion will concentrate on "traditional" pottery of the pueblos—meaning traditional materials and techniques. There are some potters doing very exciting work outside of these traditions, but that is a whole other area to examine.

The makers of traditional pottery tend to use materials local to their own pueblo (village). Acoma is known for its white clay and slip, Zia for red clay, Hopi for yellow clay, etc. The use of local materials contributes to another point of confusion about Pueblo pottery—its price. The Pueblo potter does not go to the store to buy prepared clay, tempering materials, glaze, or paint. The potter, often with a friend or relative, must go to the source to dig the clay from the ground. Time is also spent gathering the tempering, slip, and paint materials. Even fuel for the fire must be gathered and dried. Impurities are removed by hand before the clay can be ground on a metate. Paints are also prepared by hand, by grinding rocks that produce the different colors or boiling plants to produce black carbon paint.

Pueblo traditions also contribute to the variety. Each village has its own tradition about what a pot should look like. The pottery of pueblos that use essentially the same materials and techniques can look quite different. San Ildefonso tends to use matte paint on a highly polished background, while Santa Clara tends to carve the design into the pot giving a bas-relief effect. Cochiti and Santo Domingo potters use a black carbon paint, which requires

Anthony Durand, Picuris Pueblo, at Santa Fe Indian Market

a special slip material that prevents the use of fine lines in the decoration. Furthermore, Santo Domingo are not to use certain designs with religious meanings on their pottery, while Cochiti potters have no such restriction.

Varying traditions also occur within different families of a pueblo. Angela Baca from Santa Clara is known for her melon pots and her children continue the tradition, although their forms differ from their mother's. Each family at Santa Clara using the carving technique has its own style— Elizabeth Naranjo's style is similar to that of her sisters, and her daughter Betty continues the tradition—while the mother and daughter team of Jane Baca and Starr Tafoya uses a very different style of carving.

The final factor that contributes to the variety of Pueblo Indian pottery is individual innovation. This is the factor that makes the pottery so exciting at this time. Artists in virtually every one of the pottery-making pueblos are reinterpreting traditional forms, creating new styles, or even reviving old ones. Virgil Ortiz at Cochiti is reviving a figural tradition of the nineteenth century while his mother Seferina interprets the twentieth-century story-teller in a very individual way. Robert Tenorio and his sister and her husband, Arthur, and Hilda Coriz are reviving lost techniques and injecting new life into the pottery of Santo Domingo. Ida Sahmie draws upon the imagery of her Navajo ancestors to decorate her pottery, while the clay she uses, and often the vessel shapes, come from her husband's family, who are Hopi.

As an academic-turned-collector-turned-shopkeeper, my approach to the pottery is still very personal and unabashedly emotional. I think it is okay for one to like whatever one likes. I think that anyone who relies too much on the "advice" of someone else—whether an expert, the friend of a friend, or a hired consultant—is missing out on one of the greatest joys of collecting—passion. And that passion should be involved even if the collection will never consist of more than one or three pieces.

I believe that once you understand the reasons for the extensive variety of southwestern Indian pottery you will be less intimidated by it and can begin to enjoy the pottery for that very quality. You will also feel more comfortable in making your own decisions as to what to buy—and what not to buy. I think it is a very exciting time to be interested in Indian pottery.

Whatever choice appeals to you is fine as long as you understand the effort that goes into the pottery you are purchasing. Traditional potters dig the clay, dry it, sift it into powder, mix it with water; the pots are built by hand (no wheels are used), and polished, painted, and fired in an open-air fire using animal dung.

Irregularities called fireclouds are created when firing a pot, due to fuel falling against the vessel during the firing. To avoid fireclouds, many artists at Acoma use electric kilns. They have maintained the other aspects of traditional pottery, but have altered the firing stage.

A third group of potters has separated from tradition to a much greater degree. Many pots offered for sale are decorated greenware (slipcast ceramics). The pots are slip-molded and sold. The pots are purchased ready-made and then decorated with traditional designs and fired. These pots can make interesting souvenirs, but they should not be confused with traditional pottery that is very time intensive.

Acoma potter Joseph Cerno is concerned about the recent trends away from traditional techniques. He warns, "People just buy greenware and paint it with nontraditional geometric designs." He recommends that a person wanting true traditional pottery learn about what they are buying. Joseph suggests the following tests to identify greenware: Look for vertical seams. The molds on greenware often leave a small ridge that can be felt on the inside or outside of the pot. If your finger becomes chalky when rubbing the inside of a pot, this might indicate it is slipcast. A slipcast pot is extremely smooth with no imperfections or bumps. Traditional pots often

ABOVE: *Bowl, 4", by Ramona Ami, Polacca, Arizona*

BELOW: *Jar, 9", by Robert Tenorio, Santo Domingo Pueblo, New Mexico*

have a little roughness and fingerprints if burnished smooth with a stone. These details should be welcomed. Traditional Acoma slip has a slight pink cast. Any pot should have a nice ring to it when tapped just below the rim with the forefinger. A dull sound means a hairline crack somewhere. The only conclusive method of identifying a pot's origins is to break the pot and study the particles. A good way to really learn what you are getting is to visit the artist.

SANDPAINTING

Sandpainting is a fundamental part of Navajo healing ceremonies used to summon the Holy People. It creates what scholar Nancy Parezo, in her book *Navajo Sandpainting,* calls an "impermanent altar." In Navajo ceremonies, balance with nature is restored to the person who sits within a sandpainting. Religious sandpaintings use complex figures and symbols in specific arrangements that are destroyed at the end of the ceremony. Sandpainting motifs and nonreligious sandpaintings have been produced since the 1880s. Permanent commercial sandpaintings are created using ground pigments that are glued to a sand-covered wooden board.

Joe E. Tanner, Jr., owns Fifth Generation Trading Company in Farmington, New Mexico. His business is famous for carrying the finest examples of sandpainting done today. Joe states that while all sandpaintings are made with the same materials, there are certain aspects to look for when purchasing a sandpainting. Commercial sandpaintings are usually not exact copies of traditional religious sandpaintings; usually the colors are changed. There are new "pictorial" sandpaintings done today that are representations of Navajo rugs or kachina dolls or other southwestern motifs. To understand the symbolism it is helpful to cross-reference the sandpainting with the traditional ceremonial images from one of the following books: *Navajo Sandpainting Art,* by Eugene Baatsoslanii Joe; *Summoning the Gods,* by the

Museum of Northern Arizona; and *Navajo Medicine Man Sandpaintings*, by Gladys A. Reichard. Most people look for pleasant color, and symmetrical and intricate design. No type is better than another. In the end, it is a matter of personal preference.

KACHINA DOLLS

Barton Wright, author of *Hopi Kachinas: The Complete Guide to Collecting Kachina Dolls*, offers the following advice to those interested in collecting this unique art form:

Traditional kachina dolls are simply carved, almost static figures with arms held rigidly to the body and legs set solidly unbent beneath them. Action dolls are a recent development and as their name indicates, are carved as if they are in motion. Action dolls usually have stands, are more expensive, and are made solely for galleries.

Men who impersonate kachinas and dance in the plazas carve cottonwood root into replicas of their kachina appearance. They present these to infants and females of all ages. This carved and painted figure is called a tihu by the Hopis and a kachina "doll" by others. It is not a plaything, but a small part of the kachina it represents. Kachina dolls are carved by the people of Hopi and Zuni, but Zuni dolls are rarely offered for sale.

A number of carvings, represented as such, are not kachina dolls. These may be good carvings, but should not be sold or referred to as kachina dolls. These include inordinately large or small carvings, figures with removable masks, Apache mountain spirit dancers, Navajo Yei'ii bichai dancers, snake dancers, Hopi society chiefs, social dancers such as the Butterfly and Buffalo, Field Mouse, Mickey Mouse, or any figures that are not directly related to the kachina spirits. Be aware that Navajos, Anglos, and others make carvings that imitate kachina dolls in appearance.

Kachina doll, 14", by Philbert Honanie. Courtesy of Tsakurshovi, Second Mesa, Arizona

Kachina doll, 12", by Manuel Denet Chavarria, Polacca, Arizona

You would be wise to deal only with established reputable dealers. I highly recommend businesses that are members of the Indian Arts and Crafts Association. They will help you make an informed decision and avoid problems. I suggest a few simple rules that will aid you in sifting through the profusion of dolls:

♦ Decide what you wish to collect. Choosing a category will give your collection a direction.

♦ Check for good carving, proper body proportions, finished details, smooth surface and no cracks or bad wood.

♦ The material should be cottonwood root, which is lightweight. Avoid balsa wood, pine, aspen, cottonwood limbs, and other substitutes.

♦ Check painting for precise straight edges of lines and color. Look for attention to detail. Paint should not smudge or have a glossy surface.

♦ The gear or paraphernalia that the doll wears or carries may be carved, painted or purchased, but it should be present.

♦ Know the literature and be aware of variations in dolls from village to village. Try to ascertain the doll's accuracy, although this may be difficult.

♦ Establish the name, maker, and village of a doll.

BASKETS

Basketry is the oldest Native American craft. While most baskets have utilitarian purposes, such as storage, some are created for ceremonies. Today, a large category of baskets is made for the art market. Because basketmaking is one of the most time-intensive art forms, baskets sell for high prices. Even these higher prices do not provide the basketmaker with proper remuneration for her long hours. This has made baskets even scarcer. The Navajo, Apache, Paiute, Tohono O'odham, and Hopi are all famous for their unique contributions to basketry.

Steve Simpson and his family own Twin Rocks Trading Post in Bluff, Utah, and Blue Mountain Trading Post in Blanding. Steve and his brother Barry specialize in Navajo baskets. Steve says, "Navajo baskets are made of all sumac. It may not be obvious to beginning collectors, but three-rod bunch foundations are better than five. Three, being smaller, makes a finer weave. The Navajo basket designs are experiencing tremendous innovation. Variations of the wedding basket designs; interpretations of Paiute, Pima, Tohono O'odham, and Apache baskets; and new Navajo mythology baskets, based entirely on Navajo stories, are all available. It is an exciting period for Navajo basketry."

Apache baskets employ sumac with a fine three-rod base. The best work is typified by the coiled baskets of Lydia Pesata. Lydia tells us that she fears Jicarilla Apache basketry will die out because it's so difficult and time consuming that people don't want to take up the art form.

San Juan Paiute baskets are also exemplary in their use of a three-rod foundation. Like their Navajo neighbors, Paiute artists are innovative within traditional boundaries, creating new expressive designs with a superb tight weave.

Baskets, pots, and rugs at Thomas Harley Trading Company, Aztec, New Mexico (closed 1994). Hand-tinted photograph

Tohono O'odham baskets are created outside the Four Corners, but deserve discussion here because they are offered in businesses throughout the Southwest. Formerly referred to as Papago, these basketmakers have won an enormous share of the market. A few women weave willow, but the predominant material is white yucca. A wide assortment of geometric, figurative, and animal motifs is used to appeal to buyers. Tohono O'odham also produce intricately designed miniature baskets of horsehair and occasionally wicker.

Bruce McGee of McGee's Beyond Native Tradition Gallery in Holbrook, Arizona, is part of the McGee family that also has businesses in Keams Canyon and Piñon. Bruce has had a great deal of experience with Hopi baskets and shares the following:

On the Hopi Mesas baskets are still very important for ceremonial and social use. There are fewer and fewer Hopi basketmakers selling their work because it is difficult to make a living. Most weavers stick with the traditional patterns. Kachina designs seem to bring the most money.

BELOW: (Left) *Paiute butterfly basket, 14" diameter, by Rose Ann Whiskers.* Courtesy of Garland's Navajo Rugs, Sedona, Arizona. (Middle) *Navajo squash blossom basket, 14" diameter, by Elsie Holiday.* Courtesy of Blue Mountain Trading Post, Blanding, Utah. (Right) *Placing the Stars Basket, 21" diameter, by Eleanor Rock, Navajo.* Courtesy of Blue Mountain Trading Post, Blanding, Utah

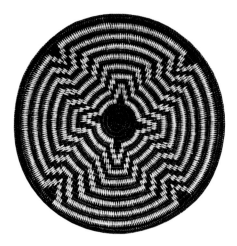
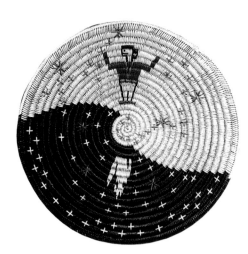

Plaited yucca sifters are made on all the mesas. In the late 1970s and early 1980s I would get a lot of wicker cradleboards. Because they did not sell well, I don't see them anymore. Rarely do we get the plaited rabbit-brush piki trays or burden baskets offered for sale, though they are still woven on the Third Mesa. The basketmakers there seem to prefer to use rabbitbrush or sumac to create the colorful flat, plaque-plaited wicker baskets with geometric whirlwind, cloud, and other patterns. Look for tightness of the weave, especially in the binding on the side of Third Mesa wicker plaques.

Distinctly different from Third Mesa are the Second Mesa baskets, which use grass and dyed yucca to create the popular and colorful coiled baskets that are so sought after. We see a lot of shallow bowls, flat plaques, and a few deep baskets. The designs include animals, geometric abstractions, and kachinas. With Second Mesa coiled baskets, notice how flat, rather than twisted, the yucca lays. Most weavers have the skills to put an additional raised feature somewhere, such as a three-dimensional rattle. This top-stitching is an extra that adds to the quality of the work.

BELOW: (Left) Cross-Legged Kachina, *Hopi coil plaque, 9" diameter, by Joyce Ann Saufkie.* Courtesy of Garland's Rugs, Sedona, Arizona. (Middle) *Hopi wicker, 12" diameter, artist unknown.* Courtesy of Garland's Navajo Rugs. (Right) Horned Toad and Arrowhead Basket, *15" diameter, by Lorraine Black, Navajo.* Courtesy of Blue Mountain Trading Post, Blanding, Utah

 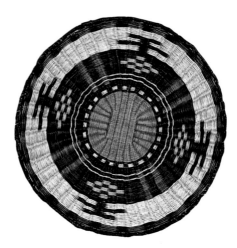 

ABOVE: (Top) Big Horned Sheep Basket, *12" diameter, by Peggy Rock Black, Navajo.* Courtesy of Blue Mountain Trading Post, Blanding, Utah. (Bottom) Yei'ii *Basket, 21" diameter, by Mary Black, Mexican Hat, Utah*

Bruce McGee suggests that when choosing any basket you consider the following:

♦ It should have a strong and pleasing shape.

♦ Is the weave tight? Usually the tighter woven baskets are preferred. Even sifters that are traditionally loosely woven are being woven tighter for the collectors' market, where they don't retain their utilitarian purpose.

♦ The designs should be symmetrical, clear, and distinct. The motifs are varied but should be well planned into the complete basket.

♦ If the colors seem too crisp, white, or new, be aware they will mellow with age.

♦ Remember that the price of the basket reflects the enormous time the basketmaker spends gathering materials, designing, and weaving the basket. Unlike rug weavers, basketmakers cannot buy commercially dyed material.

♦ Be aware of baskets that are imported. Many baskets that bear southwestern motifs are actually made in Pakistan, Africa, or elsewhere. These are cruder in technique and usually inexpensive. Sometimes they bear labels that do not state the place of origin.

FETISHES

Greg Hofmann is a trader at Turquoise Village in Zuni, an active business selling Hopi and Zuni arts and crafts. They sell more fetishes than any other place in the world. He shares his experience with Zuni fetish collecting and offers the following advice:

In recent years carved fetishes have attracted a large number of collectors. Zuni fetishes originated in small stones resembling animal forms. These found objects were said to contain the spirit of the particular animal it resembled. Since the mid-1980s fetish carving has experienced an explosion of activity with over two hundred active carvers. Fetish sizes range from four-inch sculptural display fetishes, to pocket size, down to tiny fetishes strung as necklaces. Avoid block, plastic, and manmade materials, and any fetishes that are factory-made in Taiwan, China, Mexico, or the Philippines. Also, Navajo fetishes are copies. To avoid buying misrepresentations and imitations, buy from a reputable dealer.

With so many possibilities to choose from, Greg suggests the following considerations when collecting fetishes:

♦ Try to collect the six directional fetishes in their proper colors: bear: blue, wolf: white, mole: black, mountain lion: yellow, eagle: multicolored, badger: red. (The Zuni world is divided into six directional regions each represented by a particular animal.)

♦ Try to collect old-style fetishes (see recommended books for specific shapes, details, types of stone).

♦ Collect old- and new-style fetishes other than the six directions: snake, fox, frog, turtle, rabbit, coyote, owl, deer, ram, lizard, corn maiden, buffalo, and altar dolls.

♦ Collect new carvings (that are not really fetishes): dolphin, horse, otter, seal, dinosaur, pig, elephant, turkey, skunk, insect.

♦ Collect a variety of rocks and colors: malachite, azurite, sugilite, fluorite, cedarwood, ironwood, Picasso marble and other varieties of marble. There are new kinds of stone available today that were not originally used.

ABOVE: *Lifesize Growler family animal, 27",
Sweetwater, Arizona.* Courtesy of Twin Rocks
Trading Post, Bluff, Utah

BELOW: Woman holding sheep, *woodcarving, 24",* by Johnson Antonio, Lake Valley,
New Mexico

FOLK ART

Leslie Muth's Gallery in Santa Fe specializes in Navajo folk art. This is a special passion of Leslie's, and her enthusiasm is contagious. She observes:

Anyone currently involved in collecting Navajo folk art is at a fortunate place. This art form has exploded over the past ten years, and should continue to do so for the next decade. More and more Navajos who rarely used to venture off the reservation are finding outlets for their carvings, constructions, and folk paintings. Museums are exhibiting their work and books are coming off the presses documenting it.

The Navajo way of life, which has produced this art, is in a transition stage. There is a move for the Navajo to integrate more into this country's mainstream—to have higher education, improved nutrition, and better living facilities. Much of this will be accomplished by the Navajos' leaving the reservation and the old ways behind. There won't be time or accessibility for making mud toys, found object constructions, or woodcarvings. When that happens, the only way for the Navajo to continue their artistic endeavors will be to market them at more elevated price levels than the current market, making the art more difficult to collect.

Leslie suggests Chuck and Jan Rosenak's book, *The People Speak: Navajo Folk Art,* for those who want to learn more about the subject.

JEWELRY

Mark Bahti is the owner of Bahti Indian Arts in Tucson, Arizona, author, and past president of the Indian Arts and Crafts Association. He discusses the following aspects of collecting jewelry in the Southwest:

The most important safeguard when buying any Indian craft is to exercise common sense in terms of who you buy it from and where. A roadside or swap-meet vendor can be difficult to locate or contact should there be a problem with the merchandise. Fairs run by museums are an exception to the rule, as they usually screen participants and know how to contact them again should that be necessary.

Fancy certificates of authenticity may be suitable for framing, but they are no guarantee. What they are is documentation; should the item turn out to be something other than what it was represented to be, you have proof positive of the original representation. Equally effective is having the salesperson write down on the receipt whatever claims were made that you feel are important (e.g., that it is Navajo handmade and set with natural turquoise, that it was made in the 1920s, that it was inlaid with coral).

Ignore discounts. The final price is what is important, not how high they started. A $50 bracelet is only worth $50, no matter if it was marked $100 or $200 originally.

Among the problem areas in Indian jewelry are:

♦ *Machine-made items.* This includes bench beads, which are silver beads that may be soldered together by hand, but are otherwise made with a hydraulic punch press.

♦ *Lost-wax cast reproductions.* The original handmade item is used as a model from which a mold is made. It can then be knocked off rapidly at minimal cost—with not a penny going to the Indian artist who handmade the original. It is used for copying Navajo sandcast and Hopi overlay work, as well as the silver frames for inlay work. Unless it is a sloppy cast with tiny silver bubbles in the corners or crevices here and there, they can be tough to spot. Making matters worse, the hallmark is also reproduced.

♦ *Synthetic materials.* Euphemistically called by such names as "block turquoise," they are simply colored plastic. Used in bead necklaces of the sort made at Santo Domingo Pueblo, inlay work, and even fetish carvings, materials duplicated include coral, shell, sugilite (purple), lapis (blue), spiny

ABOVE: *Hopi brooch, 1", by Homer Vance, Grand Canyon Village.* Courtesy of East West Trading Company, Santa Fe

BELOW: *Hopi pendant, 2", by Charles Willie.* Courtesy of Twin Rocks Trading Post, Bluff, Utah

oyster shell (red-orange), malachite, and an azurite-malachite blend that is sometimes represented as "stabilized azurite-malachite."

◆ *Treated materials. Generally limited to turquoise, this involves the addition of resin or dyes to harden the stone or change the color. The term "stabilized" came about because it prevents the turquoise from changing color. (Natural turquoise, in all but the hardest of grades, can absorb soaps and oils and change color over time.) Other euphemisms include "enhanced" and "fracture sealed."*

Mark is a highly regarded trader and author (*A Consumer's Guide to Southwestern Indian Arts & Crafts,* Tucson: Bahti Indian Arts, 1975). If you visit Tucson, Mark's business, Bahti Indian Arts, is at 4300 N. Campbell, telephone 520-577-0290.

PAINTING, DRAWING, SCULPTURE, AND OTHER ART FORMS

This book covers, but doesn't dwell on, these art forms. Santa Fe and the Southwest abound with the best sculptors, painters, and printmakers in the United States. Because so much already has been written on these artists, we wish to devote space to other artists, whose art forms were traditionally carried by the trading posts. In your travels you will find many other arts and crafts, such as moccasins, drums, cradleboards, flutes, and new items such as dream catchers. Suggestions about where to purchase them and learn more about them appear later in this book.

Visitors to the Four Corners area should be aware that collecting any artifacts or antiquities over one hundred years old, such as arrowheads or pottery, is illegal on public and tribal lands. Federal, state, and local laws punish those who may be tempted to pocket even a pottery sherd.

Navajo man and woman listening to juke box. Photograph by J.H. McGibbeny, Special Collections, University of Utah Library (hand-tinted)

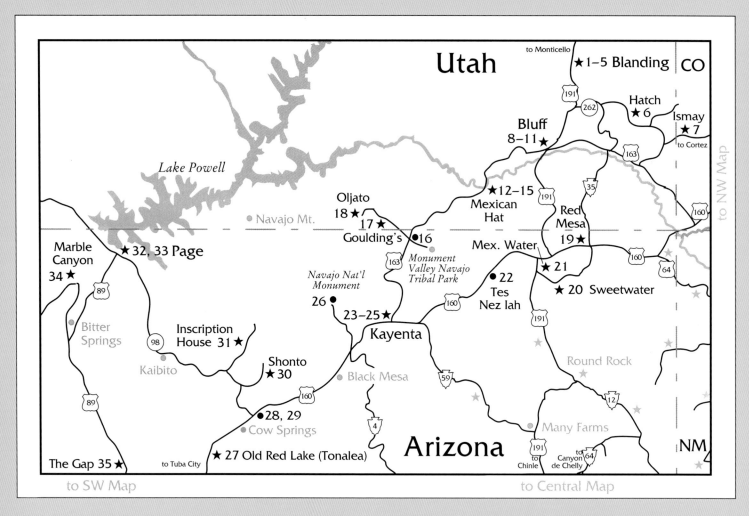

★1–5 Blanding
to Monticello
Utah
CO
191
262
Hatch
★ 6
Ismay
★ 7
to Cortez
Bluff
8–11 ★
163
Lake Powell
★ 12–15
Mexican
Hat
191
35
Red
Mesa
19 ★
160
Navajo Mt.
Oljato
18 ★
17 ★
Goulding's ●16
163
Mex. Water
Monument
Valley Navajo
Tribal Park
●22
Tes
Nez Iah
★ 21
160
★ 20 Sweetwater
64
Marble
Canyon
34 ★
★ 32, 33 Page
89
Navajo Nat'l
Monument
26 ●
23–25 ★
Kayenta
191
Inscription
House 31 ★
Bitter
Springs
98
Kaibito
Shonto
★ 30
Black Mesa
59
Round Rock
12
89
Many Farms
●28, 29
Cow Springs
4
Arizona
191
to
Chinle
to
Canyon
de Chelly
64
NM
The Gap 35 ★
to Tuba City
★ 27 Old Red Lake (Tonalea)
to SW Map
to Central Map
to NW Map

LEGEND

★ Trading Post in this chapter

★ Trading Post in other chapter

● Other site

Northwest Navajo Nation and Monument Valley

◆ ◆ ◆

The most brilliant colors in the earth are there, I believe, and the most beautiful and extraordinary

land forms—and surely the coldest, clearest air which is run through with pure light.

N. Scott Momaday, *The Names*

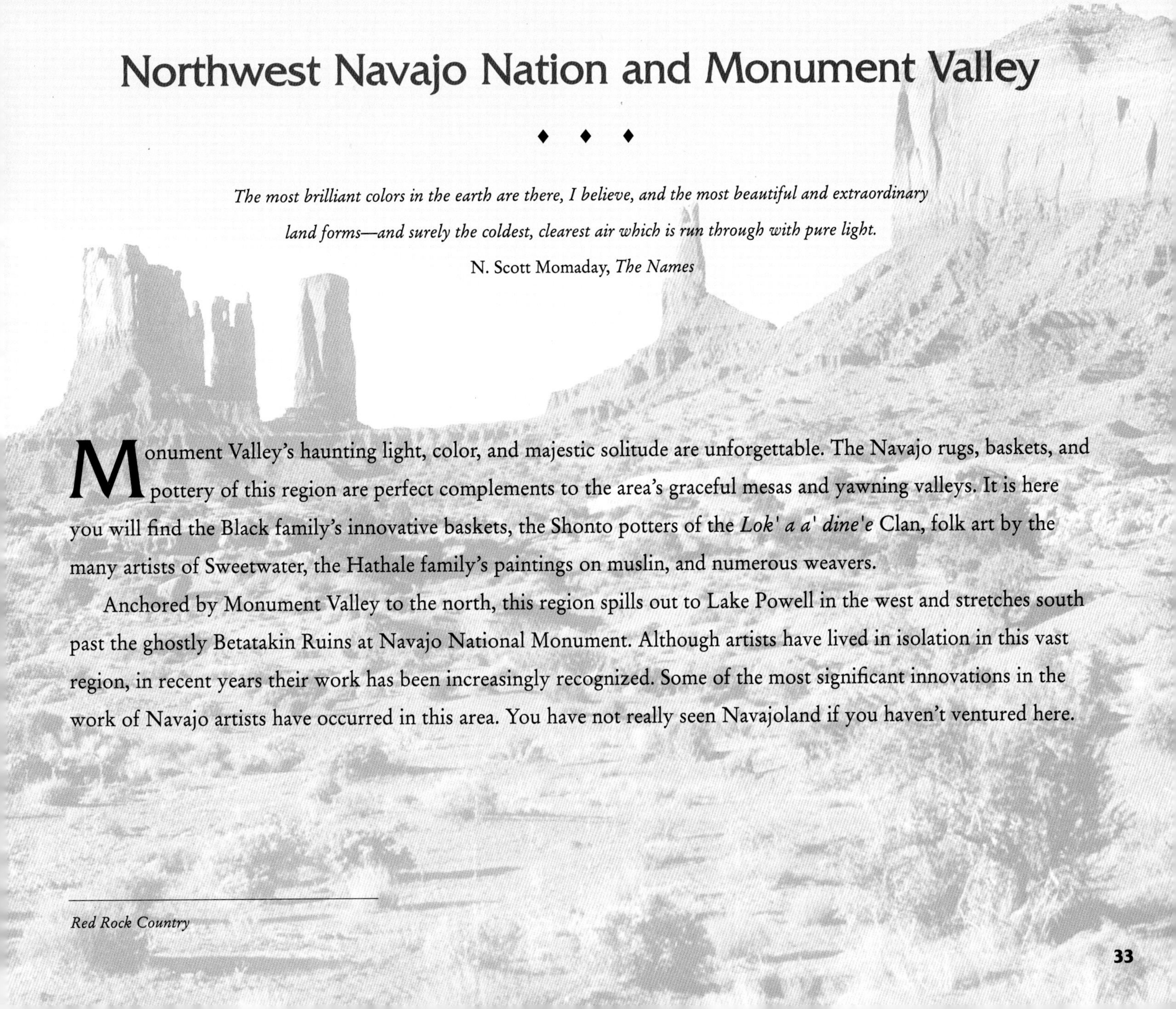

Monument Valley's haunting light, color, and majestic solitude are unforgettable. The Navajo rugs, baskets, and pottery of this region are perfect complements to the area's graceful mesas and yawning valleys. It is here you will find the Black family's innovative baskets, the Shonto potters of the *Lok' a a' dine'e* Clan, folk art by the many artists of Sweetwater, the Hathale family's paintings on muslin, and numerous weavers.

Anchored by Monument Valley to the north, this region spills out to Lake Powell in the west and stretches south past the ghostly Betatakin Ruins at Navajo National Monument. Although artists have lived in isolation in this vast region, in recent years their work has been increasingly recognized. Some of the most significant innovations in the work of Navajo artists have occurred in this area. You have not really seen Navajoland if you haven't ventured here.

Red Rock Country

THE NAVAJO NATION

P.O. Drawer 308, Window Rock, AZ
86515

520-871-6352-55, FAX 520-871-4025

NAVAJO TOURISM DEPARTMENT:
P.O. Box 663, Window Rock, AZ

520-871-6436, FAX 520-871-7381

Regional fairs are identified and located in several chapters of this book.

The Navajo Nation Fair is held in early September in Window Rock.

Most rules are common sense with respect for the privacy and customs of the Navajo people.

♦ Obtain permission before taking pictures of individuals. A gratuity may be expected.

♦ No alcohol is permitted.

♦ Do not disturb plants, rocks, or animals.

♦ Travel established routes and trails.

The Navajo Fish and Wildlife office can provide permits for hunting and fishing.

Dear Visitors:

Welcome to the beautiful Navajo Nation. We are grateful that you are visiting with us. We hope that your visit will be a pleasant and memorable one.

The Navajo Nation is larger than the State of West Virginia and has a population in excess of 250,000 Navajos. Within the Nation, there is much natural beauty untouched by man and more spectacular than many of the wonders of the world.

We invite you to spend as many days as you can with us. The Navajo People are hospitable people and are always ready to help make your stay as pleasant as possible. While you are here, take time to get to know the people, their language and culture, and visit the many beautiful places within the Navajo Nation.

Welcome and may the Great Spirit be with you on all your journeys.

— ALBERT HALE, President of the Navajo Nation

The Navajo people call themselves the *Diné* (the People). They are the largest Native American tribe in population and acreage. Over 200,000 members live on almost 25,000 square miles spreading over northeast Arizona, northwest New Mexico, and southern Utah.

BLUFF AND SURROUNDING AREA

1. **Blue Mountain Trading Post**

P.O. Box 263, Blanding, UT 84511,
1 mile south of Hwy 191

801-678-2218

Summer: M–F 8:00–6:00,
Sat 8:00–6:00

Winter: M–Sat 9:00–5:00

Owners: Simpson family

♦ M, V, D, AE, C, S, HA

An impressive basket and rug inventory are the hallmarks of this trading post. The Simpson family has employed Navajo artist Damian Jim to create unique, computer-assisted designs exploring aspects of Navajo mythology. The region's gifted artists use these designs as a springboard to

Basket, 21", by Lorraine Black, Mexican Hat, Utah. Courtesy of Blue Mountain Trading Post

create some of the most exciting and innovative art forms in the Southwest. Barry Simpson, who has lectured on basketry at the Wheelwright Museum in Santa Fe, can explain the finer points about the baskets of Mary Black, her family, and other outstanding artists of the region. Blue Mountain (and Twin Rocks in Bluff) also offer great opportunities to see innovative rugs, including mosaic pattern, Simpson Revival *Yei'ii,* and rug patterns based on traditional Navajo mythology. This post also carries pottery, books, jewelry, and sandpaintings.

B, Bk, D, J, K, P, **R**, Sp, Dye charts

2. **Thin Bear Indian Art Inc.**

1944 S. Main, 105-2, Blanding, UT 84511, 1 mile south of Blanding on Hwy 191

801-678-2940

M–Sat 9:00–6:00

Owner: Robert Hosler

◆ M, V, D, C, S, HA

The Hoslers have been here since 1973 and have been strong supporters of quality vegetal dyed rugs. The inventory includes a selection of old and new Navajo rugs (fifty to one hundred from $30 to $25,000); Paiute, Ute, Apache, Tohono O'odham, Hopi, and Navajo baskets; Hopi, Navajo, Pueblo, and Casas Grandes pottery; and bronzes by Tom Knapp.

B, Bk, D, F, **J**, K, P, **R**, S, Beadwork

3. **Huck's Museum and Trading Post**

1387 S. Hwy 191, 79-1, Blanding, UT 84511

801-678-2329, -2946

M–Sat 10:00–5:00 (hours vary)

Owners: Hugh Acton and Betty Gordon

Huck's Museum and Trading Post is a curious roadside attraction. The ranch-style log building appears to be a residence. The door opens into the trading post, which offers a limited selection of items including Ute beadwork and a few western antiques. A small admission fee allows you to enter a large room that holds an amazing amount of Anasazi artifacts.

B, J, R, Beadwork

4. **Hunt's Trading Post**

146 E. Center, Blanding, UT 84511, Hwy 191

801-678-2314

M–F 8:00–6:00, Sat 8:00–1:00

Owners: Deborah Lynn Hunt and Wayne Day

◆ M, V, D, AE, C, S, HA (one step)

The Hunt family has traded in the Four Corners area for four generations. Beside Zuni, Navajo, Hopi, and old pawn jewelry, you'll find a good selection of Paiute and Ute baskets; Pendletons; cedarberry bead necklaces; small Navajo, Pueblo, and slipcast pottery; and a large inventory of

musical cassettes and CDs. They offer espresso beverages.

B, C, I, **J**, M, P, R

5. **Purple Sage Trading Post**

790 S. Main (78-11), Blanding, UT 84511

801-678-3620

M–Sat 9:00–8:00

Owners: Brigitte and Sumner Patterson

◆ M, V, AE, D, C, T, S, HA

The inventory includes 200 artists (95 percent Navajo, some Hopi and Zuni). They carry folk art from the Sweetwater, Arizona area, and rugs from the northeast Navajo nation, (Chinle, Two Grey Hills, and Ganado). You will find rugs in the $100–$400 price range. Sumner says he likes to include some of the older weavers and this makes the prices more affordable. Also available are woodcarvings by Bernie Tohdachenny, pitch pots by Judy Addison, and necklaces by owner Brigitte Patterson. They also carry music, health food, and vitamins.

D, J, P, Pt, R, Folk art

6. **Hatch Trading Post**

Hatch, UT 87937, about 15 miles south of Blanding, UT on Hwy 191, then 15 miles east on Rt. 262

Hours variable

Owners: Sherman and Laura Hatch

Ismay Trading Post, west of Cortez, Colorado. Hand-tinted photograph

Joseph Hatch built the Hatch Trading Post in 1903, and things have changed little since then. The canopy of willows and cottonwoods makes this spot a surprising oasis in the desert. The Hatch's peacocks bark out their shrill warning when you arrive. You'll find some groceries, some Navajo clay pipes and small pots, pitch baskets, and reproduction Anasazi pottery.
B, P

7. Ismay Trading Post

391 County Rd G, Cortez, CO 81321, take Hwy 666 2 miles south of Cortez, then head west at the Hovenweep National Monument sign about 22 miles
970-565-7752
Daily: Hours indefinite
Owners: Robert and Eugene Ismay
♦ T, S, HA

John and Eleanor Ismay built this post in 1921. The building's adobe facade seems ancient and appears to loom up all at once, as if from nowhere. It stands alone in the isolated landscape near Hovenweep National Monument. Robert and Eugene main-

tain the post in its original bullpen design. A thick blanket of dust covers the horse tack, hardware, auto supplies, and few groceries. They sell Ute beadwork, cedar flutes, a few weaving tools, and a good selection of rugs that are kept in the living area. Robert sells peaches and watermelons when they are available.

The Ismays donated a number of artifacts and land to the national park system. They also have created a glittering mountain of empty glass soda bottles next to the building. The Ismay brothers are that wonderfully peculiar brand of characters that trading posts are famous for. They seem soothed by their isolation and have created a life that in many ways resembles that of their isolated Navajo and Ute customers.
I, R, Beadwork

8. Cow Canyon Trading Post and Restaurant

P.O. Box 88, Bluff, UT 84512, north end of town at the junction of Hwys 191-163
801-672-2208
Daily 9:00–6:00, evening hours when restaurant is open
Restaurant: Open evenings mid-April–mid-Oct, Th–M 6:30–9:30, reservations recommended
Bikooh Breads (bakery): Daily 7:00–2:00, closed Tues.
801-672-2482

Cow Canyon Trading Post, Bluff, Utah. Hand-tinted photograph

Owners: Liza Doran and Jim Ostler
♦ M, V, C, S, HA (one step)

We never visit Bluff without a stop at Cow Canyon for dinner. Located within the trading post, the restaurant offers a memorable dining experience. The menu is small and constantly changes to take advantage of local fresh produce. Liza tells us that her recipes are created by a group of local Navajo women who get together and put their own "spin" on gourmet recipes.

This post has a quiet, casual, time-worn ambiance. Its dark vigas and mission furniture make it seem far older than its young history would

Gladys Yellowman weaver, Twin Rocks Trading Post, Bluff, Utah

suggest. It was built just after WWII. Current owners Liza Doran and Jim Ostler stock a variety of items including mud toys, Homer Warren sandstone sculptures, old and new Navajo pottery, Navajo rugs, Navajo cooking and weaving tools, Bikooh breads (European-style breads and pastries), hairbrushes, pitch baskets, international tribal art, and a selection of well-chosen jewelry, and Zuni pottery and fetishes. They also carry a wide selection of books chosen with great care, including many titles rarely found elsewhere. Next door to the bakery is the Half-Baked Gallery, a contemporary fine arts gallery with changing thematic shows. Both Jim and Liza have a passion for and great knowledge of the Southwest. They can explain how to use a Navajo hairbrush, the fine points of Navajo pottery, or how to cook Navajo cuisine.
B, **Bk**, **F**, **J**, K, **P**, **R**, S

9. **Gladys Yellowman: Weaver**
P.O. Box 25, Bluff, UT 84512

Gladys started spinning wool when she was six. She remembers, "I picked the wool that the sheep would leave on the bushes and spin it. I started weaving with a dinner fork. My mother taught me. I still remember everything she told me. It was just like going to school. She said I could earn a living, and I raised ten daughters by weaving. My first rug

Sandstone car, 4" x 7" x 3", by Ron Malone, Sweetwater, Arizona. Courtesy of Twin Rocks Trading Post, Bluff, Utah

sold for $12. I bought my father shoes with the money. Right now I'm weaving a 4' x 6' rug to trade with a lady for sheep."

Gladys weaves traditional patterns and prefers Tree of Life and *Yei'ii bichai* rugs. She says, "When you make a *Yei'ii bichai* rug you must make the figures really neat. The eyes must be straight, arms straight, everything straight or it will affect your vision."

Gladys' daughter, Priscilla Sagg, demonstrates weaving at Twin Rocks Trading Post. Four of Gladys' other daughters also weave. Gladys is willing to teach weaving and accepts special orders for small and large rugs and sashes. She tells us her sashes are used as belts, but are also used by Navajo women when they are giving birth. She says, "We hang it above the bed for the woman to hold on to. We cover the sash with corn pollen and call it the rays of the sun. The grandmother and friends surround the bed and sing the young one into the world."

⑩ Twin Rocks Trading Post
P.O. Box 330, Bluff, UT 84512, on Bluff's historic loop, north end of town, under the Twin Rocks stone formation
801-672-2341, 800-526-3448
Daily: Summer: 8:00–7:00,
Winter: 8:00–5:00
Cafe: Summer: M–Sat 9:00–9:00,
Winter: M–Sat 9:00–7:00
Owners: Simpson family
♦ M, V, D, AE, C, S, HA

Duke and Rose Simpson traded from a gas station since the fifties. In 1989 they built this beautiful, expansive gallery. Their sons, Steve and Barry, are respected authorities on basketry, and we recommend that collectors take whatever measures necessary to visit the Simpsons' two posts. (The other is Blue Mountain Trading Post in Blanding). You won't find a better selection of baskets anywhere. The inventory includes the familiar wedding basket designs, pictorial narratives on Navajo mythology, and vibrating optical, black-and-white, abstract designs. Every visit reveals completely new motifs and ideas. The basketry of this area is creating a stir in the international collectors market. The Simpson family is currently aiming

its efforts at the creation of new innovative rugs. Working closely with local Navajo artists, the rugs are based in Navajo tradition with contemporary elements. Available are Simpson Revival *Yei'ii* rugs based upon a single standing *Yei'ii* pattern that originated in the Farmington, New Mexico, area in the early 1900s with a trader named Simpson (no relation); mosaic pattern rugs, first woven by local weaver, Anita Hathale; and Mythology rugs, many designed by Navajo artist Damian Jim.

Steve has a very large selection of Navajo folk art including the work of Bruce Hathale, the Willeto family, Silas and Bertha Claw, Dennis Pioche, Johnson Antonio, Mamie Deschillie, Homer Warren, Faye Tso, and many others who have been increasing in popularity. The large jewelry selection is chosen with a keen, informed eye for value. The Simpsons run an expansive wholesale business upstairs. The new Twin Rocks Cafe and Gift Shop is open for breakfast, lunch, and dinner.
B, Bk, **C**, D, I, **J**, K, P, **R**, S, Sp, Sv, **Folk art**

⑪ Kennedy Indian Arts
P.O. Box 39, Historic Loop, Bluff, UT 84512
801-672-2405
Owner: Georgiana Kennedy Simpson

As a child, Georgiana traveled the Navajo reservation and Pueblos of the

Southwest with her father, John Kennedy. Georgiana has covered the western states buying, trading, and wholesaling since 1990. In 1995, Georgiana, a third-generation trader, married Steve Simpson of Twin Rocks Trading Post. Her inventory includes pottery, jewelry, baskets, rugs, fetishes, and novelty items. She is enthusiastic, well educated, always on the lookout for unusual twists to traditional pieces, and enjoys working closely with artists in developing ideas. She serves on the Board of Directors of the Indian Arts and Crafts Association. Georgiana continues to work closely with her father and Kennedy Indian Arts and Crafts of Albuquerque.
♦ B, F, J, P, R

⑫ Mary Holiday Black, Sally Black, Lorraine Black, Agnes Black Gray: Basketmakers
P.O. Box 116, Mexican Hat, UT 84531

Mary Black won the Utah Governor's Award in the Arts in 1993 and in 1995 was awarded the National Heritage Fellowship by the NEA in recognition of her creativity, craftsmanship, and generosity in teaching her craft. Her daughters Sally and Lorraine Black are perennial award winners in exhibitions across the Southwest.

Mary, a member of the Bitter Water Clan, lives modestly high up on

Douglas Mesa near Mexican Hat. She learned the art of basketry at age eleven. After raising eleven children, now surrounded by her grandchildren, she continues to create innovative coiled baskets. Her daughters often weave at her house, and the family members sometimes seem to be competitively seeking new heights in innovation and virtuosity. Their baskets incorporate a wide array of motifs. Some are based on the traditional Navajo wedding basket, while others are figurative, representing traditional Navajo mythology, *Yei'iis*, fire dances, animals, or geometric abstractions.

Mary and her family are willing to accept special orders. Their work can usually be found at Twin Rocks Trading Post in Bluff and at Blue Mountain Trading Post in Blanding. Their work represents a revitalization of one of America's oldest and most beautiful art forms. Steve Simpson, of Twin Rocks Trading Post, states:

When we first opened in the 1970s, the art of Navajo basket weaving was in decline and many were speculating that it was a dying art form. Although there were a few Navajo weavers still making traditional ceremonial baskets, most of the weaving was being done by the Southern Paiute tribe.

With Mary as their tutor, however, several of her daughters, daughters-in-law, and her

Portrait of Mary Black, Basketmaker, *wood-carving, 24", by Johnson Antonio, Lake Valley, New Mexico*

son became expert basket weavers, bringing about a revival in Navajo basket weaving. Mary's children and their spouses now comprise a majority of the expert Navajo basket weavers on the northern portion of the Navajo Reservation, and are responsible for the bulk of the collectors-quality Navajo baskets currently being woven.

13. Burch's Trading Company

P.O. Box 310337, Mexican Hat, UT 84531
801-683-2221
Daily: 7:00–9:00
Owners: Phil and Susie Burch
♦ M, V, D, S

Burch's is located on the San Juan River, which divides it from the Navajo Reservation. Monument Valley is twenty minutes away. The Burch family has been here since 1988. You must make your way past groceries and general merchandise to find the arts and crafts area. This is one of the largest inventories of Navajo turquoise cluster jewelry in the Southwest. If you like the jewelry you see on traditionally dressed Navajo women, then this is the place to look. They take pawn, so their selection of older items changes. We found hatbands, an old concha belt encrusted with Bisbee turquoise, and a squash blossom necklace hammered from old mercury dimes. If you aren't overwhelmed by the turquoise jewelry here, the cafe next door continues the

Car and road through Monument Valley, 1926. Copyright Dudley Scott Archives, Grand Canyon National Park #6794

Mark said a trading post opened at this location in the 1860s. The current business sells Navajo rugs; pitch and ceremonial baskets; Apache burden baskets; Navajo, Hopi, Zuni, and Santo Domingo jewelry; and Navajo, Hopi, Santa Clara, and slip-cast pottery. If you stay at the inn, they offer a 15 percent discount on purchases, and Mark says he will give a 10 percent discount to those who ask.
B, I, J, P, R

16. Monument Valley Junction Vendors

Hwy 163 at the entrance to Monument Valley Navajo Tribal Park

More than twenty jewelry, pottery, and food vendors sell gift items here. This curious collection of temporary structures hosts a changing group of businesses. The arts and crafts tend to be of tourist quality, but there are occasional surprises. We found some exceptional pieces of jewelry. Great Navajo tacos and sun tea are available.

17. Goulding's Monument Valley Trading Post, Lodge, and Museum

P.O. Box 1, Monument Valley, UT 84536, west of Hwy 163, across from

jewelry selection. They also carry a few locally woven Navajo baskets and rugs. (Motel open April–Nov.)
B, D, **J**, M, Pt, R, Sv

14. Valle's Trading Post

P.O. Box 310216, Mexican Hat, UT 84531
801-683-2226
Daily: Summer: 8:00–8:30, Winter: 9:00–7:00
Owner: Richard and Norene Neff
♦ C, S, HA

This little post is also a trailer/RV park and laundromat. The post has groceries, propane, and a special area for arts and crafts. They sell Pendleton products; Navajo ceremonial baskets (Sally Chief's baskets are especially nice); slipcast pottery; a small selection of old pawn; Zuni, Navajo, and Hopi jewelry; about sixty Navajo rugs in the $65 to $4,000 range; sandstone carvings; and books.
B, Bk, **J**, P, **R**, S

15. San Juan Inn and Trading Post

P.O. Box 310276, Mexican Hat, UT 84531
801-683-2220, 800-447-2022, FAX 801-683-2210
Daily 7:00–9:30
Owners: Mark and Julie Sword
♦ M, V, D, AE, S, HA (three steps)

Monument Valley Navajo Tribal Park entrance
801-727-3231, FAX 801-727-3344
Daily March–Oct 7:30–9:00,
limited off-season hours
Museum: 7:30–9:00
Manager: Shirley Thomas
♦ M, V, D, AE, C, S (not overseas)
Goulding's was built by Harry and Leona "Mike" Goulding on this sparsely populated borderland known as the Paiute Strip. They started in a ten-man tent and ran the post from the 1920s to the 1960s. Harry Goulding had a unique ability for bringing the right people together. He persuaded John Ford to film many Westerns here from 1939 to 1964, and Harry was influential in the formation of the Monument Valley Tribal Park.

The present store has been open since 1989. (The old post is now the museum.) There are many John Wayne items and local crafts. They carry about one hundred rugs in the $200–$2,000 range, and rug collectors should ask to see what's not on display. Notice the rugs by Monument Valley weaver Suzie Yazzie. Goulding's sells sand-paintings from the Four Corners area, Navajo baskets, and a large stock of Navajo, Hopi, Zuni, and Pueblo jewelry. You'll find some unusual souvenirs such as videos of movies made in the Monument Valley area and nightlights with southwestern motifs.

The museum has been remodeled to add more items from Leona "Mike" Goulding's collection.
B, C, D, I, **J**, K, M, **P**, Pt, **R**, Sp, **Sv**

18. Oljato Trading Post
P.O. Box 1402, Kayenta, AZ 86033,
11 miles west of Monument Valley,
7.6 miles past Goulding's Trading Post
801-727-3210
M–F 7:00–9:00; Sat–Sun 8:00–8:00
Owner: Evelyn Y. Jensen
♦ D, C, S, HA (through back door to the curio shop)
Oljato Trading Post was opened in 1905 by John Wetherill and is registered with the Utah Historical Society. The post was originally one mile south in Arizona. This building, built in 1921, maintains an old trading post flavor with its bullpen design and general merchandise hanging from a viga ceiling. This is a quiet area with locals making up most of the clientele. Groceries are in the front, and arts and crafts are found in a gated rug room. Be sure to ask to see it. Since baskets are used by the local Navajo population, you'll find a good selection here. There is a variety of rug patterns with particularly well-crafted work by the Atenes family, pitch baskets, beadwork, cradleboards, Samuels family dolls, and pottery from the Herder family of Cow Springs. The road to this isolated post is a beautiful

Oljato Trading Post, Kayenta, Arizona

drive and one we always take when in the area.
B, Bk, D, J, P, **R**

19. Red Mesa Trading Post
HCR 6100, Box 38, Teec Nos Pos, AZ 86514, Jct Hwys 35-160
520-656-3261
Daily 7:00–10:00
Manager: Ada Fowler
♦ M, V, C, S, HA
Red Mesa is a modern building and serves as a gas and grocery source for locals. They have a rug room in the back with forty or so rugs, and unusual paintings on buckskin by

Harry Warren. Ask Ada to show them to you. They also have a case of jewelry, sandpaintings, and framed dye charts. Ada is a delightful person and enjoys promoting the local artists. Bk, J, P, **Pt**, **R**, Sp, Sv

20. The Growler Family: Animal Sculptors

P.O. Box 355, Teec Nos Pos, AZ 86514, 520-674-3616 (Emmanuel Mission)

The Growler family creates wonderful lifelike sculptures of sheep, rams, and buffalo. Parents Jimmy and Irene and daughter Ruby live near the Emmanuel Mission in Sweetwater and can be reached at the mission phone number. Ray, who is the most prolific and best known, lives near Shiprock but works at his parents' house. The figures are carved from wood with real pelts and horns added. At times they have difficulties obtaining pelts. The family produces the animals sporadically, but more often in the summer. Recently, there have been many imitations made. The Growlers' work is priced a little higher than the imitations, but worth it. You can be assured of a true "Growler" animal if you buy it from the family; at Twin Rocks Trading Post in Bluff; or the Leslie Muth Gallery, Rainbow Man, Davis Mather, or Wheelwright Museum in Santa Fe.

Memory aid on muslin with earth pigments, 12" x 10", by Bruce Hathale, Monument Valley

21. Mexican Water Trading Post

HCR 6100, Box 50, Teec Nos Pos, AZ 86514, Hwy 160 between the Jct of 191 N. and 191 S.
Daily 7:00–10:00
Owners: Ann and Morris Butts
♦ M, V, C, HA (3" step)

This post has a strong community feeling. It sells horse tack, hides, groceries, and general merchandise. They stock Anasazi beans from Dove Creek, Colorado, and local produce in season. If you are lucky, you will happen in during apricot or peach season. Arts and crafts are tucked away in a back corner of the post and include small examples of Navajo pottery, a small selection of rugs, Pendletons, cedarberry beads, arrowheads, and a small collection of Navajo jewelry. D, J, M, P, R, Cradleboards, Dye charts

22. Bruce and Dennis Hathale: Folk Artists

P.O. Box 137, Mexican Hat, UT 84531

Bruce and Dennis Hathale create depictions of traditional Navajo sandpaintings on muslin. They range from a simple figure of 10" to expansive, complete sandpaintings as large as 4' x 4'. Unlike most sandpainting artists, Bruce and Dennis do not include inaccuracies. They try to recreate the sandpaintings completely and accurately. Bruce and Dennis are the sons of Roger Hathale, a Navajo medicine man. Roger performs the Blessingway ceremony to protect his sons from harm for creating work usually considered taboo by Navajos.

The Hathale family lives in a compound on a mesa above Tes Nez Iah Trading Post and Motel. Dennis and Bruce's parents recently built a contemporary house. Bruce still lives in a traditional hogan. Mrs. Dinah Hathale and her two daughters are weavers. Dennis lives elsewhere, but can always be reached through the family.

Dennis and Bruce's muslin paintings are among the best values we've found. They grind many of the colors from materials they collect in the surrounding hills. We were amazed at their skill of drawing intricate, graceful lines with the most rudimentary tools, creating dazzling effects against all odds.

The natural pigments make these works fragile. If you buy one, handle it carefully. We suggest framing it behind glass as soon as possible. Bruce is willing to create special orders. Work is available through Twin Rocks Trading Post in Bluff, Utah; Leslie Muth Gallery, Santa Fe; Jack Beasley, Farmington, New Mexico; and Thompson River Trading Company, Durango, Colorado.

KAYENTA

 Wetherill Inn Motel

P.O. Box 175, Kayenta, AZ 86033, Hwy 163, 1.5 miles north of Jct Hwys 160-163
520-697-3231
Daily: Summer: 7:00–10:00, Winter: 8:00–9:00
Owners: G. and R. LaFont
Managers: Logan and Sally St. Clair
♦ M, V, D, AE, Diners, T, S, HA (one step)

Named after trader/explorer John Wetherill, whose post stood one block behind this building, the motel carries a selection of Navajo baskets, small Navajo and slipcast pottery, a limited selection of rugs, and a large selection of Navajo, Hopi, and Zuni jewelry.
B, Bk, D, J, K, P, R

24. Burch's Trading Company

Drawer 20, Kayenta, AZ 86033, Hwy 163
520-697-3430
M–F 9:00–5:00
Owner: Susie Burch
♦ M, V, D, AE, T, S, HA

The front porch seems to be a favorite place for local men to sit and talk in the shade. The interior looks like an old-time trading post with the arts and crafts located in an isolated room. The inventory was sparse when we visited, but there were a few Silas Claw pots among some unusual Navajo pottery.
B, Bk, D, J, P, R, Sp, S, Cradleboards

25. Holiday Inn Curio

P.O. Box 302, Kayenta, AZ 86033
520-697-3221
Daily 7:00–10:00
Owner: Leisure Properties
General Manager: LaVina Smith
♦ M, V, D, AE, C, HA

Dolls, baskets, and jewelry were the major emphases on our last visit. Check out the Navajo, Hopi, and Zuni storytellers and the selection of Navajo and Hopi woodcarvings. They also have an extensive line of local Navajo textiles, souvenir items, and jewelry.
B, **Bk, D, J**, K, P, **Sv**

26. Ledge House Indian Arts and Crafts

HCR-1, Box 2, Tonalea, AZ 86044, Hwy 160 to Hwy 564, inside the Navajo National Monument visitor center
520-672-2404
Daily: Summer: 9:00–7:00, Winter: 10:00–4:00 (closed mid-Jan–Feb)
Manager: Sally Martinez
♦ M, V, C, S, HA

This local Navajo-owned business sells only authentic quality Native American arts and crafts. They've been open since 1981. Located in the prime Navajo pottery area, they wholesale and retail Navajo pitch pots by Alice Cling, Samuel Manymules, and Susie Crank; Pueblo pottery; Hopi, Navajo, and Zuni jewelry; and about fifty Navajo rugs.
B, **J**, K, **P, R, Sp**

27. Old Red Lake Trading Post

P.O. Box 30, Tonalea, AZ 86044, 22 miles northeast of Tuba City on Hwy 160
520-283-5194
Daily 9:00–9:00
Owner: Lorenzo Fowler
♦ C, HA (back entrance)

Until its recent sale, this post had been owned by the Babbitt Brothers Trading Company since 1891. The

Old Red Lake Trading Post, Tonalea, Arizona

Arbuckle's coffee crates, it is the genuine article.

If you're looking for arts and crafts, there isn't a lot to find here. If you love historic trading posts, Old Red Lake will not disappoint you with its ambiance. We are really pleased that Lorenzo is the current guardian of this bastion of the old days.

28. Silas and Bertha Claw: Potters
P.O. Box 7416, Shonto, AZ 86054
520-283-8896

Silas and Bertha create pots that are relief sculptures and paintings.

Babbitts obtained the post as payment for a debt owed to them by then-owner Sam Dittenhoffer, who was shot in a card game. The Babbitts maintained the post to protect their investment. Jim Babbitt recalls, "In many ways I regret moving out. That old little hovel of a place was one hundred years old, no wiring to speak of, no modern-day refrigeration, just those old counters, the smell of tobacco and kerosene, sheep, wool. You know, a lot of people today would be offended by people spitting tobacco on the floor. There is nothing in existence like that."

Present owner Lorenzo Fowler grew up in Tonalea, and after time in Ganado and Polacca, he returned home. He says, "Ninety-eight percent of my clientele is local. I'm related to most of the people here in Tonalea and I really like my customers. I try to keep things the old traditional way. The Storm Pattern rug started at this post. I don't like being the middleman and trying to make money off the weavers. I line weavers up with customers and let the weavers make the extra money."

Old Red Lake Trading Post was used in the film adaptation of Tony Hillerman's *The Dark Wind*. From its unusual exterior to its wall of

Pottery by Silas and Bertha Claw, Shonto, Arizona

Silas and Bertha Claw, potters, Shonto, Arizona

They make pipes, bowls, and single-, double-, and triple-spouted vessels usually less than twelve inches high. The pottery is created in the traditional Navajo manner by Bertha and Silas, but Silas' sculptured appliqué is unique. His subjects include sheep, coyotes, horses, his neighbors, Navajo ceremonies, cacti, horned toads, and other aspects of his life near Shonto junction.

Silas' and Bertha's pots do not look like traditional Navajo pottery. The pots with their painted figures require a bit of an acquired taste. The Claws have made a traditional art form idiosyncratic and very expressive. They welcome special orders. Bertha speaks no English and Silas speaks a little. Their niece, Ella, is very helpful in taking and filling orders.

29. Alice Cling and Rose Williams: Potters

P.O. Box 7321, Shonto, AZ 86054

Alice has taken Navajo pottery to a new level of elegance and finesse. Her work has a finely polished surface and a minimum of decoration, which is the traditional Navajo way.

Alice's work has an avid following and has won numerous prestigious awards. It holds a unique place in Navajo pottery history and has attracted great interest to other potters as well. Alice's pots have placed Navajo pottery at the same level of elegance as the work of great Pueblo potters. She grew up in Shonto and still lives near her mother, Rose Williams.

Rose has been very influential in the resurgence of Navajo pottery. Her work varies from small pots to large vessels of twenty inches. She likes to create utilitarian vessels and traditional forms. Rose's generous spirit and willingness to teach the craft may have saved it from extinction. For her efforts Rose has been awarded Arizona's Living Treasure status. In recent years she has been influenced by Alice. We've noticed Rose's pots becoming increasingly finely polished by stone instead of

Rose Williams and daughter Alice Cling, potters, Shonto, Arizona

Shonto Trading Post, Shonto, Arizona. Hand-tinted photograph

corn cob, and she has even begun to use Alice's trademark red slip.

They take special orders, and you can usually find good examples of their work at their friend Bill Beaver's Sacred Mountain Trading Post or Leslie Muth's gallery in Santa Fe.

30. Shonto Trading Post

General Delivery, Shonto, AZ 86054, from Hwy 160 take Hwy 98 north 6 miles, then northeast on Rte 221 (dirt road may be a problem in snow).
520-672-2320
M–Sat 8:00–5:30
Owner: Ray Drolet
♦ M, V, D, AE, C, S, HA

This post was established in 1915 by Joe Lee and John Wetherill and has belonged to Ray Drolet's family since the 1940s. As a child Ray would help the manager stock the post shelves. Then he served as manager 1972–1991. Ray says, "Shonto is one of the few trading posts that's still authentic. It is unique because of its location. Every time I went outside, I never got tired of that view of the canyon." Shonto means "Sunlight Water." This area of the reservation is the home of the "long hairs," conservative Navajos who prided themselves in not being taken captive by Kit Carson and forced on the Long Walk to Fort Sumner, New Mexico in 1864.

During Ray's tenure at Shonto he

carried pots, saddle blankets, and baskets. He says, "The whole area between Shonto and Navajo Mountain is where Navajo and Paiute baskets are made. There are still some good weavers in the area but they are getting on in years." Today's selection of arts and crafts is still represented by Navajo baskets, an assortment of rugs, and pottery, most notably by Louise Goodman and Linda Wilson. The arts and crafts are isolated in the rug room. Ask to see them. In our travels this post was cited by trader

Mr. and Mrs. I.S. Richardson, Inscription House, 1929. Copyright Dudley Scott Archives #34, Grand Canyon National Park

John W. Kennedy, author Barton Wright, and others as their favorite.
B, P, R

31. Inscription House Trading Post

Box 5300, Inscription House, AZ 86044, from Hwy 160, take Hwy 98 north 12 miles, then northeast on Rt. 16
520-672-2651
Sun–F 8:30–5:30, closed Sat
Owners: Mae L. Townsend
♦ M & V (gas only), C

The trading post is named after the Anasazi ruins in nearby Neetsin Canyon. This trading post sells everything locals might need: food, saddles, chain saws, hats, and refrigerators. It still maintains a rug room, which you must ask to see. Mae has a great private collection of Navajo and Paiute baskets in her living quarters (not for sale). Work is available by Jim Black, an accomplished woodburner. He creates elaborate scenes on furniture and smaller items. There is also a little jewelry and other items that are made locally.

The post was established in 1929 by S.I. Richardson as a hotel for travelers between Rainbow Bridge and Tuba City, Arizona. It was made into a trading post a year later. Reuben Heflin took over in 1955, and was joined by Stokes Carson in 1958.

Carson worked here until his death in 1974 at the age of eighty-eight.

The locals will tell you the road to Navajo Mountain from here is rough. "Rough" is an understatement. The trading post at Navajo Mountain closed in 1993. Madeline Cameron operated it successfully for thirty years and sold it to Dick Johnson in 1985. We are certain that the condition of the road contributed to Navajo Mountain Trading Post's demise.

B, J, R, furniture

PAGE AND SURROUNDING AREA

32. **Dine Bí Keyah Museum at Big Lake Trading Post**
P.O. Box 1925, 1501 Hwy 98, Page, AZ 86040, 1 mile southeast of Page city center
520-645-2404
Daily: 6:00–12:00 PM,
Museum 7:00–9:00
Owners: Ross and Ruby Plasterer

Don't let the commercial exterior scare you off. Upstairs, above the groceries and general merchandise, is a fascinating museum and a crafts gallery. The museum has examples of prehistoric pottery from throughout

Storm pattern rug, 34" x 51", by Lillie Tonchin, Fruitland, New Mexico. Courtesy of Garland's Navajo Rugs, Sedona, Arizona

STORM PATTERN RUG
The storm pattern is perhaps the most easily recognized of the contemporary styles of Navajo weaving. Although there is no limit to the number of variety of colors in a storm pattern weaving, most weavers stick to red, black, grey, and white. A notable exception to this are the weavings of Lillie Touchin, who routinely uses thirty-plus shades of color in her highly collectible pieces. The storm pattern is characterized by a central rectangular design, repeated designs in the four corners tied to the central design by a zigzag lightening pattern and stylized clouds, rain, and/or water bugs filling in as the weaver sees it.
—BUZZ TREVATHAN,
Cristof's

the Southwest including work from South America and Panama, as well as Pre-Columbian, Anasazi, Tusayan, Tularosa, Sinagua, and Cliff Dweller pots. There are a couple hundred small prehistoric tools. The crafts gallery sells Navajo pottery, rugs, dolls, and some souvenir items.

D, P, Sv

33. Blair's Dinnebito Trading Post

P.O. Box 940, 626 N. Navajo,
Page, AZ 86040
520-645-3008, 800-644-3008
FAX 520-645-9256
Daily extended summer hours
Winter M–Sat 9:00–6:00
Owners: Elijah, James, and Kathy Blair

♦ M, V, D, AE, T, C, S, HA

In the past, the Blairs ran posts at Dinnebito, Kayenta, and Aneth. In the late 1940s, Dinnebito Trading Post was located north of Third Mesa on the Hopi Reservation. Competition with supermarkets priced them out of that location, changing their clientele to tourists. James still works with the same artists even though the business is now in Page. He says, "The Dinnebito-area weavers made Ganado Red, Teec Nos Pos, and Storm Pattern rugs and produced nice rugs, but they were not recognized. About 1987, I was search-ing for a new look to create attention for them. I introduced the idea of

Dinnebito black rug, 37" x 50", by Rose Dan. Courtesy of Blair's Dinnebito Trading Post, Page, Arizona

DINNEBITO BLACK RUGS

Dinnebito Black rugs are bold new rugs from an old pattern. One night in 1988 I awoke with the idea of a rug with a black background. I talked to the local weavers around Dinnebito about the idea. Rose Dan Begay created a Storm Pattern with a bold black background. Other weavers followed with Teec Nos Pos and Ganado Patterns.

—JAMES BLAIR,
Blair's Dinnebito Trading Post

using black backgrounds to replace the red of their Storm, Ganado and Teec rugs, and I was really delighted with the results." Gladys and Mary Shepherd and Rose Dan are among the many weavers creating Dinnebito Black rugs. The west side of the Navajo Reservation is also known for its bird pictorials and Storm Pattern rugs, which are well represented at Blair's.

This wholesale/retail business maintains a large inventory of Hopi kachina dolls and Hopi and Navajo pottery, including work by Lorraine Williams, Susie Williams, and Samuel Manymules. Look for Navajo, Hopi, and Paiute baskets and some fine paintings by Bill Rabbit, Carlos Begay, and James Cody. The Blairs welcome phone and mail orders.
B, **Bk**, C, F, I, J, **K**, M, **P**, Pt, **R**, S, Sp, Sv

34. Marble Canyon Trading Post

Marble Canyon, AZ 86036, 42 miles from Page on Hwy 89A
520-355-2225
Daily 6:30–9:30
Owner: Jane Foster
◆ M, V, C, S, HA

Located on the Colorado River, the original post was built by Buck Lowrey in 1927. This rustic post has a motel, restaurant, and airstrip, and serves as a stop for tourists, fishermen, and rafters. The choice of books and

The Gap Trading Post, Cameron, Arizona

contemporary Navajo, Hopi, and Zuni jewelry is particularly good. An assortment of Navajo rugs ($100–$1,600), Navajo and Santa Clara pottery, Navajo wooden dolls, and a large selection of souvenirs rounds out the inventory.
B, **Bk**, D, **J**, P, R, **Sv**

35. The Gap Trading Post

Cameron, AZ 86020, on Hwy 89, approximately 17 miles north of Jct 89-160, 50 miles south of Page
520-283-8932
Daily 7:00–9:00
Manager: Daisy Willie
◆ M, V, D, AE, C, S

The Gap was originally built around 1880 by Joe Lee. After Lee abandoned the post, trader Johnny O'Farrell built a new post nearby. After a fire in 1937, a third post, the present one, was built. Its fortresslike stone exterior was seemingly built to avoid another fire. The post is now a Thriftway, but unlike many of the Thriftway stores, The Gap has maintained a trading post personality. They carry about seventy-five rugs ($75–$1,000) by local weavers, including

Zonie Barlow, potter, Tonalea, Arizona

NORTHWEST NAVAJO NATION FAIRS

July: Todineeshzee Fourth of July Rodeo and Fair, Kayenta, AZ

October: Utah Navajo Fair, Bluff, UT

SELECTED NORTHWEST NAVAJO NATION ARTISTS/CRAFTSPEOPLE

Zonnie Barlow, P.O. Box 624, Tonalea, AZ 86044—Traditional Navajo pottery.

Shonto Begay, P.O. Box 364, Kayenta, AZ 86033—Contemporary paintings of Navajo life.

Louise R. Goodman, P.O. Box 576, Tonalea, AZ 86044—Beautiful coil pots, animal figures, and traditional Navajo pottery, famous for her large bears.

Anita Hathale, P.O. Box 1003, Monticello, UT 84535, 801-587-3018—Specializes in *Yei'ii* and *Yei'ii bichai* rugs.

Weaver Mistena Hathale, Monument Valley

Dinah and Mistena Hathale, HCR 6100, Box 62, Teec Nos Pos, AZ 86514—Weaving.

Edith and Guy John, P.O. Box 158, Teec Nos Pos, AZ 86514—Folk art: wooden owls and chickens.

the pictorial rugs for which the area is famous. (Weavers from this area make the well-known Tree of Life pattern.) Included in their inventory are Navajo and Tohono O'odham baskets, small Navajo and slipcast pottery, beadwork, wool, and replicas of Anasazi pottery. B, D, J, K, P, **R**, Sp

Sarah Lee, c/o Sweetwater Chapter House, 505-599-4250—Weaving, specializes in Storm and Two Grey Hills rugs.

Ron Malone, P.O. Box 521, Teec Nos Pos, AZ 86514—Folk art: carved sandstone cars, trucks, and other vehicles.

Rita and Betty Manygoats, P.O. Box 519, Tonalea, AZ 86044—Pottery with horned toads, Navajo life, animal figures, and other motifs.

Marjorie Sherlock and Lilly Yazzie, P.O. Box 1646, Kayenta, AZ 86033—Weaving, specialize in *Yei'ii* and Teec Nos Pos rugs.

Lulu and Wilford Yazzie, P.O. Box 891, Teec Nos Pos, AZ 86514—Folk art: wooden crows, chickens, and ceremonial figures.

Navajo hogan

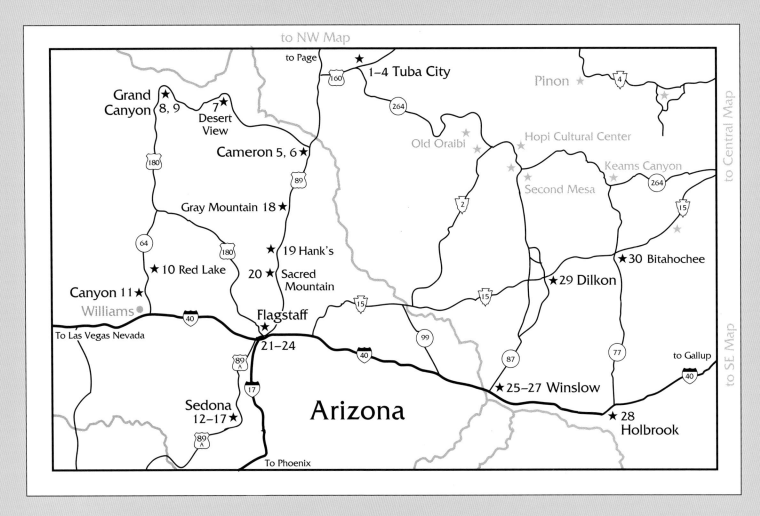

to NW Map

to Page

★ 1–4 Tuba City

160

Pinon ★

4

264

Grand Canyon 8, 9 ★

7 ★ Desert View

Hopi Cultural Center

Old Oraibi

180

Cameron 5, 6 ★

89

Keams Canyon

264

Second Mesa

15

Gray Mountain 18 ★

2

64

180

★ 19 Hank's

★ 30 Bitahochee

★ 10 Red Lake

20 ★ Sacred Mountain

★ 29 Dilkon

15

Canyon 11 ★

Williams ●

15

Flagstaff ★

40

21–24

To Las Vegas Nevada

89 A

77

to Gallup

99

40

87

40

17

25–27 Winslow ★

Sedona 12–17 ★

Arizona

★ 28 Holbrook

89 A

To Phoenix

to Central Map

to SE Map

LEGEND

★ Trading Post in this chapter

★ Trading Post in other chapter

● Other site

Southwest Navajo Nation, San Juan Paiutes, and the Grand Canyon

◆ ◆ ◆

GOD'S MASTERPIECE ON EARTH—A Cosmic Intaglio
—Vast Mountain Ranges in Captivity—
The Wonder Chasm of the World
Charles F. Lummis, *Mesa, Cañon, and Pueblo*

Over the years artists and writers have tried to capture the essence of the Grand Canyon, but it remains vast, timeless, and beyond the human scale. There is no way to prepare for it. You must go to its brink and let it accordion out before you in a rapturous array of color. At the canyon you can meet people of every nationality who have made the pilgrimage to this special place. It affects everyone differently, but leaves no one unaffected.

From the Grand Canyon the Southwest region stretches eastward across Tuba City and over otherworldly landscapes of fossilized dinosaurs and the petrified remains of ancient forests, south to the San Francisco Peaks. Flagstaff, a beautiful mountain town, offers much to the visitor, as does its neighbor to the south, Sedona. This region also includes the characteristically Western towns of Holbrook and Winslow, with their Route 66 cafes, and the isolated expanses of Leupp and Dilkon.

This region offers excellent Navajo pottery, rugs, Hopi kachina dolls, Navajo jewelry, and the finely woven baskets of Paiute women. For trading post enthusiasts Cameron, Tuba, Sacred Mountain, and the Fred Harvey Company shops at the Grand Canyon offer places to choose excellent arts and crafts, and a look into trading post history.

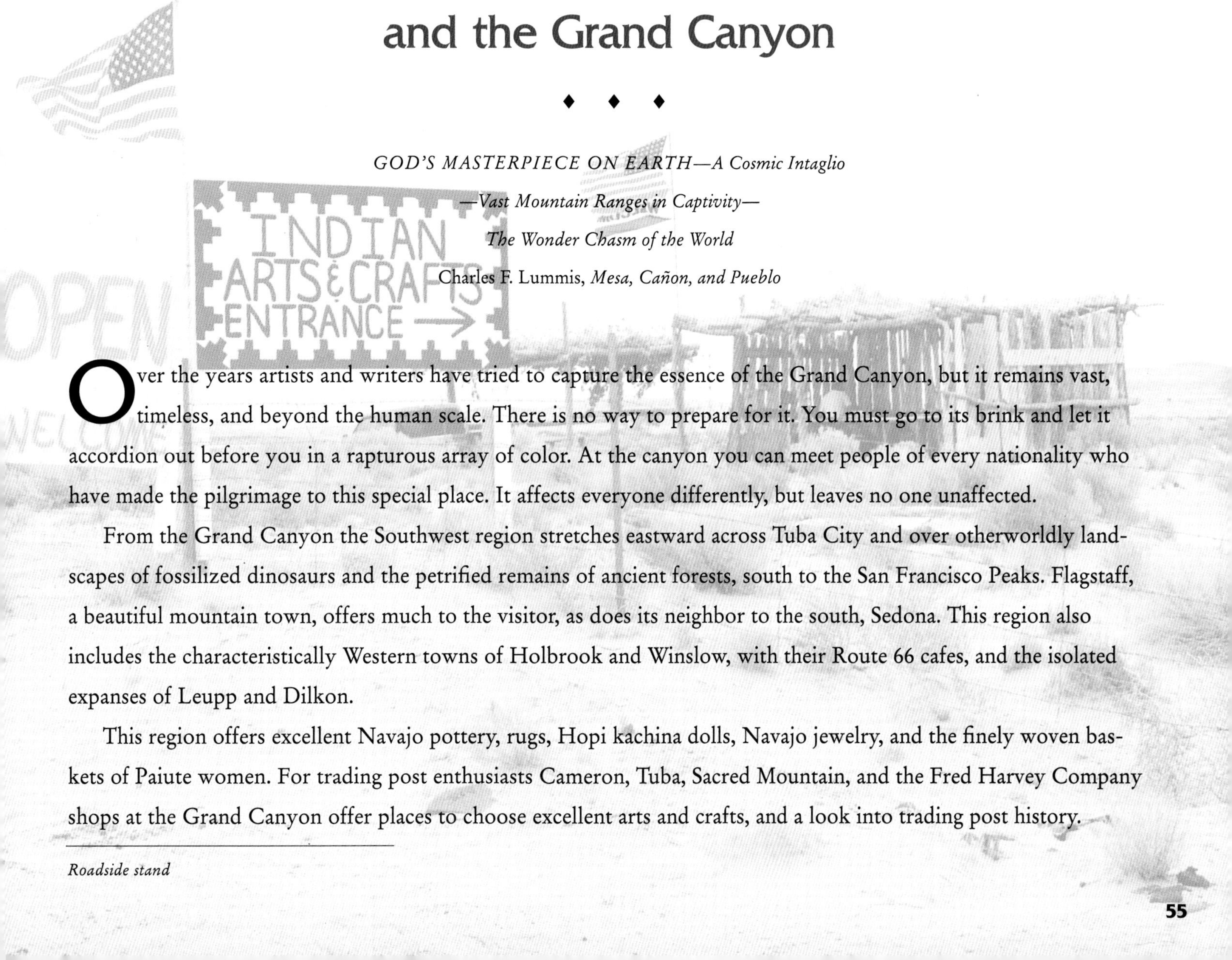

Roadside stand

TUBA CITY AND SURROUNDING AREA

1. Tuba Trading Post

P.O. Box 247, Tuba City, AZ 86045,
turn northwest towards the main part
of town at the intersection of Hwys
264-160
520-283-5441
Daily: Summer 7:00–8:00, Winter
8:00–7:00 Mountain Standard Time
Owner: Babbitt Brothers Trading
Company; manager: Janette Nuckols
♦ M, V, D, AE, C, S, HA, I

Tuba Trading Post was established
in 1870. Its present shape was designed by Samuel Preston in 1905 in
partnership with the Babbitt Brothers
Trading Company. The historic two-
story, octagonal building carries

BELOW: *Tuba Trading Post, Tuba City,
Arizona, 1910.* Photograph courtesy of James
E. Babbitt

BELOW RIGHT: *Tuba Trading Post today*

SAN JUAN SOUTHERN PAIUTES

P.O. Box 1989, Tuba City, AZ 86045
520-283-4587

Some two hundred San Juan
Paiutes live among the Navajos west
of Tuba City at Hidden Springs/Willow
Springs, and in small communities
that stretch north to Navajo Mountain.
Their history has been tragic: a 1918
influenza epidemic, corrupt politi-
cians, and land battles with the
Navajo. Government incompetence
and indifference have left these
people without a designated homeland, swallowed up by the enormous
Navajo Nation. Though small in number, the group fiercely defends and
continues its traditions and culture.

For more than a century, the San
Juan Paiutes have traded their baskets
with the Navajo. Many "Navajo" wedding baskets are actually Paiute baskets. Bill and Dollie Beaver of Sacred

Mountain Trading Post are enthusiastic
advocates for the Paiute basketmakers. Since the early seventies they
have worked to spotlight these talented artists, helping them gain the
recognition they deserve and develop
a stronger market for their work.
Anna Whiskers and the Whiskers/Lehi
family in the Tuba City area create the
lion's share of baskets. North near
Navajo Mountain, the Owl and King
families are building a reputation for
their prolific production of fine baskets. The Beavers have encouraged
the weavers to experiment and create
innovative works for the art market.
Their intricate weave, impeccable
craftsmanship, and design have made
these baskets highly sought after by
collectors. They are also purchased
by the Paiute's Navajo neighbors for
ceremonial use. Those interested in
baskets should become acquainted
with the work of the San Juan Paiutes.

general merchandise; a good selection of topical books and videos; and Pendleton blankets, including difficult-to-find limited editions. The post sells Navajo rugs ($100–$7,000) with a particularly good selection of Storm Pattern, Tree of Life, and Raised Outline; a nice assortment of Hopi kachina dolls; and a wide range of arts and crafts in a skylight-lit setting. B, **Bk**, F, **J**, K, **P**, **R**, S

2. Faye and Emmett Tso: Potters

P.O. Box 583, Tuba City, AZ 86045

Faye and Emmett Tso are active in community and political issues as well as Navajo medicine. They sell herbs across the reservation and are well respected in the Navajo community. They are also prominent potters,

Pot with Yei'ii bichai *dancers, 18", by Faye and Emmett Tso, Tuba City, Arizona*

creating a wide variety of work. They combine efforts to make enormous jars upon which Emmett applies appliqué sculptures of intricately detailed *Yei'ii bichai* dancers. Faye creates small jars, sculpted heads, canteens, and utilitarian ware with corn, *Yei'iis, Yei'ii bichai* dancers, and other motifs. Their clay is collected in an area close to the Hopi Reservation and has a yellow color that is absent from the work of the Shonto area potters. Faye adds a pigment to darken the color, so at times her pots appear a dark red.

Faye has been generous in demonstrating and teaching her crafts (she also weaves rugs). She enjoys the opportunity to share her knowledge with others and will take special orders. You can usually find some good examples of the Tso's work at Bill Beaver's Sacred Mountain Trading Post.

3. Van's Trading Company

P.O. Box 7, Tuba City, AZ 86045, 1 mile south of Tuba City on Hwy 160

520-283-5343

M–Sat 9:00–6:00, Sun 11:00–5:00

Owners: Danny and Judy Van Keuren; managers: Lucky and Shannon Mokhesi

♦ M, V, D, AE, C, S, HA

The arts and crafts department is in the southwest corner of this vast supermarket. There is a dead pawn auction on the fifteenth of every

month at 3:00. They have a large selection of Navajo rugs ($250–$2,300 with one $11,000 rug), which is especially strong in Storm Pattern and Two Grey Hills rugs. They also carry beadwork, Navajo and some Pueblo pottery, a small selection of jewelry and unusual silver objects such as boxes, spoons, letter openers, and pens. One Easter we found a large pen filled with hundreds of pastel-dyed baby chicks for sale. B, D, F, **J**, **K**, **P**, **R**, S

4. San Juan Southern Paiute Yingup Weavers Association

P.O. Box 1989, Tuba City, AZ 86045

520-283-4587

In 1985 Bill Beaver of Sacred Mountain Trading Post arranged for an exhibition of his collection of San Juan Paiute baskets at the Wheelwright Museum of the American Indian in Santa Fe. The School of American Research bought the collection, and the exhibition attracted interest. The San Juan Paiutes formed a cooperative and today sell baskets through the mail.

SELECTED SAN JUAN SOUTHERN PAIUTE ARTISTS/CRAFTSPEOPLE

RoseAnn Whiskers, Helen, or Grace Lehi, 520-283-4587, 520-283-4815—Baskets.

CAMERON

5. Cameron Trading Post and Gallery

P.O. Box 339, Cameron, AZ 85200, 25 miles southwest of Tuba City at Jct of Hwy 89N-Hwy 64
800-338-7385
Daily: Summer: 6:00–10:00, Winter: 7:00–9:00
Owners: Atkinson Trading Company and employees; manager: Mike Davis
♦ M, V, AE, C, S, HA

Cameron Trading Post was established by Hubert and C.D. Richardson in 1916, and is a must-stop for visitors to the Southwest Navajo Reservation. Cameron tries to maintain the ambiance of an old trading post while selling an array of groceries, general merchandise, western wear, and souvenirs for travelers and locals. The post continues to expand and maintains a large inventory of work by Navajo, Hopi, Paiute, Tohono O'odham, Apache, and Pueblo artists. Weaver Jean Mann often demonstrates rug weaving in the rear of the post. You should be aware of the occasional African basket or Mexican rug. Usually these are clearly marked.

The grounds are divided into a trading post (with contemporary arts and crafts, souvenirs, and dining room); motel (made of the original rock walls); terraced gardens designed by Mabel Richardson; and gallery. The original

Cameron Trading Post

hotel and trader's quarters now form the Collectors' Gallery, where you'll find a beautiful display of antique and contemporary Native American and western items available at the Collectors' Auction. There is a preview on Friday with a live auction Saturday and Sunday of that weekend. An illustrated auction catalog is available. This auction is an anticipated event for collectors across the Southwest and beyond.

Cameron is still a vital part of the region—buying wool and piñons and serving as a center for many local activities. A major part of the post is employee owned, with every Navajo clan represented. Joe Atkinson, grandnephew of C.D. Richardson, runs Cameron today. Joe is proud of the post, its operations, and employees: "We are like a large family. We share traditions, celebrations, and daily life."
B, **Bk**, C, **D**, F, I, **J**, **K**, M, **P**, Pt, **R**, S, Sp, Sv

6. Navajo Arts and Crafts Enterprise

P.O. Box 464, Cameron, AZ 85200, 30 miles south of Tuba City on Hwy 89
520-679-2244
M–F 8:00–6:00, Sat–Sun 8:00–5:00
Manager: Marilyn Reeves
♦ M, V, D, AE, C, S, HA (one step and gravel)

This small branch of the larger Navajo Arts and Crafts Enterprise in Window Rock carries commercially dyed wool, jewelry supplies, and Navajo rugs (about twenty, $150–$1,800). You will find Navajo and Hopi music cassettes; Pendletons; cradleboards; Navajo, Hopi, and Zuni jewelry; Navajo pottery; sandpaintings; and a changing assortment of arts and crafts.
B, Bk, C, **J**, P, **R**, Sp, Indian-designed t-shirts

> Cameron Trading Post is still a vital part of the community. It buys wool and piñons, provides a garden for local weddings, and throws an annual Christmas party for over four hundred people. The bridge that appears to be built of an erector set was constructed in 1911, and is the reason the post was located here.

7. The Watchtower at Desert View, Grand Canyon National Park

Hwy 64, Desert View, Grand Canyon, AZ 86023, near the east entrance
520-638-2736, trading post: 638-3150
Daily: Summer: 8:00–8:00,
Winter: 9:00–5:00, tower closes 1/2 hour before the store
Owners: Fred Harvey Company, Amfac Parks Resorts, manager: Anna Marie Galligan
♦ M, V, D, AE, C, S, HA (store only)

The Watchtower, built in 1932 by the Fred Harvey Company and the Santa Fe Railroad, was designed by Mary Elizabeth Jane Colter. The structure was inspired by the towers that haunt various ruins across the Southwest. Colter researched different sites and reflected the work of prehistoric stonemasons in her ambitious structure. Be sure to appreciate the Hopi Room's paintings by renowned Hopi artist Fred Kabotie.

The Watchtower can get crowded, and it's easy to overlook details of the densely filled interior and the overflowing inventory of Zuni fetishes; Navajo and Pueblo pottery; Hopi kachina dolls; Navajo rugs; and Hopi, Navajo, and Tohono O'odham baskets. Five display cases reflect the building's circular design and offer an array of jewelry, including old pawn.

Desert View Watchtower, Grand Canyon. The Watchtower is the creation of architect Mary Elizabeth Jane Colter. Her visionary work at the Grand Canyon also includes Hopi House, Hermit's Rest, the Lookout Studio, Bright Angel Lodge, and the Phantom Ranch

---

The Watchtower contains intimate details, beautiful little niches, and wonderful objects. Repeated visits will reveal new surprises. It also offers reflectoscopes to observe the canyon in greater detail. Allow plenty of time to view Colter's architectural achievement. The canyon can produce its own weather, so if you plan to visit in the winter, call ahead. Storms can close the road.
B, Bk, F, **J, K, P, R**, S, **Sv**

8. Verkamp's

P.O. Box 96, Grand Canyon, AZ 86023, on the South Rim opposite El Tovar Hotel
520-638-2242
Daily: Summer: 8:00–7:00,
Winter: 9:00–6:00
President: John Verkamp III
♦ M, V, AE, S, HA

John George Verkamp was the first curio dealer at the Grand Canyon, selling goods from a tent store in 1898. The present building, built in 1906, is on the National Register of Historic Places. It retains its Mission-style interior and displays a variety of collectable souvenirs and Native American arts and crafts. Among the inventory are some unusual finds: Havasupai baskets, Maricopa pottery, Apache beadwork, a selection of mineral specimens, Apache beaded necklaces, and an impressive jewelry selection that includes Hopi overlay, Navajo sandcast, contemporary Navajo inlay, Zuni, and Santo Domingo work. Third-generation John and Michael Verkamp note that

---

Verkamp's, South Rim, Grand Canyon Village

Main sales room, Hopi House, 1905. Photograph courtesy of Grand Canyon National Park #11,426

their staff is experienced with the stock and can provide information about the area. Be sure to notice the 1907 painting of the Grand Canyon by Louis Akin and the 535-pound meteorite discovered near Meteor Crater, Arizona.

B, Bk, D, **J**, K, **P**, **R**, S, Sp, Sv, Mineral Specimens

9. Hopi House

#1 Main St., Grand Canyon, AZ 86023, next to El Tovar Hotel

520-638-2631 (central switchboard)
Daily: Summer: 8:00–8:00,
Winter: 8:00–6:00
Owner: Fred Harvey Company; manager: Angie Kenoyer
♦ M, V, D, AE, C, S, HA (ramp can be set up), Diners

The Hopi House was designed by architect Mary Jane Colter for the Fred Harvey Company in 1905 to serve as the main sales area for Indian arts and crafts at Grand Canyon Village. Built by Hopi workers in the

style of pueblo buildings at Old Oraibi, the Hopi House served as a place where visitors could watch traditional potters, weavers, and silversmiths at work. Until the thirties, craftspeople such as Nampeyo lived and worked on the premises. Today the rambling series of rooms displays a cornucopia of goods from contemporary Native American crafts to work from South America. There is a large selection of Hopi, Navajo, Apache, and Havasupai baskets, rugs, Zuni fetishes, woodcarvings, pottery from every pueblo, and jewelry. If you venture to a remote back corner, you will find a tiny room with some dazzling older jewelry and other items. Remodeling in 1995 allows visitors on the second story gallery, which had been closed to the public since 1955. The kiva remains closed.

Elizabeth Compton Hegemann, in her book *Navajo Trading Days*, states:

> *Hopi House itself was a deluxe curio or Indian crafts shop. No Japanese-made Indian curios were handled (if such were produced at this time [1920s]) nor were the Denver and Albuquerque mass-produced items of Indian silver jewelry. Only true handmade silver jewelry from the Navaho, Zuñi, or other tribal silversmiths was sold, and the Fred Harvey name was protection enough for any buyer.*

B, Bk, D, I, **J**, **K**, **P**, **R**, **S**, Sp, Sv

Canyon Trading Post, Williams, Arizona

10. Red Lake Campground and High Country Mercantile

Hwy 64, Williams, AZ 86046, 10 miles north of Williams
520-635-9122; 800-581-4753 (reservations only 6:00–10:00 PM)
Daily 6:00–9:00 (hours vary)
Owner: Joseph Petrillo;
manager: Sharon Post
♦ M, V, D, T, S, HA (one step)

Sharon and Joseph run a friendly little store that supplies travelers and campers with groceries, gas, and propane. They also have unusual leather medicine bags, Pendleton blanket material, crystal beadwork by Alice Tso Begay, Navajo rugs by local weaver Mary Bighorse Knight, treasure bead jewelry by Bobby Esplaine, woodcarvings by Harold Spencer, Casas Grandes pottery, Mexican throws, two cabinets of jewelry, and other unusual items created by local artisans. They also carry locally made reproductions of Santo Domingo depression jewelry.

In the Southwest, treasures are found in obscure places. It would be easy to rush by this little modern structure. We suggest a stop.
J, P, R, S

11. Canyon Trading Post

64 Sunset Strip, Williams, AZ 86046, milepost 190, Hwy 64
520-635-2787
Owner: Mitch M. Sobczak
Daily: Sunrise to sunset
♦ M, V, D, AE, T, S, HA (ramp next to restaurant)

This enormous sprawling business is really a family operation. Mitch, originally from Poland, came to the United States in 1980. After four years in Chicago, he came to the Southwest and rented this post. He cooks Polish sausage, bakes his own bread, and serves Polish dishes in an intimate cafe that is lined with license plates and mounted longhorns. He loves to chat with visitors and insists that you try his latest culinary efforts.

The curio shop is an expanse of souvenirs that includes Mexican weavings, tarantulas and rattlesnakes mounted in resin, old sandpaintings, wildlife drawings by Alfred Watchman, and a large display of minerals and fossils. The same curious Navajo wooden dolls, carved coconut heads, and petrified wood bola ties might well have been contemplated by visitors here in the 1950s.
D, J, R, Sp, Sv

SEDONA

12. Hoel's Indian Shop

9440 N. Hwy 89A, Sedona, AZ 86336, 10 miles north of Sedona
520-282-3925
Daily 9:30–5:00 (call ahead)
Owner: Nita Hoel;
managers: David and Carol Watters
♦ M, V, AE, C, S

Hoel's Indian Shop was started by Don Hoel in 1950. This shop continues its reputation for high-quality, handmade southwestern items. Pots are all handmade, and slipcast pottery is not sold here. They usually have work by Joseph Lonewolf, Maria

Martinez, and Nampeyo. They stock many Navajo rugs and are particularly proud of the natural dyed rugs by Lillie Taylor in a variety of patterns including pictorials with faces and pottery. Also represented are jewelers Thomas Curtis, Boyd Tsosie, Carl Clark, Al and Kee Nez, Charles Morris (overlay), and Cheryl Yestewa (hand-cut and polished turquoise and coral beads), and Hopi carver Michael Talahytewa. All jewelry is made with natural stones, and Carol Watters says they carry the most beautiful turquoise in the Southwest. Baskets include new Hopi coilwork and old collectables from the Apache, Tohono O'odham, and Pima tribes. Hoel's has a good reputation for securing high-quality work, and they welcome phone orders.
B, J, K, P, R

13. Garland's Indian Jewelry

P.O. Box 1848, Sedona, AZ 86339, at Indian Gardens, 4 miles north of Sedona on Hwy 89A,
3953 N. Hwy 89A
Daily 10:00–5:00
520-282-6632
Owner: William (Bill) Garland

♦ Unspecified credit cards,C, S, HA
Garland's stone exterior opens into a lodgepole viga and cedar interior that is an ideal setting for one of the finest jewelry selections in the Southwest. They buy direct from top artists. We were dazzled by Jesse Monongye's

Bill Garland in front of Garland's Indian Jewelry, Indian Gardens in Oak Creek Canyon, Arizona

channel and mosaic jewelry, work by Carl Clark, Henry Shelton, walls of concho belts and bolas, and sixty trays of rings. Available is the prize-winning silver hollowware of White Buffalo along with a surprising amount of rare museum-quality work by artists like Zuni carver Leekya Deyusa, fabulous old squash blossom necklaces, and a fine selection of paintings. Bill, who owned Garland Steel in Phoenix, opened this store in 1985. His wife's father was a trader at Old Red Lake in Tonalea. Out on the south side of the building is a fascinating photographic history of this location when it was named Indian Gardens.

The jewelers we interviewed speak glowingly of Bill. Jesse Monongye reflects, "You feel that Bill really believes in you and your work. He pays what I ask and he always comes through when times are really tough. He wants me to do the very best work I can produce." Indeed, Jesse's words are reflected in the inventory. It has the exalted feeling of work done at the artists' full potential.

Don't hesitate to ask Bill questions about the work or the artists. He speaks with a delight usually reserved for someone showing photos of their grandchildren. This is a great place to stop, and its location in Oak Creek Canyon is beautiful.
B, Bk, J, P, Pt

14. Jesse Monongye: Jeweler

(available at Garland's Indian Jewelry)
6102 E. Charter Oak Rd., Scottsdale, AZ 85254
602-991-2598, FAX and business

Jesse was born and grew up in the Two Grey Hills/Newcomb area. He remembers, "I loved growing up there. My friends and I would ride bareback and have jackrabbit stampedes. That area is beautiful. I try to use the colors and sunsets of my youth in my work today." Jesse's work is regarded by many as the most ambitious and innovative jewelry being created today. His mosaic work is unparalleled in its precise elegance, and his materials are always the finest available.

When asked how much planning goes into his work he answers, "My grandmother was a weaver. She told me that spiritual thought is what counts. If you draw out your design you release it. Because of this she always worked with a very rough diagram instead of a finished drawing. I agree with her so I like to work from one stage to the next in my work without a drawing of the design."

Jesse has established his studio in

Jesse Monongye, Jeweler, Santa Fe Indian Market. "Craftsmen make the same designs and that can burn them out; artisans keep changing and never burn out; they keep themselves challenged. They constantly improve themselves." —JESSE MONONGYE

Scottsdale. His work is available there, at Santa Fe Indian Market, and at Garland's Indian Jewelry in Sedona. He welcomes special orders and inquiries.

15. Garland's Navajo Rugs

P.O. Box 851, Sedona, AZ 86339, 411 Hwy 179
520-282-4070
M–Sat 10:00, Sun 11:00–5:00
Owner: Dan Garland
♦ M, V, C, S, HA

If you're an established collector or someone just learning about Navajo rugs, you can't find a better place to stop than here. Open since 1976, Garland's Navajo Rugs has the largest selection of historic and contemporary weavings in the country. Thousands of rugs are hung by category and size in a vast showroom. The visitor can rapidly see many rugs as easily as turning pages in a book. This is a great place to learn about the various patterns and variations possible within each pattern. The staff is friendly, knowledgeable, and patient. You will never feel pressured here. Artists come from all over the Navajo reservation to sell their work, ranging in price from $200 to $30,000. Garland's has a good relationship with the artists, resulting in excellent-quality rugs at fair prices. Many fine kachina carvers are also represented, with more than 200 dolls on display. We were very impressed with those of

Bird pictorial rug, 36" x 25", Daisy Nockideneh, Cedar Ridge, Arizona. Courtesy of Garland's Navajo Rugs, Sedona, Arizona

Arthur Holmes. Ask to see the Antique Collector's Room containing pottery, artifacts, old wearing blankets, rugs, and baskets.

Dan's father, Bill, owns Garland's Indian Jewelry, four miles north of Sedona. The two shops complement each other and represent one of the best inventories of Indian arts and crafts in the country. If you have specific interests, be sure to ask. The inventory is so vast that it's easy to miss items. **B**, Bk, **K, P, R**

16. Many Hands Gallery

P.O. Box 10089, 301 Hwy 179,
Sedona, AZ 86339
520-282-1060
M–Sat 11:00–5:00, Sun 12:00–4:00
Owners: Ken and Cathy Osborn
♦ M, V, D, C, S, will accommodate HA

The emphasis of this gallery is jewelry, pottery, and kachina dolls. They represent artists from the fourteen pottery families documented in Rick Dillingham's influential book, *Fourteen Families in Pueblo Pottery.* They also carry work by Navajo, Hopi, and other Native American jewelers including the Yellowhorse family, Boyd and Richard Tsosie, Andy Kirk, Lionel Yellowhorse, Al Nez, and others.

J, P, K

17. Blue-eyed Bear

299 N. Hwy 89A, Sedona, AZ 86336
520-282-1158
M–Sat 9:00–5:30, Sun 10:00–5:00
Manager: Bud Johnson
♦ M, V, AE, S, HA

Blue-eyed Bear is particularly proud of their impressive selection of Navajo jewelry, featuring Ray Tracey, Robert Taylor, Brian and Alvin Tso, and Jimmy King, Jr.

Bk, **J**, P, R, Sp

HIGHWAY 89 NORTH OF FLAGSTAFF

18. Gray Mountain Trading Post

P.O. Box 29100, Gray Mountain, AZ 86016, on Hwy 89, 8 miles south of Cameron
520-679-2203
Daily: Summer: 6:00–10:00,
Winter: 7:00–8:00
Managers: Randy and Patty Wolff, and Gloria Begay
♦ M, V, D, AE, C, S, HA

This post is heavily stocked with souvenir items, books, cards, and

Trader Bill Beaver, Sacred Mountain Trading Post, north of Flagstaff, Arizona

videos to appeal to Grand Canyon travelers. They also carry about 150 Navajo rugs ($80–$2,000) with an emphasis on the Storm Pattern preferred by the local weavers. Navajo, Hopi, and Zuni jewelry shares the display case with some interesting old pawn and Hopi kachina dolls.

B, Bk, D, **J**, K, P, **R**, **Sv**

19. Hank's Trading Post

HC 33, Box 446-A, Hwy 89N,
Flagstaff, AZ 86004, 17 miles south of Cameron
520-679-2357
Daily 8:00–10:00
Owners: Joe Freeman and Peggy Bradford
♦ M, V, C, HA

This business combines a gas station, bar, grocery store, and arts and crafts business. The Freemans bought it in 1988. A post has been on this site since 1963. The inventory of horse tack, saddles, Pendletons, beadwork, rugs, and interesting stone inlay knives is aimed at local clientele. Hank's also carries some local alabaster sculpture, slipcast pottery, and paintings.

B, D, J, K, P, Pt, S, Sp, Sv

20. Sacred Mountain Trading Post

HC-33, Box 436, Flagstaff, AZ 86004, on Hwy 89N, about 20 miles north of Flagstaff
520-679-2255
M–Sat 9:00–5:00, Sun 10:00–5:00,

Sign for Sacred Mountain Trading Post, north of Flagstaff, Arizona. Hand-tinted photograph

Winter: closed Sun
Owners: Bill and Dollie Beaver
♦ T, S, HA

Sacred Mountain Trading Post was opened by the Blevins family in 1915. Bill Beaver took over in 1960 and still operates the post. Bill fell in love with Navajo pottery while working at Chaco Canyon in the forties. In 1951 he worked at Shonto Trading Post, where he befriended the Shonto-area potters. When he moved to Sacred Mountain, he continued enthusiastically to promote the Shonto potters. He remembers:

Tom Bahti of Tucson bought some of the first pieces. Things really took off when Grover Turner took the pots on the road, increasing sales. When he returned with unsold pots and orders for others, Navajo pottery was affected by the dollar market for the first time. Potters made work for specific orders, creating a profusion of work that sold well. The potters made animal figures and pots with the traditional biyó *design around the collar.*

The Navajo wedding vase with its two spouts is considered to be an object immediately associated with the Navajos. Surprisingly, Bill said these were first created in 1972. In the 1970s, pottery was being embellished with a wide variety of motifs including corn, scenes from Navajo life, and assorted animals, but horned toads continued to sell the best.

> **Bill Beaver needs to be singled out and recognized for the revival of Navajo pottery. He was very significant, he did it all, and really encouraged the potters. He also worked hard to get the Paiutes the recognition they deserve and to establish the distinction between them and the Navajos.**
> **—JAMES E. BABBITT, Babbitt Brothers Trading Company**

Alice Cling reacted to the pottery embellishment. Bill calls Alice "the Nampeyo of Navajo pottery" (referring to the famous Hopi potter). Alice refined and simplified her own work, burnishing the pots to a rich sheen. Decoration was sometimes added, but always in moderation. Alice's work drew enormous attention. Interest in Navajo pottery has grown ever since.

At Sacred Mountain you will find wooden shelves deeply stacked with the work of the Claws, the Manygoats family, Lorena Bartlett, Alice Cling, Faye Tso, Louise Goodman, Lorraine Williams, Rose Williams, and other Navajo potters.

Navajo pottery is increasing in popularity. It captures the viewer with its rich amber pitch surface and fire-clouds. It continues to be one of the best values in southwestern arts and crafts. A visit to Sacred Mountain Trading Post allows you to survey the best work being created today and to meet one of the reservation's most influential, modest, and charming traders. Bill also carries Hopi, Navajo, and Paiute baskets, Hopi kachina dolls, and bead supplies.
B, J, **K**, **P**

FLAGSTAFF

21. **Museum of Northern Arizona**
Rte 4, Box 720, 3001 N. Fort Valley Rd., Flagstaff, AZ 86001, Hwy 180 to the Grand Canyon
520-779-1703 (shop); -5213 (bookstore)
Daily 9:00–5:00
Manager: Steven Pickle (shop); Bonnie Shattuck (bookstore)
♦ M, V, D, AE, C, S, HA

The museum, which has collections in archaeology, ethnology, geology, biology, and fine arts (see resource section for more information), also includes a fine shop and bookstore.

The bookstore carries every title imaginable that relates to the Colorado Plateau, from popular titles to obscure scholarly studies. We found books here that we did not find elsewhere. The staff is knowledgeable and friendly.

The Museum Shop extends a 10 percent discount for members and tours. The inventory is carefully chosen with an eye for quality, and represents a well-rounded view of the Southwest. You will find Hopi, Navajo, Zuni, and antique jewelry; a nice selection of Navajo rugs ($50–$12,000); Zuni fetishes; Navajo folk art; Navajo, Hopi, and Apache baskets; alabaster and bronze sculpture; Hopi kachina dolls; Hopi pottery by Dextra Nampeyo and Steve Lucas; paintings by Baje Whitethorne and C. Begay; and occasional one-of-a-kind items. The flat metal sculptures of Joe Lester are very interesting. The museum sponsors impressive exhibitions, allowing the shop to secure top-quality items.
B, D, F, J, K, P, Pt, R, S, t-shirts

22. **Winter Sun Trading Company**
107 N. San Francisco, Ste. 1, Flagstaff, AZ 86001
520-774-2884
M–Sat 9:00–7:00, Sun 10–4
Owner: Phyllis Hogan; manager: Jonathan S. Day
FAX 520-774-0754
www.wintersun.com
◆ All credit cards, C, T, S, HA
Open since 1976, Winter Sun carries Hopi, Zuni, and Navajo arts and crafts, but their main focus is traditional Hopi kachina dolls. Manuel Denet Chavarria, Larry Melendez, Tay Polequaptewa, Fred Ross, Tayron Tsavadawa, Philbert

Honanie, and Danny Denet are represented. Also available are rattles, musical instruments, cedar beads, mud toys, Zuni fetishes, Hopi baskets, and Navajo pottery. An herb shop, with lotions, soaps, and dried herbs, is located in the back of the store. Phyllis is very knowledgeable about Native American herbal remedies.
B, F, J, I, **K**, P

23. **Four Winds Traders**
118 W. Old Route 66, Flagstaff, AZ 86001
520-774-1067
T–Th 9:00–5:00, F 9:00–6:00, Sat 9:00–4:00
Owner: Steve Causer
◆ M, V, D, AE, C, HA
This is not a tourist-oriented business but a pawn shop with 80 percent Indian customers. They carry some old baskets and pottery, but their main stock is jewelry. New items include diamonds and gold jewelry and one of the larger inventories of Native American music in the Southwest.
B, C, **J**, P, **Pawn**

24. **Puchteca Indian Crafts**
20 N. San Francisco, Flagstaff, AZ 86001
520-774-2414
M–Sat 9:00–5:00, Summer: Sun 10:00–4:00
Owner: Steve Beiser
◆ M, V, D, C, S, HA

This twenty-year-old business in downtown Flagstaff carries a variety of work including pottery by Alice Cling, Frog Lady, and the Nampeyo family; Paiute baskets; Hopi kachina dolls; Navajo rugs; and paintings by Harrison Begay and Baje Whitethorne. Owner Steve Beiser has an eye for quality, which is reflected in his inventory.
B, I, J, K, P, Pt, R, S

Babbitt Brothers sign on what is now a sporting goods store, downtown Flagstaff

Billy Betoney, Navajo jeweler, Winslow, Arizona

WINSLOW, HOLBROOK, AND SURROUNDING AREA

25. Billy and Betty Betoney: Jewelers

HC 63, Box 458, Winslow, AZ 86047

Billy and Betty collaborate on their jewelry. He does the silverwork, and she cuts the stones in the manner learned from her parents, who were also jewelers. Billy strives for originality, and in addition to his jewelry he enjoys doing large masonry, murals, and cutout metal signs. They welcome special orders and inquiries.

26. Jimmy and Clara Wilson: Potters

HC 61, Box 70, Winslow, AZ 86047

Jimmy doesn't like to wholesale his pots, so to buy one you must track him down at home, at Santa Fe Indian Market, or possibly at a Navajo fair. His work ranges from inexpensive pipes to large, elaborately decorated vessels. Clara, his wife, also makes small animals. Jimmy began making pots with Clara around 1976. He recalls, "Faye Tso told us to come visit her in Tuba City. She told us to learn it. So we stayed up most of the night learning. She gave us a traditional pot, blessed it, initiated it, and told us to take it home, keep it safe, and never sell it. That is how I began."

Jimmy was born in Leupp in 1935. There isn't any trading post open in Leupp now, but Jimmy remembers the old Sunrise Post: "Old trader McGee would see me herding sheep, and always stop and give me candy, pop, or a bag of oranges and apples. We all liked him. His son took over after him. When he left, people tore the old place down."

Jimmy's pottery is a fine example of the evolution that Navajo pottery has made from utilitarian ware in the 1960s to almost exclusively art pottery in the 1990s. At a recent Santa Fe Indian Market, Jimmy told us he was excited to spend his pottery earnings on a ram for his sheep herd. Jimmy, Clara, and their daughter Laura Blake, also a potter, welcome special orders.

27. Bill Dixon: Painter

2700 Mountain Dr., Winslow, AZ 86047

520-289-0174

Bill, whose work is available at McGee's in Holbrook, is a Navajo painter who deals with subject matter from all tribes. He is particularly interested in pre-Columbian Indians and their symbolism. Using a combination of traditional motifs, abstraction, and realism, Bill works in oil, preferring 24" x 36" to mural size. His work is also available at Honani Gallery at Second Mesa, Arizona.

28. McGee's Beyond Native Tradition Gallery

2114 E. Navajo Blvd., Holbrook, AZ 86047, off I-40, east end of town

520-524-1977

Summer: M–F 8:00–8:00, Sat 9:00–4:00; Winter: M–F 9:00–6:00, Sat 10:00–4:00

Owners: Bruce, Ferron, and Ron McGee and Johnny Kay; manager: Bruce McGee

♦ M, V, D, AE, C, S, HA

Bruce McGee and his family, who are also at Keams Canyon and Piñon, opened this business in 1990 as a showplace for Native American art. The front of the building is designed in traditional pueblo style and the interior is a contemporary gallery with blond oak and whitewashed cases. One of this business's strengths is Hopi crafts. We were impressed with the hard-to-find Hopi wicker by Doris Tawahongva; pottery by the Nampeyo family, Stephen Lucas, and Alton Komalestewa; and kachina dolls by Cecil Calnimptewa. Stock includes both Hopi and Navajo weaving. The McGees are proud of the work of Sarah Begay, who developed the "Beyond Native Tradition" sampler rug, which contains up to thirty-two small rugs on a traditional background ranging from 2' x 3' to 9' x 12'. Howard Nelson creates contemporary jewelry from gold, silver, and gemstones with designs that reflect tradition. Another treat is the work of local painters Richard Gorman and Bill Dixon and sculpture by Harold Davidson, Tomas Dougi, and Doug Hyde. Bruce also has unique collections for sale such as the works collected by Ray Manley.

Bruce is part of the McGee family, whose interest in Native American art began at Keams Canyon around 1940. He states, "I was raised as one of the two Anglo children at Keams until the

Detail from oil painting, 24" x 36", by Bill Dixon, Winslow, Arizona. Photograph courtesy of the artist

fifth grade, and until the age of six, I thought I was Indian." Bruce's babysitter was Fanny Nampeyo, and he considers Nellie Nampeyo his grandma. Bruce says, "When buying art, do it because you love it, not as an investment, and you'll never go wrong."
B, Bk, **J, K, P, Pt, S**

29. Dilkon Trading Post
HC 63 Box F, Star Route, Winslow, AZ 86047, 35 miles north of Winslow and I-40, located 0.5 mile south of Hwy 15 near the junction with HC61
520-657-3342

It's true the landscape forms the mind. If I stand here long enough I'll learn how to sing. None of that country & western heartbreak stuff, or operatic duels, but something cool as the blues, or close to the sound of a Navajo woman singing early in the morning.
—JOY HARJO, *Secrets from the Center of the World*

M–F 8:00–7:00, Sat 9:00–7:00
Owners: Darlene Begaye
♦ T, HA
This out-of-the-way structure was built by J.W. Bush in 1919 and is located in an area with unusual geological formations. The bunkerlike post serves the local community and sells some jewelry and Navajo wooden dolls.   D, J

30. Bitahochee Trading Post
P.O. Box 3218, Indian Wells, AZ 86031, off Hwy 77, 0.25 mile south of Jct with Hwy 15
M–F 9:00–7:00, Sat 9:00–3:00
♦ T, S, HA
The main attraction here is the picturesque old buildings and setting. Cows stroll alongside the gas pumps

69

adding to the laid-back feel of the post. Besides gas and groceries, there is a limited selection of pottery, jewelry, and beadwork. We found a good selection of blankets from the Navajo Textile Mills in Mesa, Arizona, that are 100 percent sheep wool in Navajo and Hopi designs.

P, J, Beadwork, **Blankets**

SOUTHWEST NAVAJO NATION FAIRS:

September: Southwestern Navajo Nation Fair, Dilkon, AZ

October: Western Navajo Fair, Tuba City, AZ

SELECTED SOUTHWEST NAVAJO AND HOPI ARTISTS/CRAFTSPEOPLE

Norman Bia, P.O. Box 3159, Indian Wells, AZ 86031—Jewelry.

Daisy Cody, P.O. Box 2991, Tuba City, AZ 86045—Rugs.

Harold Davidson, 452 Shonto Trail, Flagstaff, AZ 86001, 520-525-1318—Sculpture.

Dilkon Trading Post, north of Winslow, Arizona. Hand-tinted photograph

David Dawangyumptewa, P.O. Box 3327, Flagstaff, AZ 86003, 602-779-3881—Hopi/Navajo painter (gouache, 23K gold leaf, handmade paper, contemporary/traditional).

W.B. Franklin, Roanhorse Productions, P.O. Box 477, Flagstaff, AZ 86002—Contemporary painting (acrylic, oil, mixed media), alabaster and marble sculpture.

Arthur D. Holmes, Sr., P.O. Box 1642, Tuba City, AZ 86045, 520-283-4446—Large, elaborate-action Hopi kachina dolls.

Delbridge Honanie, 1819 N. Turquoise Dr., Flagstaff, AZ 86001, 520-779-5500 (Lorraine Honanie, messages)—Hopi kachina dolls.

Wilson Jim, P.O. Box 871, Holbrook, AZ 86025—Navajo jewelry.

Lucinda Jody, P.O. Box 315, Winslow, AZ 86047—Rugs.

Laura Maloney and Rose Maloney, P.O. Box 234, Cameron, AZ 86020—Weaving, specializes in Storm Pattern.

Crecinda Namoki, P.O. Box 1484, Tuba City, AZ 86045, Hopi kachina dolls.

Ned Nez, P.O. Box 7034, Winslow, AZ 86407-7034—Jewelry.

Third phase chief blanket revival rug, 34" x 36", by Elsie Wilson, Ganado, Arizona. Courtesy of Garland's Navajo Rugs, Sedona, Arizona

Redwing Nez, P.O. Box 3300, indian Wells, AZ 86031, 520-654-3393—Navajo paintings.

Laurence Numkena, P.O. Box 2804, Tuba City, AZ 86045—Hopi kachina dolls.

Loren Phillips, P.O. Box 3044, Tuba City, AZ 86045—Famous for detailed action Hopi kachina dolls.

Susie Slowtalker, P.O. Box 5081, Leupp, AZ—Rugs, specializes in Storm Pattern.

THIRD PHASE CHIEF BLANKET REVIVAL RUGS

Sometimes these are referred to as Hubbel revivals. In the late 1800's Lorenzo Hubbell encouraged weavers in the Ganado area to recreate classic period blankets. Many weavers used the newly introduced Germantown dyes to create revival rugs of brilliant color. today the revival rug is created across the reservation. Weavers see these early revivals with bright Germantown colors and are in essence creating revivals of revivals.
—DAN GARLAND, Garland's Navajo Rugs

Ervin Tso, P.O. Box 3422, Flagstaff, AZ 86003, 520-607-2347—Contemporary one-of-a-kind jewelry (silver/gold, turquoise).

Baje Whitethorne, 5250 N. Hwy 89, Flagstaff, AZ 86001, 520-526-0063—Navajo paintings.

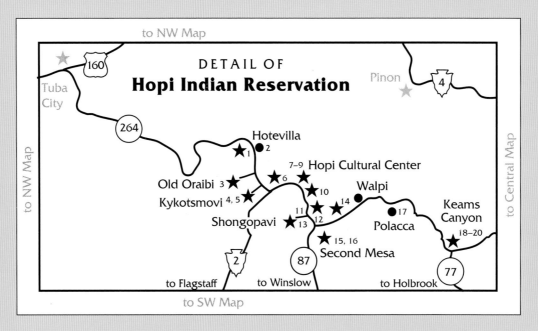

DETAIL OF
Hopi Indian Reservation

LEGEND
★ **Trading Post in this chapter**
★ **Trading Post in other chapter**
● **Other site**

Hopi

◆ ◆ ◆

Scarlet bluffs gather here to drink and watch deer trip down in dusk.

Everything arrives perfectly in time, including snow clouds that bless the earth.

And the moon, the blind eye of an ancient mountain lion who shifts his bones on a starry branch.

Joy Harjo, *Secrets from the Center of the World*

Loloma!

On behalf of the Hopi people, I welcome you to our beautiful homeland. The Hopi have occupied these mesas and surrounding area since time immemorial. In more recent dimensions, the village of Oraibi, is considered the oldest, most continuously inhabited village in the United States.

This arid desert is an oasis of our rich agricultural traditions, cultural values and practices which live on, despite many strong outside influences. This legacy is portrayed in detailed works of unique Hopi art and craftsmanship. May your visit to the "Center of the Universe" be one of fulfillment of our simple way of life.

—Ferrell Secakuku, Chairman, The Hopi Tribe

Aholi and Eototo, lithograph, 18" x 24", by Lowell Talashoma. Courtesy of McGee Traders, Keams Canyon, Arizona

THE HOPI TRIBE
P.O. Box 123, Kykotsmovi, AZ 86039
520-734-2441
**CULTURAL PRESERVATION
OFFICE: 520-734-2441, ext. 202**
Traditional ceremonies are held
throughout the year with no approx-
imate dates.
Walking tour of village of Walpi
(Jct of US 164–AZ 264),
520-737-2262 or 520-737-2670,
daily 9:00–4:30

♦ No photography, videotaping,
sketching, or hiking

The Hopi Tribal government has
no authority over villages or ceremonies. Contact the village chief or
community development office to
obtain information and permission
to attend any ceremonies or enter
a village. The following is a list of
villages and phone numbers, if
available:

**PONSI HALL: 520-737-2262
MISHUNGNOVI: 520-737-2520
SIPAULOVI: 520-737-2570
SHUNGOPAVI: NA
KYKOTSMOVI: 520-734-2474
OLD ORAIBI: NA
HOTEVILLA: 520-734-2420
BACAVI: 520-734-9360
MOENKOPI UPPER/LOWER:
520-283-6684**

OLD ORAIBI, HOTEVILLA, AND KYKOTSMOVI

1. **Monongya Gallery**
P.O. Box 287, Old Oraibi Village,
AZ 86039
520-734-2344, -2544
M–Sat 9:00–5:00, Sun 10:00–4:00
Owner: Von Monongya
♦ M, V, AE, C, S, HA
This gallery sits isolated on the
west end of Hopiland, but it's worth
seeking out. In a modern gallery setting, Von Monongya has assembled an
impressive selection of more than 200
kachina dolls done by established
carvers and by younger artists. If you
plan to purchase a kachina doll, we
recommend that you look here before
you make a final decision.

Monongya's engages in wholesale
and retail.
B, Bk, C, **J**, **K**, **P**

*Tawaquoptewa, Chief of Old Oraibi, Hopi
Kachina doll carver.* Photograph by J.H.
McGibbeny, courtesy of Special Collections,
University of Utah Library (hand-tinted)

2. Rick Honyouti: Furniture, Cedar Chest Maker

P.O. Box 994, Hotevilla, AZ 86030
520-734-2528

Rick is a carpenter by trade. He warmly reflects, "I helped my dad make all sorts of projects. He taught me a lot. He could take some old wood crates and turn them into beautiful things." Rick started to make peyote boxes and containers for ceremonial clothes and shawls. Soon his creativity spread to benches, cedar-lined blanket chests, coffee tables, and a wide assortment of custom work. He has

Rick Honyouti and his cedar chests, Hotevilla, Arizona

an impeccable design sense and intuitively creates softly stained designs to fit each piece. He is a member of the Greasewood Clan and his brothers carve kachina dolls. Although a newcomer to the art market, Rick shows a mature elegance in his work that is rapidly creating a healthy reputation for him. Rick takes special orders and is willing to do custom design work. He can ship his work anywhere.

3. Old Oraibi Crafts

P.O. Drawer 193, Old Oraibi Village, AZ 86039
Daily 9:00–6:00, hours vary in winter
Owner: Sandra Hamana

This is the home of the Hopi dawa and kachina wall decor made by Sandra Hamana and her son, Rod Davis. The artwork represents facial features of various kachinas and radiates outward in colorful geometric patterns. They make miniature dawas as bola ties and pins. Also for sale are beaded hat bands, gourd rattles, coiled and wicker baskets, and Anthony Honahnie's prints and watercolors. They carry unusual double-faced Hopi overlay pendants and beautiful charm bracelets by Dorothy Koyasyousie.

This business opened in 1987. As in the rest of Old Oraibi, the building has an ancient elegance. Old Oraibi is conservative and wishes to maintain its quiet traditional ways. Visitors are asked to park at the shop and ask for

information before visiting the village.
B, Bk, K, **J**, K, P, Pt

4. Sockyma's Arts and Crafts

P.O. Box 96, Kykotsmovi, AZ 86039
M–Sat 9:00–5:00
Owners: Michael C. Sockyma, Sr., and Theodora Sockyma
♦ M, V, D, AE, C, S, HA (difficult)

The Sockymas opened this retail-only business in the mid-fifties. They specialize in custom designs and overlay work made from sterling silver or 14K gold. The entire family makes jewelry, and at least one of them will likely be at work at a sunlit bench when you visit. They seem to be lost in their craft at times as they work the small labyrinth sawcuts. The jewelry here is meticulous and first rate. Inexpensive carved gourd earrings by Annette Sockyma, kachina dolls made by daughter Michele, pottery from First Mesa, and music cassettes round out the inventory. We especially enjoyed the jewelry displayed among beautiful pot sherds from the area. Theodora is a Hopi medicinewoman and is well known in the area for her traditional healings.
Bk, C, **J**, K, P

5. Calnimptewa's Gallery

P.O. Box 37, Kykotsmovi, AZ 86039
520-734-2406
Summer: M–F 9:00–6:00,
Sat and Holidays 10:00–6:00

Winter: M–F 10:00–5:00,
Sat 9:00–5:00
Owner: Cecil Calnimptewa, Jr.

♦ M, V, C, S, HA

Cecil Calnimptewa is a kachina doll carver of great reputation and respect. A visit to his modern gallery is an opportunity to purchase a kachina doll direct from the carver.

Besides Cecil's beautiful carving, you will also see kachina dolls by other carvers, medium-sized alabaster Navajo sculpture, flutes, Rick Honyouti's superb blanket chests, and other work that Cecil believes in. Cecil opened his gallery in 1981, and the inventory changes over time. He wholesales and retails.

B, I, J, **K**, P, Pt, R, S, Sv

SECOND MESA

6. Hopi Arts and Crafts Silver Craft Cooperative Guild

P.O. Box 37, Second Mesa, AZ 86043
Daily: Summer: 8:00–6:00,
Winter: 8:00–5:00
Executive Director: Milland Lomakema, Sr.

♦ M, V, AE, C, S, HA, I

Many of the finest Hopi jewelers started their careers with the guild. Overlay jewelry is the focus. There is a tremendous selection, and there is an informative pamphlet available on overlay jewelry and its symbolism.

Many jewelers can be found at work here, and they are eager to educate visitors in the steps of production. All work other than jewelry is made in the artisans' homes and brought here for retail.

There is a permanent display in many of the cases with jewelry by master jewelers from the guild's collection. Some old copper pieces are particularly interesting. The cases also contain an array of Hopi pot sherds.

The guild sells wholesale, but advance application is advised.

B, **J**, K, P

7. Hopi Cultural Center

P.O. Box 67, Second Mesa, AZ 86043
520-734-2421

Artists can often be found selling items in the parking area of the Center. Carvers sell kachina dolls from their trucks, and women offer small souvenir items. The Center, opened in 1972, has motel rooms (reservations are necessary) and a restaurant open 7 AM to 9 PM with inexpensive Hopi and American dishes. Shops in the Center (listed below) offer a variety of items.

8. Hopi Cultural Center Museum

(at the Cultural Center)
P.O. Box 7, Second Mesa, AZ 86043
520-734-6650
M–F 8:00–5:00, weekends 9:00–3:00,
closed weekends in winter
Admission fee

Weaver Selina suggests that you look for clean cutting, soldering, and finish in overlay jewelry. He says, "Art talks to the people for you. My designs are always my own, and I create each piece as good as I can make it."

The museum offers a glimpse into the Hopi peoples' history on the three mesas.

B, J, K, P

9. Bear Strap

P.O. Box 683, Second Mesa, AZ 86043,
in the Hopi Cultural Center, shop #2
Daily 9:00–6:00
Owner: Violet Laban

◆ M, V, AE, C, S, HA

Unlike the other shops at the cultural center, this shop carries work from other pueblos, and Tohono O'odham, and Plains Indians. The business was very open about including Zapotec weavings of Navajo designs. Pendleton blankets, silver supplies, and assorted gift items round out the small inventory.

B, J, K, P, R

10. **Is-Ka-Sok-Pu**
(The Burping Coyote)
P.O. Box 329, Second Mesa, AZ 86043, 1.5 miles east of the Hopi Cultural Center
520-734-9353 or 9361
Owner: Iva Lee Casuse
◆ M, V, C, S, HA (with difficulty)

This business operates out of a 16' x 20' building. Owner Iva Lee Casuse is very enthusiastic, and she is proud to be the source of Leonard James Hawk's work. Hawk creates contemporary designs that incorporate turquoise, coral, sugilite, lapis, and opal. Hawk is originally from the Yakima Tribe of Washington but currently lives at Second Mesa with his family. His designs have a refreshing, bright, clean quality.

You will also find gourd rattles, a large selection of Hopi overlay jewelry, kachina dolls, and an ever-changing collection of traditional and contemporary jewelry. Prices are

Kachina dolls, Tsakurshovi, Second Mesa, Arizona. Hand-tinted photograph

set, and negotiating is discouraged. Wholesale and retail.

J, K, P

11. **Selina Hopi Silver Arts**
and Crafts
P.O. Box 726, Second Mesa, AZ 86043
Daily: Summer: 8:00–7:00,
Winter: 9:00–5:00
520-734-6695
Owners: Weaver and Alberta Selina
◆ M, V, C, S, HA (3 steps)

Weaver Selina has been a jeweler since 1967. He moved into his modern studio/shop in 1993. He sells

overlay jewelry of impeccable design and execution. The Selinas' inventory also includes kachina dolls, rattles, pottery, coil and wicker plaques, baskets, textiles, and books on Hopi. They have set prices and discourage bargaining; wholesale and retail.

B, Bk, J, K, P

12. **Tsakurshovi**
P.O. Box 234, Second Mesa, AZ 86043, located 1.5 miles east of the Hopi Cultural Center on Hwy 264
520-734-2478
Daily: Summer: 8:00–6:00,

Winter: 9:00–5:00

Owners: Janice and Joseph Day

Opened in 1988, this small shop should not be missed. It is the home of the "Don't Worry—Be Hopi" t-shirt. The Days are true advocates for the old-style kachina dolls. This shop avoids flashy work and has chosen to carry work with integrity and strong ties to tradition. It is a popular emporium for locals who shop here for *quotsvi* (culinary ash that Janice says is better than baking soda), deer hooves, piki bread (a very thin blue corn bread made from water, ash, and corn), kilts, rattles, sashes, shoulder shells, pelts, Hopi coiled baskets, plaques and yucca sifters, and Native American Church paraphernalia. Ron Preston, who is half Hopi, half Apache, is a good friend of the Days and makes traditional arrows, shields, rattles, bags, and amazing war bonnets for the shop.

The walls of Tsakurshovi are lined with kachina dolls by Manuel Chavarria, Clark Tenakhongva, Philbert Honanie, and Bert Tsavadawa. If you are not familiar with the resurgence of old-style dolls, this is the place to be baptized into the fold. Even if you don't purchase a thing, Joseph will supply you with a few great jokes before leaving. The Days have created a shop that has a wonderful energy and a personable atmosphere.

B, Bk, J, **K**, P

13. Dawa's

P.O. Box 127, Shungopavi, Second Mesa, AZ 86043

520-734-2430

Daily 8:00–5:00

Owner: Bernard Dawahoya

♦ T, C, S (no pottery or kachina dolls), HA

This family business opened in 1960. A back room exhibits Bernard's beautiful jewelry. The front room features daughters Carol and Berna's charming Christmas ornaments, and Carol's dance tablitas (she will make them to order). Bernard's wife Alice helps with the jewelry and also makes coiled baskets. She does not take special orders but instead says they are something she does when she is in the mood. If you are lucky you might find one nearly finished when you visit.

B, J, K, P

14. Honani Crafts Gallery

P.O. Box 221, Second Mesa, AZ 86043, Just off Hwy 264, 0.25 mile west of Hwy 87

520-737-2238

Daily: Summer: 8:00–6:00,

Winter: 8:00–5:00

Owner: King Honani

♦ M, V, C, S, HA, I

King Honani's retail/wholesale gallery carries a full inventory. The gallery is especially proud of the spectacular gold jewelry. Much of the work on display was made in the jewelry studio next door, and the gallery encourages visitors to ask questions and watch the jewelers at work. They also carry Navajo and Zuni jewelry, pottery, and Hopi textiles. We found the staff to be friendly and helpful. There are set prices here and bargaining is discouraged.

B, Bk, **J**, K, P, Pt, Sv, Hopi textiles

15. Hopi Gallery

P.O. Box 316, Second Mesa, AZ 86043, Jct Hwys 264-87

Kachina doll carver Lowell Talashoma, Second Mesa, Arizona

Daily: Summer: 8:00–6:00,
Winter 8:30–5:00
Owner: Phil Sekaquaptewa

♦ M, V, D, AE, C, S, HA

Phil runs a retail/wholesale business and says he is willing to negotiate on prices. In addition to his fine contemporary jewelry, you will find local crafts and piki bread.

He also stocks items usually purchased by the locals: skunk, bobcat, and fox furs; rattles; musical rasps; cottonwood; and shells. He also sells bows and arrows that are popular with children. Phil silversmiths on the premises and can be observed from the gallery area.

Bk, F, I, **J**, K, M, P

16. Lowell Talashoma: Kachina Doll Carver

P.O. Box 693, Second Mesa, AZ 86043
520-737-2371

Lowell carves intricate sculptures of kachinas that are animated with strong gestures. Lowell reflects on his childhood:

Born in 1950, I spent my early years in Salt Lake City. I carved a rifle from a magazine picture. Then I carved boats and I'd sail them in the park. I lived with a couple in the LDS placement program. In fourth grade my mother took me home. When I first saw the kachina dances I was amazed. Everything seemed so crystal clear. I saw men carving and made my first kachina doll when I was ten or eleven.

Lowell talks with a mystical choice of words that make you feel he has one foot in this world and one foot in another. He speaks eloquently about the diverse pantheon of kachinas, pointing out particular traits and details. He has what he calls "a natural artistic talent" for drawing, designing, and carving. Lowell hopes to pursue galleries for his work with larger, more ambitious pieces. He enjoys the challenge of detailed carving. While we hope he will continue with printmaking, drawing, and painting, Lowell says that the market seems to prefer the carvings. You can see Lowell's work at McGee's Indian Art Gallery in Keams Canyon, Garland's Navajo Rugs in Sedona, McGee's Beyond Native Tradition Gallery in Holbrook, or purchase work directly from Lowell at his home just south of Sekakuku's Grocery Store at Second Mesa. He does not usually have finished work available, but welcomes commissions and mail orders.

POLACCA AND KEAMS CANYON

17. Manuel Denet Chavarria: Kachina Doll Carver

P.O. Box 271, Polacca, AZ 86042
520-737-9457

Kachina Doll, 12", Manuel Denet Chavarria, Polacca, Arizona

Hopi coil plaque, 8" diameter, artist unknown.
Courtesy of Sacred Mountain Trading Post,
Flagstaff

Manuel makes simple, hand-carved,
traditional-style kachina dolls. "My
tools are basic: Knife, rasp, and hand-
saw. I try to look into the past through
museums and books," says Manuel,

*but I also add my own personality to them.
We can no longer use illegal feathers, so we
find legal feathers that look similar and
miniaturize them. I first started carving at
fifteen. I learned from my godmother,
Otille Jackson. She taught me her way. It
was the sixties' style, where they painted
the doll a solid white, added color, leather,
shells, yarn, and turquoise. I call it the
'Otille style.' She taught me to never leave
home without my tools and that this skill
would make it so I would never go hungry.
This was how she raised her family. Now
I carve full-time.*

Manuel's work is available at
Garland's Navajo Rugs in Sedona,
Winter Sun in Flagstaff (they have
produced a small book on his work),
and at Tsakurshovi on Second Mesa.
Manuel adds,

*old-style dolls rely on finishing and paint-
ing. The skill is creating a clean finish and
clear, straight lines. Contemporary dolls rely
on carving. Our old-style dolls are more
like three-dimensional paintings. When I
finish a doll I sometimes put it away and
don't look at it anymore. If I look at them
I begin to see the doll's unique personality
and become attached. Then I don't want
to sell it.*

Manuel welcomes commissions
and special orders.

18. **Adelle Lalo-Nampeyo: Potter**
P.O. Box 1077, Keams Canyon, AZ
86034

Adelle is a direct descendant of the
famous Hopi potter Nampeyo, whose
work inspired the revival of Hopi pottery at the turn of the century. Adelle
prefers to work with the elements of
the family tradition, incorporating
three traditional designs. She started
when she was twenty years old by
watching her mother and grandmother. She enjoyed it from the very
beginning. From morning to late
afternoon she strains the clay, sands,
polishes, and paints or shapes the
forms. Sizes range from miniature to

as large as a customer wants. Occasionally someone will order a piece
from a book, but Adelle is most
proud of her work from the family's
heritage. Adelle prefers to sell out
of her home, but you can find her
work at many shops in the Southwest
and at the Eight Northern Indian
Pueblos Artist and Craftsmen Show.
She is pleased to do mail orders and
commissions.

19. **McGee's Indian Art Gallery**
P.O. Box 607, Keams Canyon, AZ
86034, Hwy 264
520-738-2295, FAX 520-738-5250
M–F 9:00–6:00, Sat–Sun 9:00–3:00
Winter (Nov 1–Apr 1): M–F
9:00–5:30, Sat 9:00–3:00
Owners: McGee and Sons

Jar, 9" diameter, by Adelle-Lalo Nampeyo,
Hopi. Courtesy of Palms Trading Company,
Albuquerque

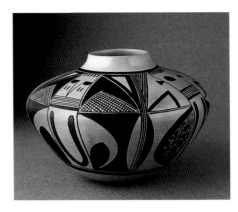

Manager: Ron McGee

♦ M, V, D, AE, C, S, HA (difficult with 7 steps), I

The McGees bought the post in 1937 and have a thriving retail and wholesale business. Ron is the third generation McGee at Keams with father Cliff McGee and uncle Bill McGee running it before him. As laws made the policies of the old trading post obsolete, the McGees have shifted to an art gallery orientation that has proved very successful. The McGees specialize in Hopi jewelry, especially gold and silver combinations. Ron buys over fifty kachina dolls a week and offers an astounding diversity. He also stocks a wide selection of Hopi basketry, Navajo rugs ($165–$2500), and traditional and contemporary jewelry from Hopi (including unusual gold jewelry), Navajo, Santo Domingo, and Zuni. We were impressed with Rick Honyouti's blanket chests and the original prints by Neil David Sr. and Lowell Talashoma. The gallery will take special Hopi pottery, jewelry, or kachina doll orders on request.

Many of the artists we spoke with were very complimentary of Ron McGee mentioning the importance of his encouragement on their work and artistic development.

The gallery is adjoined to a grocery store, restaurant (try the pie or hand-dipped ice cream), motel, and gas

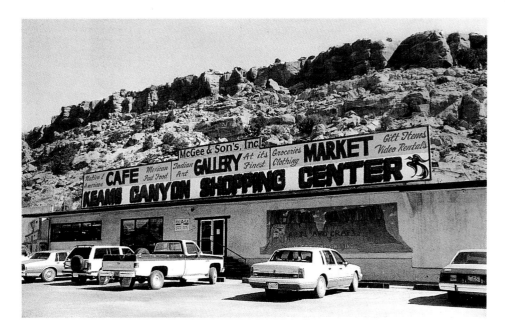

McGee's Indian Art Gallery, Keams Canyon, Arizona

station (mechanic on duty). McGee's can provide tourist information, and schedules and rules for Hopi dances.

Keams Canyon is named after trader Thomas Keam who first opened a trading post in the canyon in 1875; he was one of the Southwest's most influential traders. In 1889 he moved from the canyon to the present site of the McGee's gallery.

B, Bk, F, **J**, **K**, P, R, Sv

20. Ida Sahmie: Navajo Potter

P.O. Box 835, Keams Canyon, AZ 86034

Ida was born in 1960 in Pine Springs. Her grandmother was a well-known weaver. In 1975 she met her husband Andrew in Gallup. Andrew, who carves kachina dolls, is the son of Priscilla Namingha and a direct descendant of the famous Hopi potter Nampeyo. Of her first pot in 1980, Ida says, "It was really primitive, big, and heavy. I left it at Priscilla's house and someone came and bought it. I was very surprised." Her second

Ida Sahmie, potter, Keams Canyon, Arizona

Yei'iis get angry when they get put in the fire. Mom said they would make me go blind. Now I'm having problems with my eyes and ears. I've had a Night Chant Blessingway sung for me. I'm planning to have a *Yei'ii bichai* dance done for me, but it is expensive and lasts nine days."

Ida worked with computers in a nine-to-five job, but demand for her pots was so great that she returned to the mesas, where her husband's family lives. Her pottery is created in a traditional manner, using clay and pigment from the mesas that she digs herself, and beeweed for her strong black colors. Her work is at once innovative and traditional. Robert F. Nichols

group of pots was sold to Bruce McGee at McGee's Indian Art Gallery at Keams Canyon. She reflects, "Bruce was really a big supporter. He encouraged me to continue in those early days."

Ida's work is unique because it marries Hopi pottery technique with design that is unmistakably Navajo. Her family in Pine Springs is not completely supportive of her use of *Yei'ii bichai* dancers and *Yei'iis* on her pottery. Ida says, "My mother and grandmother warned me that the

in Santa Fe maintains a wonderful selection of her pots and is one of her biggest advocates. McGee's Indian Art Gallery in Keams Canyon still has a few pieces. Ida is also willing to accept commissions and mail orders. In a time when political pressures have created some animosity between Navajo and Hopi, it is wonderful to see a marriage and art form between the cultures work so beautifully.

B E L O W : (Top) *Overlay bracelet by Gary and Elsie Yoyokie, Hopi. Pins* (Right and left), *Beauford and Dinah Dawahoya, Hopi Pueblo;* (Bottom) *Hopi pendant, 2", by Charles Willie.* Courtesy of Twin Rocks Trading Post, Bluff, Utah

SELECTED HOPI ARTISTS/CRAFTSPEOPLE

Ramona Ami, P.O. Box 349, Polacca, AZ 86042, 520-737-2541—Traditional Hopi pottery.

Karen Kahe Charley, P.O. Box 1047, Keams Canyon, AZ 86034, 520-738-5195, 520-737-2278—Pottery.

Neil David, Sr., P.O. Box 257, Polacca, AZ 86042—Painting and drawing.

Wallace Hyeoma, P.O. Box 272, Second Mesa, AZ 86043—Kachina dolls.

Gloria Kahe, P.O. Box 1096, Keams Canyon, AZ 86034, 520-737-2563—Pottery.

Wilmer Kaye, P.O. Box 1225, Zuni, NM 87327—Kachina dolls.

Alvina Rae Kewanyama, P.O. Box 412, Second Mesa, AZ 86043—Baskets.

Les Naminga, P.O. Box 595, Ramah, NM 87321, 505-783-4559—Pottery and painting.

Loren Nampeyo, P.O. Box 270, Polacca, AZ 86042—Pottery.

Delbridge Philip, P.O. Box 290, Second Mesa, AZ 86043—Jewelry.

Myron Sekakuku, P.O. Box 978, Keams Canyon, AZ 86034, 520-737-2318—Jewelry.

Hon Kachina, *12", by Köcha Hon Mana, Hopi.* Courtesy of Palms Trading Company, Albuquerque

Eloy Talahytewa, P.O. Box 389, Polacca, AZ, 520-737-2606—Kachina dolls.

Milson Taylor, P.O. Box 337, Kykotsmovi, AZ 86039—Jewelry.

Gary & Elsie Yoyokie, P.O. Box 340, Kykotsmovi, AZ 86039, 520-734-2552—Overlay jewelry.

THE HOPI CATALOG

P.O. Box 508, Kykotsmovi, AZ 86039

520-734-6646

FOUNDER: Rebekah Masayevsa

COST: $1.00

For those not fortunate enough to visit the Hopi mesas or for those haunted by artwork they saw on a past visit, Rebekah Masayevsa offers the Hopi Catalogue. The mail-order catalogue offers Yungyapu wicker plaques, kachina dolls, colorful dawas, jewelry, pillows and shirts, coiled plaques, and pottery. Also included are offset prints and well-chosen children's items. The inventory will change as new catalogues are produced.

Rebekah has chosen items that reflect the spirit of the Hopi people and will appeal to diverse tastes. The beautiful, sixteen-page catalogue is unique and provides the artists with a year-round income as opposed to the roller coaster seasonal fluctu-ation of tourist sales. Rebekah is willing to take special orders. She can also be found at The Hopi Shop, the Hyatt Regency, Gainey Ranch, 7500 E. Doubletree Ranch Rd., Scottsdale, AZ 85258, 602-991-3388, ext. 5606.

B, Bk, J, K, P, Sv

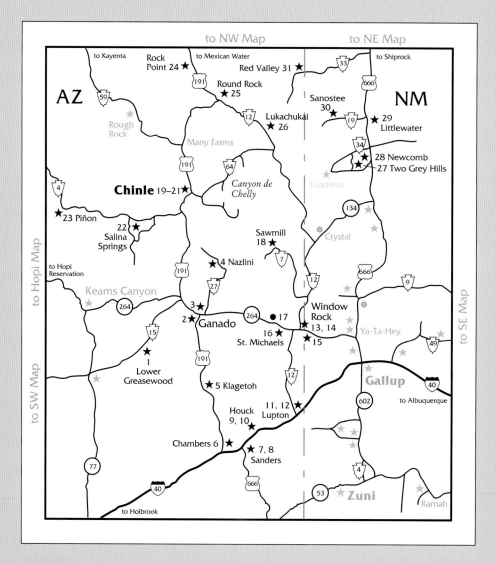

LEGEND

★ **Trading Post in this chapter**

★ **Trading Post in other chapter**

● **Other site**

Central Navajo Nation and Canyon de Chelly

◆ ◆ ◆

You cannot travel very long through Navajoland without stubbing your toe on the Anasazi.

You can feel these things the children speak of, for the wind carries voices:

Every conversation, every sigh uttered by the "long-time-ago people" circulates above you.

Perhaps that's why the clouds move so quickly in the Southwest.

—Terry Tempest Williams, *Pieces of White Shell: A Journey to Navajoland*

The Central Navajo Nation area has a plenitude of well-known tourist magnets: Canyon de Chelly, Hubbell Trading Post National Historic Site, the Painted Desert, and Petrified Forest National Park. This is the heart of Navajo weaving country and the Navajo trading post. This area gave birth to the best-known Navajo rug styles, including Ganado Red, Two Grey Hills, Crystal, Chinle, Burntwater, Wide Ruins, and others. You will find a diverse group of arts and crafts here, but nowhere will you find so many quality weavers. In this region the traders and the weavers jointly evolved and created a business enterprise that continues to hold a special mystique.

Allow extra time to venture into the landscape of this region. Sculpted sandstone forms and dense wooded areas of fir, piñon, and juniper appear among endless oceans of golden grass, torn by rock crags that explode into the sky. The dirt road that meanders between Red Valley and Lukachukai, with its view from the Chuska Mountains towards Shiprock, caused western author Louis L'Amour to declare the area his favorite place. Explore some of the less-beaten paths and always ask questions and converse with the locals. They can provide you with an intimate portrait that you could never obtain in any other way.

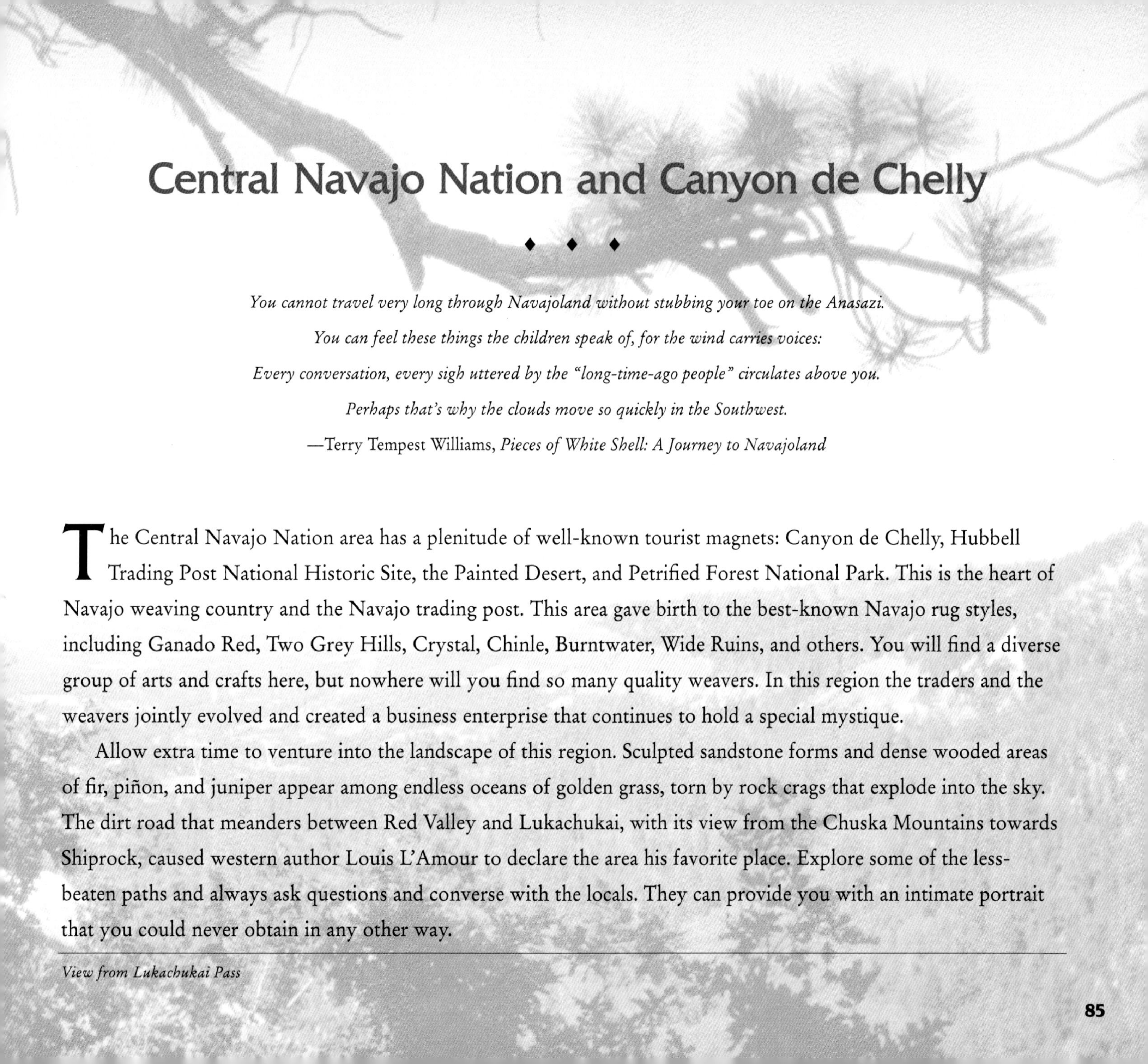

View from Lukachukai Pass

> Their remote posts were oases in the desert, landmarks in an unmarked wilderness. They were bankers, doctors, interpreters, school teachers, art agents, representatives of an encroaching White civilization to the Indians, and champions of Indian tribes against an inimical government.
> —FRANK WATERS, *Masked Gods*

Cross Canyon Trading Post (closed), Ganado, Arizona

GANADO AND SURROUNDING AREA

1. Greasewood Trading Post

1 Hickman Blvd., Ganado, AZ, on Rte 15, 25 miles south and west of Hubbell Trading Post
520-654-3302
Daily 7:00–9:00
Owner: John Hickman
♦ M, V, C, S, HA

Greasewood is a series of old buildings where cows wander around the gas pumps. Owner John Hickman has a generous handshake and is the epitome of the southwestern gentleman. John says, "We're open seven days and long hours. Old posts have been closing because the owners won't respond to the people's needs. We do our best to do so here." You won't find much in the way of arts and crafts here, but it's worth stopping by to say hello to John. He can point out the original part of the building and tell how Lorenzo Hubbell originally opened this post. They carry a nice selection of Pendletons.

2. Hubbell Trading Post National Historic Site

P.O. Box 388, Ganado, AZ 86505, 1 mile west of Ganado
520-755-3477 (historic site), -3475 (visitor center), -3254 (rug room)
Daily: Summer: 8:00–6:00, Winter: 8:00–5:00
Manager: Bill Malone
♦ M, V, D, AE, C, S, HA

In 1883, construction began on the building that houses Hubbell Trading Post, named for Lorenzo Hubbell, the most significant and successful of all the traders in the Southwest. This continues to be a working post under Bill Malone's guidance. In 1967 it became a national historic site; profits from the

Brenda Spencer, weaver, holding one of her Wide Ruins rugs at Hubbell Trading Post National Historic Site, near Ganado, Arizona

post go into the national park system.

Bill Malone is friendly, knowledgeable, and well respected. He can usually be found in his corner niche buying rugs from weavers. When asked about his philosophy, Bill said, "I try to pay the weavers the most I can and still sell the rug." This philosophy has provided the post with an impressive rug room ($90–$30,000). You will also find jewelry, baskets, and Pendleton blankets.

Hubbell Trading Post is the gem of Navajo trading posts. It remains unchanged, with saddles, pans, and

Trader Bill Malone, Rug Room, Hubbell Trading Post National Historic Site

Ganado rug, 41" x 29", by Ruby Hubbard. Courtesy of Garland's Navajo Rugs, Sedona, Arizona

rope hanging from the ceiling. An old wood stove provides heat. The old bull pen area carries groceries, general merchandise, wool, and pottery. In the morning you will find some of the Southwest's finest weavers bringing their recent creations to Bill.

The visitor center has weaving and silversmith demonstrations. You can also tour the Hubbell home. Built in 1900, it remains unchanged, with original furnishings and impressive art collection. (Note the Maynard Dixon paintings.)

If you wish to experience a genuine trading post atmosphere, this is about as close as you'll come to a turn-of-the-century experience. You might also find a Ganado Red rug that you can't leave behind.
B, Bk, J, K, M, P, **R**, Sv

3. Round Top Trading Company
P.O. Box 209, Ganado, AZ 86505,
0.5 mile north of Hwy 264
520-755-3480
Daily 8:00–5:00

Originally built in the early 1900s by a trader named Schillingberg, this post no longer deals in arts and crafts. It is a convenience store selling gas, groceries, Pendletons, and straw cowboy hats.

GANADO AND KLAGETOH RUGS

Ganados are one of the best-known Navajo rugs. They have a deep red background with a complex single or double diamond-shaped geometric pattern in black and white. They range from 2' x 3' to 9' x 12'. Hubbell sold them through his catalog earlier this century and they still are one of our most popular rugs. Klagetoh rugs vary from Ganado only in the fact that they use a predominant grey background.

—BILL MALONE, Hubbell Trading Post

BURNTWATER RUGS

In Burntwater rugs, design takes over the rug; sometimes there is no background at all. In the early eighties excellent Burntwater rugs had six to twelve colors. Today weavers may use forty to sixty colors. Burntwater rugs are based on the designs of Ganado or Two Grey Hills rugs, but use pastel colors. The weavers use vegetal dyed wool and like using so many colors because they can use leftover wool. I've seen them use a ball of wool the size of a marble.

—BRUCE BURNHAM, R.B. Burnham and Company Trading Post

ABOVE: *Nazlini Trading Post, Nazlini, Arizona*

LEFT: *Burntwater rug, 50" x 37", by Betty A. Roan, Klagetoh, Arizona.* Courtesy of Garland's Navajo Rugs, Sedona, Arizona

4. Nazlini Trading Post

Thriftway 273, Nazlini, AZ 86540
520-755-3886
Daily 7:00–9:00
Manager: Shirley Bydonnie

The drive to Nazlini is beautiful and capped by a magnificent view as you clear the final ridge before descending into Nazlini. The post, devoured by the Thriftway empire, has been reduced to a convenience store. (Not all Thriftways are so.)

5. West Sun (Old Klagetoh Trading Post)

#1 Klagetoh, Ganado, AZ 86505, 14 miles south of Ganado on Hwy 191
520-652-3260
Daily 6:00–10:00

There are no arts and crafts sold here. The old post has become a convenience store selling gas, groceries, and feed, and fixing flat tires. A series of old buildings from the original compound surrounds the feed store in the rear.

6. Chambers Trading Post

P.O. Box 129, Chambers, AZ, 86502
on Hwy 191 north of I-40
520-688-2538, -2228 (gallery)
Daily 7:00–10:00
Owners: Tony and Julie Konheiser
♦ M, V, D, AE, T, C, S

The Konheisers opened this wholesale/retail business in 1976. Tony is willing to negotiate on prices and can do so in English, German, French, and Navajo. They recently built a separate, new Santa Fe–style gallery (9:00–5:00). They carry a good selection of Pottery (notice pots by Frogwoman, Sylvia Navatsie, and local Elmer Delmor) and old Plains beadwork. Tony and Julie

are proud of the jewelry of Clement Nalwood and Paul Arviso, and the gallery's collection of Northwest coast ivory carvings. They have a somewhat small, but well-chosen selection of Navajo rugs. Particularly impressive were the Wide Ruins rugs of Annie Bonnie and Bertha Tishie. The inventory is chosen carefully and is supportive of local artists. They also sell gas and groceries from this charming wood-plank–floored building next door.

B, D, **J**, K, **P**, **R**

7. Painted Hills Trading Post

P.O. Box 366, Sanders, AZ 86512, 0.5 mile north of I-40 at Sanders exit
520-688-2111
M–F 8:00–5:00, Sat 8:00–12:00
Owner: Virginia Burnham
♦ C, S, HA

Virginia Burnham bought this post in 1992 from Don Jacobs, Sr., who opened it after leaving Burntwater Trading Post in 1982. He is well known for helping to develop the Burntwater rug style. This is a small post that sells dead pawn, baskets, and weavings (about fifty). Virginia and her husband also own Burnham Trading Post.

B, D, I, J, R

Wide Ruins rug, 27" x 41", by Marjorie Spencer. Courtesy of Garland's Navajo Rugs

---

WIDE RUINS RUGS

Wide Ruins rugs are more complicated than the other banded rugs, Chinle and Crystal. The wool is vegetal dyed with rich, deep colors. Sally Lippincott Wagner's critical eye helped develop the Wide Ruins rug. In the forties she started a weaving school and the Wide Ruins pattern naturally evolved from the Chinle pattern Cozy developed.

—BRUCE BURNHAM, R.B. Burnham and Company Trading Post

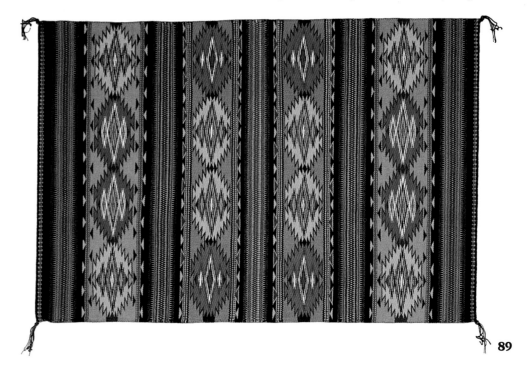

R.B. Burnham and Company Trading Post, Sanders, Arizona. After you pass the groceries and the wool you will discover the gallery area where Bruce presents a unique line of Navajo-made furniture.

8. R.B. Burnham and Company Trading Post

Box 337, Sanders, AZ 86512, just
south of I-40 on Hwy 191 at
Sanders exit
520-688-2777
M–Sat 8:00–6:00
Owners: Bruce and Virginia Burnham
♦ M, V, C, S, HA

You will not encounter anyone who
loves trading more than Bruce Burnham. He is a fourth-generation trader
whose great-grandfather traded from a
wagon in Kirtland, New Mexico. His
grandfather and father traded in the
northeastern and southeastern parts of
the Navajo Reservation. Bruce settled
into Sanders in 1970 and has been in
the current building since 1974, with
an impressive gallery added in 1992.

Bruce has been instrumental in
creating the New Lands style rug and
influential in recent changes in the
Burntwater rugs. Weavers across the
reservation know of Burnham's selection of vegetal-dyed wool in hundreds
of colors. When you walk through the
room, it is like walking in the sleeve of
a wool sweater. This large selection of
colors allows weavers to use up to
sixty colors to create the newer
Burntwater rugs. Bruce is currently
working on reproducing Germantown
rugs from the 1860s to 1910. He is
matching the original vivid colors and
fine texture of Germantown wool
with newly produced wool from
Germantown, Pennsylvania. Bruce
and Virginia also offer beginning,
intermediate, and advanced weaving
seminars with Navajo instructors
upon request.

After you pass the groceries and
the wool, you will discover the gallery
area where Bruce presents an exclusive
line of Navajo-made furniture that is
comfortable and beautiful. He carries
a good selection of cradleboards, some
dead pawn, limited-edition prints, and
Northwest Coast items.

> I always call it dubious vegetal dyed
> wool. The weavers dye the wool in a
> tub and never get the same color
> twice. They never empty the tub.
> They use vegetal dyes, but all sorts
> of other things too, such as rusty
> baling wire, batteries, or construction paper. You never know. When a
> weaver comes in and shows me a
> nice color, I give them 100 skeins to
> dye for us. Over the years we have
> been able to build up our wool
> selection this way.
> —BRUCE BURNHAM

The Burnhams are remodeling to accommodate the thousand book titles in their inventory. They have been taking them to trade shows and selling mail-order. Bruce is a treasury of information on trading posts, weaving, and Navajo culture. Don't miss an opportunity to visit him.

B, **Bk**, C, D, J, K, Pt, **R**, S, **Furniture**, **Wool**

9. Ortega's Indian City Arts and Crafts

P.O. Box 137, Houck, AZ 86506, exit 351 off I-40
520-688-2691
Daily 6:00–7:30
Owner: Armand Ortega
♦ M, V, D, AE, S (no breakable items), HA

This store carries Tohono O'odham and Mexican baskets, dye charts, imported beadwork, cradleboards, and dead pawn.

B, D, I, **J**, K, M, P, Pt, **R**, S, Sp, Sv

10. Querino Canyon Trading Post

P.O. Box 489, Sanders, AZ 86512, located in Houck, 5 miles from Sanders exit, on I-40 to Querino 0.5 mile north, or take Hwy 66 and go east 1 mile
Daily 7:00–8:00
Owner: Earl Taylor

Earl says he may have had four or five tourists stop here since opening in 1990. He has been a trader for twenty-

two years and presently operates a general merchandise, grocery, and wholesale jewelry business. Earl is particularly proud of Lukachukai silver needlepoint artist Victor Begay's work. Mr. Taylor points out that his ninety-six-year-old mother made the benches in the store for the customers to sit and chat. **J**

11. Ortega's Chaparral Trading Post/Indian Galleria

P.O. Box 406, Lupton, AZ 86508, 16 miles west of Gallup on old Route 66
520-688-2477
Daily 7:00–6:30
Owner: Armand Ortega
♦ M, V, D, AE, S, HA

Ortega's has covered the Southwest with its billboards. Like many other businesses, they claim that they wholesale to the public. This business seems designed for tourists seeking film, postcards, and souvenirs.

B, D, J, **Sv**

12. Fort Yellowhorse

P.O. Box 18, Lupton, AZ 86508, Lupton exit off I-40
520-688-2462
Daily 7:00–5:00 (flexible)
Owner: Juan Yellowhorse
♦ S, HA (difficult)

This is one of those kitsch-ridden businesses that still haunt old Route 66. The Arizona-New Mexico border runs through the store, which inhabits

There are four kinds of traders. The Takers are those that move in and take, take, take, from the Navajos. The Missionaries are those sent by the church. The givers are the traders that work with the Navajo to improve livestock, elevate their rugs, and help them increase their income. The new type of trader is the Hogan-Hopper. He trades from his tailgate and only wants the cream of the crop. He is not part of the community. As a trader, I buy rugs from the grandmothers even though their eyesight is failing and the quality isn't as good, because it's the grandmas that teach the young people to weave. It is difficult for traders to continue buying Grandma's rugs if they don't also get high-quality rugs. The Hogan-Hopper puts this chain of culture in jeopardy.

—BRUCE BURNHAM

Traders Mr. and Mrs. G. Kennedy (center) at Canyon de Chelly, 1916. Photograph courtesy of John W. Kennedy

an old hogan. The proplike fort was built in the seventies. There are dinosaur tracks, wagon rides, and some ruins. In the early 1900s, Harry Miller, an author, ran a business here. He had a small zoo and lived here until he shot the postmaster of Gallup. As expected, there is a wild collection of souvenirs, including tarantulas, scorpions, and black widows in plastic. A few Navajo rugs sit amongst the Mexican weavings. Don't stop here for arts and crafts, but for the zany signage that is a throwback to the glory days of Route 66.

P, R, **Sv**

WINDOW ROCK AND SURROUNDING AREA

13. **Navajo Arts and Crafts Enterprise and Museum**
P.O. Box 160, Window Rock, AZ 86515, on the corner of Rt. 12 and Hwy 264
520-871-4095
Summer: M–Sat 9:00–6:00,
Winter: M–F 8:30–4:30
Manager: Raymond Smith
♦ M, V, D, AE, C, S, HA, I

The Navajo Nation runs this sprawling business. Inside is a display of a wide selection of rugs in all patterns, Pendletons, jewelry (over 100 bola ties), jewelry supplies, silver spoons and buttons, beadwork, posters, an unusual selection of shirts and hats, and an impressive group of miniature rugs. The large inventory is always changing. Take some time to explore the many display cases.

B, **J**, P, **R**, Sp,

14. **Navajo Nation Museum, Library and Visitors' Center**
P.O. Box 9000, Window Rock, AZ 86515, in the same building as the Navajo Arts and Crafts Enterprise
520-871-6673, -6675
Call for hours.
♦ S, HA

The Navajo Nation is building an expansive new museum nearby. Until it's finished, they will operate this small, interesting display. The museum explores the history of the Navajo, early trading posts, Navajo artifacts, basket weaving, jewelry, and a section of contemporary sculpture, painting, and pottery.

The giftshop occupies the entryway and contains a large inventory,

---

Howard Begay, silversmith, Navajo Arts and Crafts Enterprise and Museum, Window Rock, Arizona

including some obscure titles. They publish a twelve-page catalogue and take mail and phone orders.
Bk, C, Sv

15. Griswold's Inc.

HC33 Box 423, Gallup, NM 87301, off Hwy 264, 200 yards on the NM side of the NM-AZ border
505-371-5393
M–Sat 9:00–5:30
Owners: Russ and Glenda Griswold
♦ M, V, D, AE, C, S, HA

This wholesale/retail business opened in 1988 on the site of the old Lucero's Trading Post. If you're a rug collector, ask to see the rug room. They stock between 100 and 250 rugs in the $40–$3,000 range. The front display area is in the old bullpen design. You will find cradleboards, Pendletons, buckskins, and jewelry including some old pawn.
B, D, J, **P, R**

16. St. Michaels Historical Museum and Bookstore

P.O. Box 680, St. Michaels, AZ 86511, on Hwy 264 west of Window Rock
520-871-4171
Memorial Day–Labor Day 9:00–5:00

The small museum was originally the first mission building (1898). The museum opened in 1977 and offers a glimpse of the early days at St. Michaels Mission. The museum includes a 6' x 7'

St. Michaels' Mission, St. Michaels, Arizona

weaving of the crucifixion created in 1936 by Adyan Yazzie; some Navajo artifacts; and an early chapel.

In the forties, St. Michaels secured a printing press and began publishing books, pamphlets, and posters about Navajo ceremonies, language, and other aspects of the culture. Many of these books were created by Father Berard Haile and are well known to scholars. Surprisingly, many of these early publications can still be purchased at the bookstore. The bookstore publishes a list and will mail order.
Bk, Sv

17. Tom Yazzie: Sculptor

P.O. Box 562, Fort Defiance, AZ 86504
520-729-5197

Tom Yazzie has been carving small (twelve inches or less) meticulously detailed sculptures that celebrate Navajo culture since the fifties. He has documented Navajo ceremonial life with diligence and a respect that imbues each carving with a special unique magic. The Navajo Nation Museum in Window Rock has a large collection of Tom's sculptures.

Whether a carving of a single figure or a large Navajo nativity scene, Tom's work is always a labor of love and exudes a charm that collectors find irresistible (see photo page 142).

18. Sawmill Trading Post
P.O. Box 8, Sawmill, AZ 86549, about 15 miles north of Window Rock on Rte 7
520-729-2661
M–F 8:00–6:00, Sat 8:00–12:00

This post has been remodeled and little of the old post is still visible. The post serves the local Navajo population and sells gas, groceries, general merchandise, and operates a post office. This area is the home to some fine weavers of Crystal and miniature rugs. They are available at wholesale prices.   R

CHINLE AND SURROUNDING AREA

19. Navajo Arts and Crafts Enterprise
P.O. Box 608, Chinle, AZ 86503, on Hwy 191
520-674-5338, FAX 520-674-5339
M–F 8:00–6:00, Sat 8:00–5:00
Manager: Anselm Harvey
◆ M, V, D, AE, C, S, HA

Sawmill Trading Post, Sawmill, Arizona, circa 1993

A smaller retail branch of the Window Rock enterprise. They carry a full line of jewelry supplies and will negotiate on prices.   B, Bk, J, P, R

20. Garcia's Trading Post
Navajo Rt. 7, Chinle, AZ 86503 (at Holiday Inn)
520-674-5000
Daily 7:00–10:00
Hotel manager: Kurt Berridge
◆ M, V, D, AE, C, S, HA

Hubbell and Cotton located a post here in 1886, and around 1900 Camille Garcia opened Garcia's Trading Post on the same site. The original building has been cannibalized into a modern structure with carpet, muzak, and an antiseptic gift shop atmosphere. The typical line of gift shop items is available. The one notable item was pottery by local Navajo potter Helen Burlow. When you drive by, notice the surreal emerald green lawns placed amid the desert landscape.
P, **Sv**

Skinwalker, woodcarving, 18", by Robin Wellito, Nageezi, New Mexico

21. **Thunderbird Lodge Gift Shop**

P.O. Box 548, Chinle, AZ 86503,
near the mouth of Canyon de Chelly
National Monument
520-674-5841, -5842
Daily: Summer: 7:30–9:00,
Winter: 7:30–8:00
Owner: Mary Jones
♦ M, V, D, AE, C, S, HA

Samuel Day originally opened this
post in 1902. It passed hands until
George Kennedy took over in 1916.
His son, John William Kennedy,
remembers:

In those days they didn't have tourist
accommodations on the reservation, so buy-
ers or salesmen working on the reservation
had to rely on their trader friends for food
and lodging. Often we boys had to give up
our room for the night and go sleep on the
counter of the trading post. We wrapped up
in the large quilts for sale in the store and
managed to be fairly comfortable. One of
the early salesmen was a man by the name
of Switzer who traveled for the Fred
Harvey Company. He usually brought a lot
of coral, which he traded for Navajo rugs.
This accounts for the Navajos' early interest
in the red beads.

Cozy McSparron named the
Thunderbird Lodge in 1925, and during his tenure he helped create the
Chinle rug pattern that is still very
popular with weavers in the area. You
will see a good selection of them in
the gift shop.

The original post is now the cafete-
ria (the food is quite good). The gift
shop is housed in the building to the
north and has a very complete inventory. The rug selection usually
includes at least 700 rugs in all styles
($10–$4,500). The shop also carries
Navajo pottery (Lorraine Williams,
Betty Manygoats, and Louise
Goodman), local beadwork, Anasazi
pottery reproductions, Rena Juan's
woodcarvings, and an enormous selection of souvenirs. Mary Jones and
her staff are friendly, knowledgeable,
and able to arrange truck tours of
Canyon de Chelly. This is a retail-
only business; negotiating prices is
discouraged but has been known to
occur on rugs and high-priced items.
B, Bk, D, F, J, K, M, P, **R**, Sp, Sv

> I was always fascinated by a
> Malpai bowl that was on the
> counter in the trading post at
> Chinle. Apparently it came from
> some prehistoric ruin. My father
> kept Bull Durham tobacco and
> cigarette papers in it so when the
> Indians came into the store, they
> could roll a cigarette and sit and
> smoke before they started doing
> business.
> —JOHN WILLIAM KENNEDY,
> Kennedy Indian Arts and Crafts

22. **Salina Springs Trading Post**

Chinle, AZ 86503, take Indian Route
4 (5 miles south of Chinle) 14 miles
east from Rt. 191. At Cottonwood,
take the road 3 miles south. This dirt
and very sandy road goes up some
hilly terrain; we suggest 4WD vehicles.
The alternate "paved" road is not
recommended.
M–F 8:30–5:30, Sat 8:30–2:30
Owner: Joe Cline
♦ HA (difficult due to deep sand)
Author Frank Waters told us this

Yei'ii bichai *dancers at Salina Springs Trading*
Post, Chinle, Arizona, 1935. Photograph
courtesy of Joe Cline (hand-tinted)

was his favorite trading post. Joe Cline has been here since 1993. He sells groceries and a few locally made items and plans to expand the post to sell rugs and offer a laundromat. The most notable aspect of Salina Springs is the dramatic location. Swirling white and yellow cliffs stretch upward on each side of the building. The road meanders up steep grades to reach the pass where the post sits.   R

23. Piñon Trading Post

P.O. Box 437, Piñon, AZ 86510, approx. 35 miles east of Hwy 191 on Rt. 4
520-725-3257, -3335
M–F 8:30–7:30, Sat 9:00–4:00, Sun 9:00–3:00
Owners: McGee Traders Inc.; manager/owner: Ferron McGee
◆   M, V, AE, C, S, HA (most of the store)

The Piñon post was opened by Hubbell and Cotton in 1916. The evidence of their occupancy is a bust of Hubbell, the original safe with "Hubbell" emblazoned on it, and the original store floor and walls. Piñon is one of the old bastions of the trading business, and still extends credit and buys rugs. Ferron McGee fondly recounts his childhood in the area: "I loved growing up at Keams Canyon and working at Piñon. I remember Dad [Cliff McGee] dressing up like Santa Claus and we'd go out to the hogans

and give out candy and toys. I raised my kids out there too."

Ferron's passion for trading posts has made him an authority. He enjoys giving seminars on the subject and, along with his family, is planning a trading post museum with his photo archive and collection.

The remodeled front porch of Piñon is usually bustling with the local Navajo clientele chatting, smoking, and exchanging local news. Inside you will find families eating bowls of mutton stew, Navajo tacos, pizza, ice cream, and Mexican dishes from the newly opened restaurant. The post also features gas, a laundromat, a car wash, hardware, a variety store, Big A auto parts, and a convenience store. The arts and crafts center carries many Ganado Red, Klagetoh, Burntwater, and unusual Dinnebito Black rugs that were developed by Elijah Blair at Dinnebito. Ferron says: "When Dinnebito Trading Post moved to Page, Arizona, in 1992, the weavers that sold the Dinnebito Black rugs to Blair began to bring them to us. They are incredible rugs." Piñon also has some unusual multipatterned traditional rugs.

Piñon sells jewelry, wool, Pendleton blankets, Navajo baskets, small wooden *Yei'ii bichai* sculptures, and some one-of-a-kind items created by locals. Piñon is out of the way, and that may be why the post has retained its charm. **B**, J, P, **R**, S

24. Navajo Evangelical Lutheran Mission

P.O. Box 304, Hwy 191, Rock Point, AZ 86545
520-659-4202
Daily 8:00–5:00
Manager: Clara Tohtsonie
◆   C, T, HA (4 steps)

The store at the mission is a good place to see locally made and gathered items, including sashes and rugs, Navajo folk art, and silver-and-turquoise jewelry. They also carry a selection of religious books in Navajo and English. Prices are retail and negotiating is discouraged.
B, Bk, P, R

25. Round Rock Trading Post

(Thriftway 272)
Round Rock, AZ 86547
520-787-2230
Daily 7:00–10:00
Manager: Richard Yazzie
◆   M, V, C, S, HA

Behind this picturesque post is the building that housed the original 1887 post built with thick adobe walls and vigas. The current post, though owned by Thriftway, still has a nice ambiance. When we visited they had Pendletons. Most of their business is local, so gas and groceries are the big attraction here. Be sure to ask if they have items in the vault that might be of interest.
J, P, R

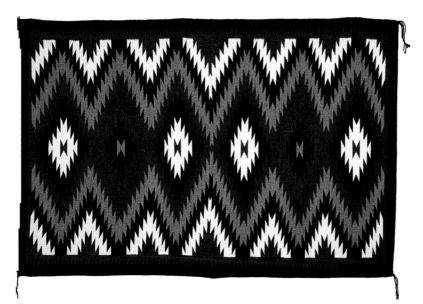

ABOVE: *Eyedazzler rug (serrated diamond), 37" x 57", by Sarah Begay, Piñon, Arizona.* Courtesy of Garland's Navajo Rugs, Sedona Arizona

BELOW: *Raised outline rug (New Lands Rug), 32" x 49", by Metilda Yazzie, Coal Mine Mesa, Arizona.* Courtesy of Garland's Navajo Rugs

EYEDAZZLER RUGS

Eyedazzlers were influenced by new Mexican serapes. When traders introduced brightly colored Germantown wool in th late 1800s, Navajos took to it with great success creating rugs of great optical brilliance. Today we see revivals of the eyedazzlers by weavers in the Red Mesa and Teec Nos pos areas, and weavers in the Piñon area creating black, white, and red serrated pattern eyedazzlers. In the eighties no one bought them, but today there is a resurgence of interest and they sell quickly.

—DAN GARLAND, Garland's Navajo Rugs

NEW LANDS RUGS

When weavers moved over here from Coal Mine Mesa, they were creating raised outline rugs. I thought a Burntwater would look great in outline so we tried that. i brainstormed with Malone and McGee. We thought the outline technique was more effective with diagonal designs, so we encouraged weavers to use patterns similar to Teec Nos Pos patterns. The name New Lands was just something I called them because the area the weavers lived was new to them.

—BRUCE BURNHAM, R.B. Burnham and Company Trading Post

26. **Totsoh Trading Post**
P.O. Box 218, Lukachukai, AZ, 90
miles north of Gallup
520-787-2281
M–Sat 8:00–8:00
Owners: Bradley H. and Victoria Blair
♦ M, V, AE, C, S, HA
  The original Lukachukai Trading
Post was opened in the twenties one
mile north. The Blairs opened the
present shop in 1984, which offers
food and gas. You must ask to see the
crafts room upstairs. Totsoh specializes in *Yei'ii* rugs and Navajo wedding
baskets. These are good quality rugs
by weavers such as Nora Allen and
Louise Bia.
  The surrounding countryside is
beautiful with redrock cliffs to the
south and spectacular views from
mountain passes. Occasionally the
Blairs will arrange horseback rides
into the mountains.
B, P, **R**, Sv, Wool

HIGHWAY 666 FROM TOADLENA TO RED ROCK

27. **Two Grey Hills Trading Post**
Tohatchi, NM 87325, approximately
23 miles south from Shiprock on Hwy
666, to Newcomb or Rt. 19. The post
is 6 miles from the highway.
505-789-3270
M–Sat 8:00–6:00, Sundays by appt.

*Pictorial rug, 38" x 42", by Geanita John,
Many Farms, Arizona.* Courtesy of Garland's
Navajo Rugs, Sedona, Arizona

PICTORIAL RUGS
Pictorials vary in size and com-
plexity. They give us a view of
the weaver's daily life. They can
include anything that interests
the weaver: animals, plants,
hogans, vehicles, neighbors, or
deities. They are a true Navajo
folk art. The color is usually
quite strong. There are not many
weavers creating them and there
is a lot of media attention and
interest, so the rugs don't stay
around long.
—DAN GARLAND, Garland's
Navajo Rugs

◆ M, V, C, S, HA (with difficulty)
Owner: Les Wilson

This is the home of the famous Two Grey Hills rug. Originally built in 1897 by the Noel family, June 19, 1997 is the post's one-hundredth birthday. Les Wilson bought it in the early eighties, and he continues to carry the rugs that made this post famous. Prices range from $400 to $5,000 and include rugs made with handspun wool and increasingly rare, finely woven tapestries. There are usually 50–100 rugs in stock; you must ask to see the rug room. The front area sells food, gas, and local crafts.

An old painting of the post hangs on the wall, showing the front of the post, which is now the rear of the building. The Wilsons work hard to encourage the local weavers. They buy children's weavings and tell us that the inventory changes all the time, with the largest selection in the winter months.
B, D, J, P, **R**, Sp, Weaving tools, Fleeces, Navajo toys

28. Newcomb Trading Post
Hwy 666, Tohatchi, NM 87325
505-696-3325
M–Sat 8:00–6:00
Owners: R.B. and Grace Foutz

The view towards Two Grey Hills from the former Toadlena Trading Post, Tohatchi, Arizona

This is a local grocery and video store. R.B. Foutz is the son of R.B. Foutz, Sr., who originally opened the Sheep Springs Trading Post south of here.

29. Littlewater Trading Post
HCR 4, Box 400, Littlewater, NM 87420, on Hwy 666, 10 miles north of the Burnham turnoff
Daily: 7:00–10:00, Winter: 7:00–9:00
Owner: Cora Johnson
◆ M, V, S, HA

Littlewater specializes in Two Grey Hills and Crystal rugs, hand-built and slipcast pottery, kachina dolls, jewelry, Navajo mud toys, bead-work, sandpaintings, and Navajo bas-

kets. Propane, gas, and groceries are also available.
B, D, F, I, J, **P**, Pt, **R**, Sv

30. Sanostee Trading Post
P.O. Box O, Sanostee, NM 87461
505-723-2478
Daily 7:00–8:00
Owner: Navajo Nation Shopping Center

The old post burned in 1986, and the post now occupies a new building. They are a gas and grocery convenience store.

31. Red Rock Trading Post
P.O. Box 100, Red Valley, AZ 86544, 22 miles west of Hwy 666 on Hwy 13

Two Grey Hills rug, 25" x 39", by Dorothy
Lowe, Two Grey Hills, New Mexico.
Courtesy of Garland's Navajo Rugs

TWO GREY HILLS RUG

The colors of Two Grey Hills rugs are always grey, brown, tan, black, or white. This is because the wool is undyed and hand-spun in the natural sheep color. The design is in a complicated single or double diamond shape and a black or dark border. Many of the Two Grey Hills weavers create tapestries (rugs woven with in excess of ninety strands per square inch).
—LES WILSON, Two Grey Hills Trading Post

including old tablitas and a beautiful old Navajo blouse.

The post buys livestock, piñon nuts, wool, and mohair. Behind the post is an amazing barn built in 1920, with a unique interior system of supports and beams well worth a look. Jed Foutz also runs the Shiprock Trading Post and Broadway Pawn in Farmington. He has a flair for dramatic display and an eye for quality that was trained by growing up in a trading family.
B, K, J, P, R, Sp

Mary Owens, weaver, Sanders, Arizona

520-653-4555
M–Sat 7:30–7:30
Owner: Jed Foutz
♦ M, V, D, AE, C, S, HA

The old refurbished post stretches out behind the convenience store front. You must ask to see the arts and crafts room, which occupies the old structure. The stone walls and dramatic lighting reveal an old banner from the Gallup Ceremonial, fox pelts, and some *Yei'ii* and Storm Pattern rugs from Red Valley. There are some exceptional pieces on display

CENTRAL NAVAJO NATION FAIRS

August: Central Navajo Nation Fair, Chinle, Arizona

September: Navajo Nation Fair, Window Rock, Arizona

SELECTED CENTRAL NAVAJO NATION ARTISTS/CRAFTSPEOPLE

Jerry D. Begay, Chinle, AZ, 520-674-5427—Navajo jewely.

Leroy Begay, P.O. Box 331, Piñon, AZ 86510, 520-725-3225—Contemporary Navajo jewelry based on old styles with an updated feel.

Rena Begay, P.O. Box 69, Piñon, AZ 86510, 520-725-3225—Weaving, specializes in chief's blankets.

Irene Clark, 505–777–2437—Weaving.

Sadie Curtis, P.O. Box 424, Ganado, AZ 86505—Weaving.

Galena Dineyazhe, P.O. Box 863, Chinle, AZ 86503, 520–674–5417—Weaving.

Nusie Henry, P.O. Box 469, Crownpoint, NM 87313, 505-786-5678—Traditional/contemporary jewelry; gold and silver inlay, turquoise, lapis, opal, etc.

Gene Jackson, P.O. Box 1662, Chinle, AZ 86503—Navajo jewelry.

Lillian Joe, P.O. Box 449, Navajo, NM 87328—Weaving, specializes in Burntwater rugs.

Isobel John, P.O. Box 637, Many Farms, AZ 86538—Weaving, specializes in Pictorial rugs.

Jake Livingston, P.O. Box 252, Houck, AZ 86506, 520–688–2369—Navajo jewelry, sculpture, saddles.

Mary S. Owens and Ethel Nez, P.O. Box 340–1097, Sanders, AZ 86512—Weaving.

Betty Roan, P.O. Box 262, Chambers, AZ 86052—Weaving.

Brenda and Marjorie Spencer, P.O. Box 133, Chambers, AZ 86502—Weaving, specialize in Wide Ruins.

Andrew Tsihnahjinnie, P.O. Box 694, RRDF, Rough Rock, AZ 86503—Painter.

Ervin Tsosie, P.O. Box 72, Mexican Springs, NM 87320—Navajo jeweler.

Elsie Jim Wilson, P.O. Box 494, Ganado, AZ 86505—Weaving.

Playing Cards, *14" x 24", by Andrew Tsihnahjinnie, Rough Rock, Arizona*

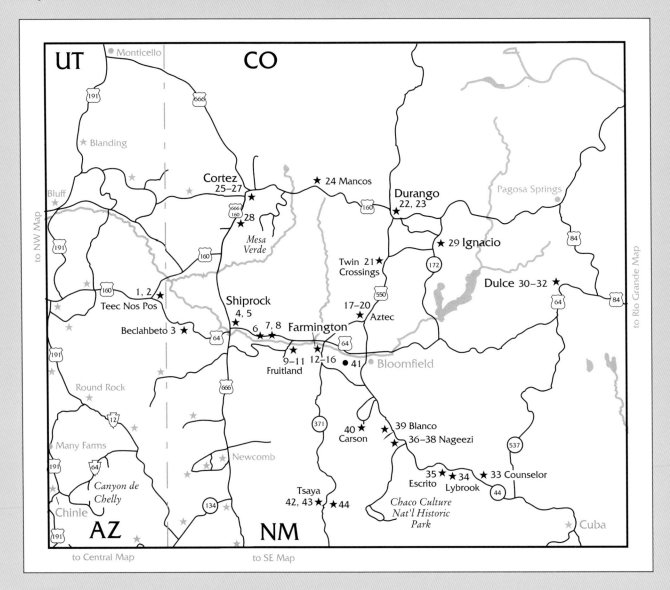

UT

CO

Monticello

191

666

Blanding

Bluff

to NW Map

191

160

Cortez
25–27

★ 24 Mancos

666
160

28

Durango
22, 23

Pagosa Springs

84

to Rio Grande Map

160

Mesa
Verde

160

★ 29 Ignacio

550

172

Dulce 30–32 ★

84

Twin 21 ★
Crossings

160

1, 2 ★

Teec Nos Pos

Shiprock
4, 5 ★

17–20
★ Aztec

64

191

Beclahbeto 3 ★

64

6 7, 8 Farmington

64

Bloomfield

9–11 12–16
Fruitland

● 41

666

Round Rock

12

Many Farms

191

64

Canyon de
Chelly

Newcomb

371

40 ★
Carson

39 Blanco

36–38 Nageezi

537

35 ★ ★ 34 ★ 33 Counselor
Escrito   Lybrook

44

Tsaya
42, 43 ★ ★ 44

Chaco Culture
Nat'l Historic
Park

Cuba

Chinle

191

AZ

134

NM

to Central Map

to SE Map

LEGEND

★ Trading Post in this chapter

★ Trading Post in other chapter

● Other site

Northeast Navajo Nation, Four Corners, Southern Ute, Ute Mountain Ute, and Jicarilla Apache

◆ ◆ ◆

Cerulean skies and deep vinaceous bands of sandstone become places of power.

Pit houses dug in the earth and cliff dwellings hanging on ledges still house the Anasazi spirit.

Listen. You may hear music inside their ancient earth architecture. I have—I think.

Terry Tempest Williams, *Pieces of White Shell: A Journey to Navajoland*

The prehistoric ruins at Mesa Verde National Park attract a large number of tourists to the Cortez-Durango area, but often visitors miss the rest of the Four Corners. This is a territory of many hidden surprises. It is also the heartland of Navajo sandpainting and home to a large number of talented Navajo weavers and folk artists.

The Teec Nos Pos–Shiprock area produces quality rugs in many diverse styles, such as figurative *Yei'ii* and *Yei'ii bichai* rugs that resemble sandpaintings, the Teec Nos Pos rugs with bright, busy, geometric shapes. You will also find a large selection of old and new jewelry and other traditional artwork.

What is unique about the Four Corners area is the folk artists. In the late sixties Jack Beasley began trading in Farmington. He actively encouraged artists to create toys of their youth and to explore their Navajo roots. This resulted in a dazzling array of artistic production. For instance, Navajo woodcarvers in the past often created work heavily influenced by Hopi kachina dolls and culture. Beasley has motivated these new carvers to create sculptures that are profoundly Navajo. The work is figurative, inspired by personal experiences, acquaintances, and the artist's community. The carvings are done primarily from cottonwood root found on the banks of the San Juan River. The

St. Luke's Cemetery near Carson Trading Post

pieces are stained or painted with a matte finish. The result is work of great integrity, humor and beauty. This area is home to carvers Johnson Antonio, Lawrence Jacquez, Dennis Pioche, Delbert Buck, Harrison and Rena Juan, Bob Beyale, and the Willeto family. Mamie Deschillie also makes her home here. She creates paintings, mud toys, and whimsical cardboard cutouts of animals and people that are painted and covered with fabric.

The folk artists of this vicinity have attracted a great deal of attention in the last few years. Collectors are drawn to their works, which at times defy traditional classification. If you are unfamiliar with these artists, you are in for a pleasant surprise. Creativity is alive and well in this region and very accessible. We are always surprised by the new artists we find when we visit.

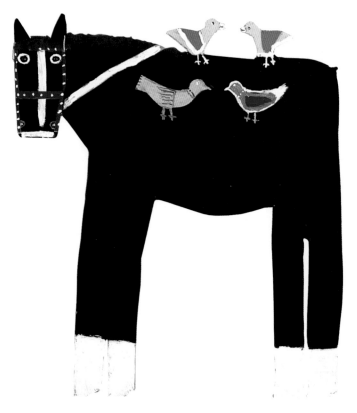

Cardboard cutout, 36" x 31", by Mamie Deschillie, Fruitland, new Mexico

SHIPROCK AND SURROUNDING AREA

The Shiprock area produces the highest quality and quantity of sandpaintings in the Southwest. The styles and character vary greatly—everything from refrigerator magnets to works of art valued at several thousand dollars.

Teec Nos Pos rug, 38" x 56", by Bertha Tom, Teec Nos Pos, Arizona. Courtesy of Garland's Navajo Rugs, Sedona, Arizona

1. Teec Nos Pos Trading Post

P.O. Box 940, Teec Nos Pos, AZ 86514
520-656-3224
M–F 8:00–6:00, Sat–Sun 8:00–5:00
Owners: Kathleen Foutz and John McCulloch

♦ M, V, C, S, HA

H.B. Noel established this post in 1905. Progressive Mercantile bought the post in 1913, and operated it until Russell Foutz bought the business in 1959 (he owns the Foutz Indian Room in Farmington, New Mexico). Russell's daughter Kathleen and son-in-law John McCulloch are the current owners. This area is well known for its weaving and you will find a good selection here. Rug prices range from $50 to $10,000. In addition to rugs you will find peyote ceremonial supplies, Navajo folk art, pottery, and other crafts. You must ask to see the rug room. Teec Nos Pos continues in a traditional trading post spirit, buying livestock, wool, and mohair. There is a cafe on the premises. B, J, P, **R**, Sp, folk art

2. Foutz Teec Nos Pos Arts and Crafts

Box 113, Teec Nos Pos, AZ 86514
520-656-3228

TEEC NOS POS RUGS

Teec Nos Pos rugs have wide borders, and are colorful, with patterns resembling oriental rugs. Every weaving family has its own particular bold and energetic pattern. The name comes from the Teec Nos Pos Trading Post which was established near Shiprock in 1905. They are the most collectable Navajo rug today ranging from $100 to $5,000.

—RUSSELL FOUTZ,
Foutz Indian Room

A single wagon-load of goods was often enough to give a trader his start. Leaving Wingate or Defiance Station, the trader drove his four-horse or ox team across the desert or into the mountains. Purposely he avoided any region where another white man had located . . . he would choose his place and open negotiations with the tribe's nearest head men.
—FRANK MCNITT, *The Indian Traders*

Summer: Daily 10:00–6:00,
Winter: M–Sat 9:00–5:00 (closed November–March 1)
Owner: Bill Foutz
♦ M, V, AE, C, S, HA (except for rug room), I

The business has been in this building since the mid-sixties. Bought by Bill Foutz about 1988, it is associated with his post in Shiprock. The two stores work together and Bill can find any item for you. The Foutz family influence is found throughout the Southwest. They originally settled in this area as Mormon polygamists. Their early history is covered more extensively in the book *Rugs and Posts*, by H.L. James.

This post has approximately 200 rugs for sale in the $50–$3,500 range. They also carry a selection of Cochiti drums, yarn, and Pendleton blankets. B, I, J, P, **R**, Sp, Sv

The first quarter of the century was the "golden age" of the trading posts, when for a brief span, the integrity of Indian work and Indian thought achieved its only recognition. It was the trader who made this possible, and it is these old-timers I remember with a boy's love and respect for their high traditions.
—FRANK WATERS, *Masked Gods*

3. Beclahbeto Trading Post
Shiprock, NM 87420, 18 miles west of Shiprock on Hwy 64
520-656-3455
M–F 8:00–6:00, Sat 8:00–3:00
Owner: Brent Foutz
♦ M, V, C, S, HA

Yei'ii rug, 33" x 54", by Virginia Nakai, Shiprock, Arizona. Courtesy of Garland's Navajo Rugs, Sedona, Arizona

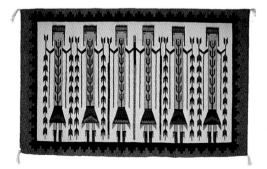

Beclahbeto Trading Post is a place where you can "water up" and share a story or two. We greatly enjoyed Lloyd, Brent, and E.J.'s humor. The Foutz family has been at this location since 1957 and in the trading business since the 1920s. It is a basic building and offers a line of general merchandise. They usually have 10 to 50 ($100–$4,000) rugs in the vault, and you must ask to see them.
B, J, **R**

YEI'II RUGS
The *Yei'ii* rugs are usually woven in the Lukachukai/Shiprock area, The *Yei'iis* are shown facing forward. Although the *Yei'ii* rugs are also a form of Sandpainting rug, there is less reluctance from weavers to create them. Therefore we see more of them. The recent ones seem to have more pattern, detail, and an increasing number of colors.
—JED FOUTZ, Shiprock Trading Company

Rug room, Shiprock Trading Company, Shiprock, New Mexico

4. **Shiprock Trading Company**
P.O. Box 906, Shiprock, NM 87420,
State Hwy 64
505-368-4585
M–Sat 8:00–7:30
Owner: Jed Foutz
♦ M, V, AE, C, S, HA, I

This bustling, active store serves the population of Shiprock. Ninety-five percent of their business is the local Navajo population. Wending your way past the aisles of food, beads, and sandpainting supplies, you will eventually come to the jewelry and book counter. You must ask to enter the hidden back rooms that house a large assortment of arts and crafts, rattles, Growler family animals,

> If you look with the mind of the swirling earth near Shiprock you become the land, beautiful. And understand how three crows at the edge of the highway, laughing, become three crows at the edge of the world, laughing.
> —JOY HARJO, *Secrets from the Center of the World*

Sandpainting rug, 50" x 49", by Bertha Teller, Chinle, Arizona. Courtesy of Garland's Navajo Rugs, Sedona, Arizona

SANDPAINTING RUGS

They are a pictorial rug and they use the designs of ceremonial sandpaintings. The colors have specific meanings. The backgrounds are usually a sand or grey color. Our Shiprock area has always been the center for them as the few families that made them live here. They are still one of the hardest rugs to find. Although sandpainting on board is now commonplace, in weaving it maintains many taboos and many Navajos are still very bothered by it.

—Jed Foutz, Shiprock Trading Company

some antique items, and dead pawn from the reservation. The back rooms were once the original trading post's rug rooms. They are an inner sanctum of solitude in an otherwise lively store.

B, J, P, **R**

5. Foutz Trading Company

P.O. Box 1894, Hwy 64, Shiprock, NM 87420
505-368-5790
Summer: M–Sat 9:00–5:30,
Winter: M–Sat 9:00–5:00
Owner: Bill Foutz
♦ M, V, AE, C, S, HA, I

Bruce M. Barnard opened his orig-inal post at this site in 1905. Bill Foutz opened for business in 1979, and he's usually in a whirlwind of activity, talking on the phone and buying rugs from weavers. The beautiful building houses a well-displayed collection of rugs, including pictorials by the Nez family, raised outline by Margie and Rose Dougi, and a variety of styles by Anita Tsosie and other weavers of this area. Bill also has an expanded selection of pottery, carved greenware, and Navajo pottery, including work by Lorraine Williams, Lorenzo Spencer, and occasionally Alice Cling and Rose Williams. Lorraine Williams told us that Bill bought her first pot and encouraged her to continue, for which she is most thankful. Much of the pottery is stored in a back room, and collectors should ask to see it. Bill has broadened his folk art inventory to include Lawrence Jacquez and Lorenzo Reed in addition to other fine Navajo wood carvings by Harrison Juan, Rena Juan, and Bob Beyale. These are also found in the back room so you must ask to see them. Bill also carries beadwork, wool, and craft supplies.

B, D, **P**, **R**, S, Sp, folk art

FARMINGTON AND SURROUNDING AREA

6. Hogback Trading Company

3221 Hwy 64, Waterflow, NM 87421
505-598-9243
M-Sat 8:00–5:00
Owner: Tom Wheeler
♦ M, V, C, S, HA, I

The Hogback Trading Post moved into its current circular building in 1986. The original post, located across the highway and slightly west of the new location, opened in 1871. The old building still has a lot of charm even though it is in ruins. Old paintings grace its exterior. Tom Wheeler is the fourth generation of traders at Hogback. In the upstairs space you will find a small museum featuring the family collection. The original trader, Joseph Wheeler, was a blacksmith and a wheelwright and was among the first Anglos in the Farmington area.

The new post is a well-designed, ten-thousand-square-foot, two-story contemporary hogan with a selection of 250 to 300 rugs ranging from $90 to $9,000. In addition, you can find other arts and crafts.

B, I, **J**, K, P, **R**, S, Sv

The ruins of the old Hogback Trading Company, Waterflow, New Mexico, across the highway from the new building

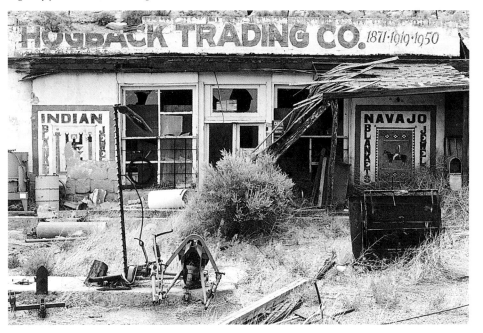

7. Bob French Navajo Rugs

P.O. Box 815, Waterflow, NM 87421, on Hwy 64, 15 miles west of Farmington
505-598-5621
M–Sat 8:00–5:00
Owner: Bob French
♦ M, V, AE, D, C, S, HA

If you enjoy Navajo rugs, Bob French's business is a must-stop. He has been at this location since 1976, and he also offers Black family baskets, Pendletons, and craft supplies in a modern setting. Weaving, however, is obviously his first love. He has an inventory of 500 to 600 contemporary rugs ($75–$10,000). Bob is very

Charlie Dickens, Big Rock Trading Post, Waterflow, New Mexico

knowledgeable about Navajo weaving and is willing to answer questions. He has been a trader since 1942 and worked at Teec Nos Pos, Fruitland, and Beclahbeto.

B, Bk, I, J, P, **R**, K

8. Big Rock Trading Post

P.O. Box 98, Waterflow, NM 87421
505-598-5184
M–F 8:00–5:30, Sat 9:00–5:30
Owners: Chuck and Charlie Dickens
● M, V, C, S, HA

An enormous white propane tank advertises Big Rock Trading Post. Chuck Dickens bought and rebuilt the current structure in 1968 and runs the business with his son, Charlie. They have a small museum consisting of their personal collection of saddles and other cowboy and Indian items. They do a thriving pawn business, sell a line of general merchandise to the

Hatch Brothers Trading post, Fruitland, New Mexico, has the traditional bullpen layout, old counters, and impeccably stocked shelves. Hatch will deny it, but we suspect that he stocks these shelves with an artistic eye for each item's color and visual beauty. Hand-tinted photograph

local population, and have a notable collection of old and new jewelry. We always enjoy its atmosphere of horse tack, galvanized tubs, rope, and other hardware hanging in every conceivable space.   B, **J**

9. Fruitland Trading Post
P.O. Box 328, No. 5 Road 6677, Fruitland, NM 87416
505-598-5991
M–F 8:00–6:00, Sat 8:00–1:00
Owners: Smalley Enterprises
♦ C, S, HA (through the back)

For the history-minded traveler, a stop at Fruitland Trading Post is obligatory, for this post opened in 1886. Among the groceries and general merchandise, look for sandpaintings, rugs, Navajo, Hopi and Pueblo pottery, kachina dolls, woodcarving, cradleboards, and jewelry. The real reason to stop here is for the atmosphere. An old creaking screen door, the large front porch, Schilling coffee clock, and an old pawn charge box can transport you to another time when people moved more slowly. Be sure to

notice the photograph of the post from earlier in this century.

You are very close to the Hatch Brothers Post. Ask for directions here. B, J, K, P, Pt, Sp

10. Hatch Brothers Trading Post
36 Riverside Drive, Fruitland, NM 87416
505-598-6226
M–Sat 8:00–5:00
Owner: R.S. Hatch
♦ S, HA

The Hatch Brothers Trading Post is one of our favorite stops. R.S. Hatch built this post in 1949 and still operates it. He chose this site because it was at the intersection of two wagon roads and between two fords on the San Juan River. With the main highway a half-mile away, you could say it was chosen for its seclusion and beauty too, because both are in abundance. Sunset light streams through the windows, and the charming country store atmosphere is undeniable. Original Arbuckles coffee advertising, scales, and a pack string device add to the timeless feeling of this post. Above the entrance is an unusual painting of skinwalkers attacking a hogan, which Hatch said was painted in the fifties.

We run into people across the Southwest who exclaim the virtues of this post and have bought rugs here. Hatch offers collectors a wide range of rugs, Black family baskets, concha belts,

Mamie Deschillie with a cardboard sculpture, Fruitland, New Mexico

and Navajo pipes. Cedar flutes sit among ax handles, enamel cups, and plates. Hatch builds collections of sixteen very old Navajo pots and baskets that he sells as collections. When asked why sixteen pots or sixteen baskets, he said, "Well, I just arrived at it." Collectors of antique pots and baskets should ask to see whatever collection is in progress. He comes across some magnificent pieces.

B, I, **P, R**

11. Mamie Deschillie: Folk Artist

P.O. Box 1305, Fruitland, NM 87416
505-327-3042 (daughter Jane Jones)

Mamie was born in 1920 and didn't begin to do artwork until the 1980s. At the insistence of trader Jack Beasley, she began to create mud toys and cardboard cutouts of animals and her Navajo neighbors. Mamie Deschillie's mud toys are not fired, but sun dried. They are very fragile. You can distinguish her work from that of Elsie Benally's by the noses Mamie adds. She infuses her work with a whimsical humor that has won her a wide audience. Mamie recently began making paintings as well. Her work can be seen at Jack Beasley's in Farmington, Thompson River Trading in Durango, and Leslie Muth Gallery and the

Rainbow Man in Santa Fe. Mamie welcomes special orders. Her daughter, Jane Jones, is very helpful in taking orders and shipping items.

Portrait of Mamie Deschillie, Folk Artist, *woodcarving, 24", by Johnson Antonio, Lake Valley, New Mexico*

12. Russell Foutz Indian Room

301 W. Main, Farmington, NM 87401
505-325-9413
M–Sat 9:00–5:00
Owner: Russell Foutz;
manager: Larry Comer
♦ M, V, AE, C, S, HA, I

Russell Foutz is a third-generation trader, also owning Russell Foutz Indian Room in Scottsdale, AZ. In the fifties, Totah Curio and E.P. Woods Indian Room were combined into the present business. (Totah Curio was owned by Willard Leighton of Notah Dineh in Cortez.) Serious collectors should ask to see the rug room and, if it is not busy, ask to see the museum room, which has some unique items that collectors will enjoy. The back room has a wonderful display of photographs of the Foutz family's early days at Teec Nos Pos.

In the Indian room you will find an exceptional bounty of old and new jewelry, cradleboards, an occasional Johnson Antonio carving, and, of course, rugs.

B, D, **J**, K, P, **R**, S, Sp, folk art

13. Beasley Manning Trading Company

111 E. Main, Farmington, NM 87401
505-327-5580
Hours variable
♦ M, V, D, AE, C, S, HA

Jack Beasley opened his trading company in 1968. He has been referred to as the "grandfather of Navajo folk art" for encouraging and guiding folk artists Mamie Deschillie, Elsie Benally, Johnson Antonio, and others. He was one of the first to see the intrinsic value of Navajo folk art, and his efforts have brought much attention to the artists in recent years.

Jack usually has a good selection of work by Mamie Deschillie, Johnson Antonio, Elsie Benally, the Hathale brothers, the Willeto family, and others. Any serious folk art collector would be well advised to stop by.

Jack's finely trimmed mustache, Western dress, and hospitality are a perfect accent to his stories and folk art offerings. Jack is much more than just another trader. His encouragement, vision, and hard work have ensured a place for him in the history of the Southwest. These artists who once sold their work as souvenirs are now fixtures in the international art market. Once, their work could only be found in Jack's storefront. Now it's shown in Santa Fe, New York, Los Angeles, and Europe.

Folk art

14. Fred Carson Trading Company

113 E. Main, Farmington, NM 87401
505-326-4115
M–F 9:30–5:30, Sat 9:00–3:00
Owner: Fred Alan Carson
♦ M, V, AE, D, C, S, HA

Third-generation trader Fred

Carson displays wonderful photographs that document the family's trading history. Fred's grandfather, Fred Carson, Sr., originally traded south of Gallup. His father, Fred Carson, Jr., traded at Nazlini from 1937 to 1952. He was also at Toadlena, Naschitti, Oljato, and Apache Mercantile on the Jicarilla Apache Reservation. Fred Carson III was at Nazlini from 1971 to 1979 and opened this business in Farmington in 1994.

Fred sells Jicarilla, Pima, and Navajo baskets; and jewelry. Fred suggests that collectors of Navajo rugs stop in. He is willing to sell rugs from the family's collection; some are as large as fifteen feet and are quite old. The shop is retail/wholesale.

Fred carries an extensive line of Navajo folk art including work by Dan Hot, Betty Manygoats, Delbert Buck, Ron Malone, Guy and Edith John, Wilford and Lulu Yazzie, Johnson Antonio, Rena Juan, Mamie Deschillie, and Ray Growler. Fred and his mother, Thelma, enjoy talking about the family's earlier trading days, and their stories are spellbinding.
B, J, R, **Folk Art**

15. Jack's Boots, Saddles, and Shoe Repair/Hank's Pawn
312 W. Broadway, Farmington, NM 87401
Jack's 505-325-2652,
Hank's 505-326-5019

Owners: Edna Guillory and Leland Noel (Jack's); Hank Foutz (Hank's)
M–Sat 9:00–6:00
♦ M, V, AE, C, S, HA

Jack's Boots and Saddles is a *very* Western store, chock full of spurs, boots, hats, horse tack, western clothing, and anything else the working cowboy might need. We especially like Herman Tsosie's custom rodeo chaps. Leland Noel can usually be found behind the counter. He has an array of quirky puzzles that he has made and his sleight-of-hand tricks will entertain nearly anyone. Leland spent time working at Piñon, Keams Canyon, and Polacca trading posts.

Hank's Pawn is in the rear of the store.
B, I, J, P, S, Sp

16. Fifth Generation Trading Company
232 W. Broadway, Farmington, NM 87401
505-326-3211
M–Sat 9:00–5:30
FAX: 505-326-0097
Owner: Joe E. Tanner, Jr.
♦ M, V, D, AE, C, S, HA, I

Joe Tanner, Jr., has been in business since 1987, opening his retail operation in 1993. His contemporary, well-displayed business offers the best sandpaintings we have encountered. Of special merit are the sandpaintings by Rosie Yellowhair, Herbert Ben,

Sr., Diane Thomas, and Eugene "Baatsoslanii" Joe. He also carries fine Tohono O'odham miniature horsehair baskets, including the work of Karen Antone. We found a wide range of handmade Navajo, Hopi, and Zuni Indian silver-and-turquoise jewelry. Joe said that this area has a large quantity of alabaster sculptures because it is taught at Shiprock High School. We were also impressed with the enormous selection of drums available in unusual shapes that could be easily used as coffee or end tables. Fifth Generation also houses a large selection of Native

Trader Jack Beasley, Beasley Manning Trading Company, Farmington, New Mexico

Tohono O'odham horsehair basket, 4.5" diameter, by Karen Antone. Courtesy of Fifth Generation Trading Company, Farmington, New Mexico (hand-tinted photograph)

Sandpainting, 24" x 24", by Rosie Yellowhair. Courtesy of Fifth Generation Trading Company

American artifact reproductions, such as bows and arrows, peace pipes, rattles, tomahawks, and quivers.
B, I, **J**, P, **S**, **Sp**

17. Ambrose Teasyatwho Studio and Gallery

119 S. Main, Aztec, NM 87410
505-334-6937
Owners: Ambrose and Elnora Teasyatwho

Navajo/Hopi sculptor Ambrose Teasyatwho, and his wife, Navajo weaver Elnora opened this family business in 1996. Ambrose describes his work as modern wood sculpture carved from a single piece of cotton-wood representing Hopi kachina figures or other Native American themes. He has taught several local carvers about his style of woodcarving. Elnora is known for her pastel, vegetal-dyed, La Plata style rugs. Call about weaving demonstrations at the studio.

18. West Chaco Gallery

105 West Chaco St. (upstairs), Aztec, NM 87410
505-334-6035
T–Sat 12:00–5:00 or by appt.
Owner: Ron Pease and Dawn Schmidt
♦ V, C, T, S

This gallery shows contemporary and traditional Native American art in addition to custom framing. Navajo/Hopi carver Ambrose Teasyatwho, and Navajo carvers Lawrence Jacquez and Lawrence Yellowhair exhibit here. Ron and Dawn also manage the Native Images Gallery, owned by artist Dan Stolpe, which is a print studio located in the same building (505-334-0417 messages).

19. Kiva Trading Post

624 Ruins Rd., Aztec, NM 87410
505-334-2949
Daily: Summer: 9:00–6:00, Winter: 9:00–5:00 (hours vary)
Owner: Robert Burnside
♦ M, V, D, AE, C

Kiva Trading Post is one of the

shops near the entrance to Aztec Ruins National Monument. While carrying souvenir items, the shop also carries about 50 to 100 rugs from $200 to $4,000.

B, J, K, P, **R**, S, Sv

20. Aztec Ruins Trading Post

70 County Rd. 2900, Aztec, NM 87410, at Aztec Ruins National Monument
505-334-2943
Daily Summer: 9:00–6:00,
Winter: 9:00–5:00
Owners: Tom and Barbara Roberds
♦ M, V, C, S, HA (with some difficulty)

This post was opened in 1930 by Verda Josey and was later purchased by Bob Leighton, who is now at Notah Dineh in Cortez. The Roberds bought the post in 1986. It is an interesting shop that offers Tohono O'odham and Navajo baskets; Navajo, Acoma, Jemez, Santa Clara, and slipcast pottery; and 20 or so Navajo rugs ($300–$3,000).

There is a small museum on the premises as well. Old Navajo, Pueblo, and Anasazi pottery, metates, old baskets, fossils, rifles, hunting trophies, and western collectables line a display wall of the post. The Roberds welcome and enjoy people. This is a retail-only business, and bargaining is discouraged.

B, Bk, D, F, **J**, M, **P**, R

DURANGO AND SURROUNDING AREA

21. Twin Crossings Trading Post

1929 Hwy 550 South, Durango, CO 81301, 17 miles south of Durango
970-259-5835
Daily 5:00–8:00, Winter 8:00–7:00
Owner: Brent Bennion
♦ C, HA

The new owner is remodeling and has plans to carry work by local Hopi, Navajo, and Ute artists. It is a watering hole between Farmington and Durango

SINGLE FIGURE YE'II RUG
R.T.F. Simpson was an active trader in the Farmington, New Mexico, area around 1900. His Navajo wife, Yadesbah, wove large, beautiful, single Ye'ii rugs. In 1991 we encouraged some weavers to revive these unusual rugs. The weavers' designs have evolved into unique forms of self expression.
—STEVE SIMPSON,
Twin Rocks Trading Post

and sells more lottery tickets than any other location in Colorado.
Restaurant

22. Thompson River Trading Company

140 W. 8th St., Durango, CO 81301
970-247-5681
Daily 10:00–6:00 or by appt.
Owner: Jack Antle
♦ M, V, C, S, HA (through the back door)

Single Figure Ye'ii rug, 40" x 64", by Marjorie Dee. Courtesy of Twin Rocks Trading Post, Bluff, Utah

Jack Antle has been in this location since 1990 but has been trading since 1968. In his small storefront he has accumulated an impressive presentation of Navajo folk art including the work of Johnson Antonio, Dennis Pioche, Harrison and Rena Juan, Dan Hot, Mamie Deschillie, the Benallys, and a wide assortment of paintings by the Hathale family. Jack is also very knowledgeable about old baskets and offers museum quality baskets from the Southwest, California, and the Northwest coast. He also carries beadwork, some old pottery, flutes, and unusual items that he uncovers in his travels. He might have a silver-adorned Navajo blouse, an old Navajo rattle, or good advice on local trout fishing. Jack obviously loves the work that he sells, and we highly recommend a visit to his unique shop.
B, D, I, J, K, P, R, **Folk Art**

23. Toh-Atin

145 W. 9th St., Durango, CO 81301
970-247-8277
Summer: M–Sat 9:00–9:00,
Sun 10:00–6:00
Winter: M–F 9:00–6:00, Sat 10:00–6:00
Owners: Jackson Clark II and
Antonia Clark

Toh-Atin Gallery, Durango, Colorado, with alabaster sculpture by Ricky Nez in foreground

♦ M, V, AE, D, C, S, HA, I
This business was begun in 1957 by H. Jackson Clark who, as a result of attempting to collect on some traders' bad debts, traded Pepsi Cola for Navajo rugs. Clark's entertaining book, *The Owl in Monument Canyon*, describes this beginning and other trading stories from 1930 to the present.
The gallery is located off Durango's Main Avenue and is run by Jackson's son, J.C., and daughter, Antonia. It is known for weaving. Here you'll find work by Theresa and Helen Begay,

Jack Antle, Thompson River Trading Company, Durango, Colorado

Bessie and Laverne Barber, Ella Rose Perry, and Isabel John. The gallery represents a group of weavers who create Burnham rugs and tapestries. These new rugs, developed in the early eighties, are reminiscent of the Two Grey Hills style in their layout and their use of handspun wool. Bright accent colors and pictorial elements are woven into a tightly compressed design. The name comes from Burnham, New Mexico, where the Barber-Begay family of weavers used to live. Toh-Atin is the best place to inquire about their work.

We were also impressed by the beautiful display of Pueblo pottery. You can get a good education about the stylistic differences of the pueblos from looking at this selection. While carrying some estate jewelry, the gallery emphasizes contemporary jewelers such as Andy Lee Kirk, Ben Knighthorse, Jimmie Poyer, Orville Tsinnie, Jeanette Dale, and Jimmie King, Jr. All turquoise is untreated. B, Bk, **J**, **P**, Pt, **R**, S, Sv, Folk Art

24. **Mud Creek Hogan**
38651 Hwy 160 West, P.O. Box 269, Mancos, CO 81328
970-533-7117
Mar 1–Nov 1: 7:00–6:00

Enromous arrows stop visitors at Mud Creek Hogan in Mancos, Colorado. Hand-tinted photograph

Yei'ii pot, 14", by Lorraine Williams, Cortez, Colorado

Owners: Bill and Judy Countess
♦ M, V, D, AE, C, S, HA
  Mud Creek Hogan offers arts and crafts and original Anasazi pottery. There is also an assembly of animal pelts and skulls, including skulls of snapping turtle, coyote, badger, and bear. This is the *only* place where we have seen mountain man toothpicks for sale. (If you visit, be sure to ask for the story behind them!) The Mud Creek Hogan also carries gift items, including a wide selection of local food products.
B, I, J, M, P, R, Sp, Sv

25. **Lorraine Williams: Potter**
405 W. 7th St., Space 7, Cortez, CO 81321
970-564-9639
Lorraine learned how to make pottery in 1984 from her mother-in-law, Rose Williams.
  Her work is ever-changing with new motifs. Sacred Mountain Trading Post near Flagstaff, Packards and

When I started, I made traditional Navajo pots. One day when I was polishing a pot, I scratched it. To hide the scratch, I made a one line design around the pot. I liked it and added more and more designs. I used horned toads, but my father said that they were one of our sacraments and should not be burned, so in his honor, I stopped. I now use *Yei'iis* and *Yei'ii bichai* dancers. Some people don't think I should use them, but I feel good about it. When I do them I feel serenity, comfort, and feel good about myself. I don't draw out the designs ahead of time. I like to pick up my screwdriver and just begin to draw on the pot and see what happens.
—LORRAINE WILLIAMS, potter

Leslie Muth Gallery in Santa Fe, and Twinrocks Trading Post in Bluff, Utah, carry her work. Lorraine attends Santa Fe Indian Market and will take special orders.

26. **Mesa Verde Pottery and Gallery Southwest**
27601 U.S. Hwy 160 E., P.O. Box 9, Cortez, CO 81321
970-565-4492
Memorial Day–Sept: Daily 8:00–7:00, Sept–May: M–Sat 8:00–5:00
Owners: Scott and Jay Tipton; gallery director: Sandra Stockdale
♦ M, V, D, AE, C, S, HA, I
  Scott and Jay Tipton have been at this location since 1981. The large modern building houses their cast pottery operation. The pottery sells in the $9–$22 range. They also carry a large Pueblo pottery selection with many museum-quality pieces dating from 1910. Their inventory represents over four hundred potters, including Maria Martinez, Joseph Lonewolf, Christine Naranjo, Greg Garcia, Effie Garcia, the Naranjo family, and the Fragua family. They also have a children's room full of inexpensive gift items. The owners are amiable and enjoy answering questions. (You might ask about the arrowhead over the door to the office.)
B, J, **P**, R, S, Sv

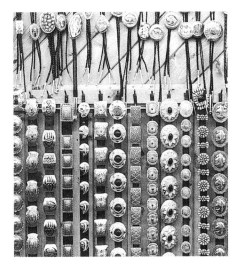

Bolos and conchas, Notah Dineh Museum, Cortez, Colorado

27. Notah Dineh

345 W. Main, Cortez, CO 81321
970-565-9607
M–Sat 8:00–6:00, Sun 10:00–6:00
Owner: Robert Leighton;
manager: Gregg Leighton
♦ M, V, D, AE, C, S, HA

Robert Leighton has been trading since the fifties and opened Notah Dineh in 1961. They moved into this new location in 1992 and maintain a large inventory. They have developed a 3,200-square-foot museum on the premises that houses their collection of baskets, jewelry, pottery, Ute and Navajo beadwork, two impressive Simpson *Yei'ii* rugs, and Winchester rifles in a trading post atmosphere.

Two hundred and fifty weavers supply Notah Dineh, which has approximately 400 rugs in stock. The rugs are priced at $40 per square foot or from $100 to $5,000. The store has one of the largest inventories of cradleboards in the Southwest, and a wide range of contemporary and old rugs and exceptional beadwork. We were impressed with watercolors by the Toddy Brothers and the finely tuned pencilwork of Wilton Charley.

Gregg Leighton is a wealth of information, and serious collectors should express particular interests.
B, Bk, C, I, **J**, K, M, **P**, Pt, **R**, S, Sp, Sv

28. Burch's Sleeping Ute Trading

158 Hwy 160, Cortez, CO 81321
970-565-3534
Daily 6:00–12:00; pawn hours:
M–F 8:00–6:00, Sat 8:00–5:00
Owners: Danny and Cheryl Rudder
♦ M, V, AE, HA

The Rudders are part of the Burch family with a post at Mexican Hat. This trading post sells groceries and gas. A small but interesting selection of jewelry, including some old pawn, local beadwork, and beadwork supplies can be found in the gift shop upstairs.
B, C, **J**, P, R

Notah Dineh Museum, Cortez, Colorado. Hand-tinted photograph

UTE TRIBAL LANDS

 Southern Ute Cultural Center and Museum

P.O. Box 737, Ignacio, CO 81137, next to the casino in Ignacio
970-563-9583, -4649 (gift shop)
Summer (May 15–Sept): M–F
9:00–6:00; Sat–Sun 11:00–3:00; Winter:
T–F 10:00–5:30, or by appt.
Director: Helen Hoskins;
gift shop manager: Orin Box
♦ I

Owned by the Southern Ute Tribe, the museum contains permanent and temporary exhibitions about the tribe based on creation stories and seasonal point of view. The museum, which charges an entry fee, presents a multimedia slide show, contemporary exhibitions, and historical artifacts. The gift shop sells Ute art and beadwork; Navajo, Zuni, and Pueblo jewelry; and Pueblo pottery. Group tours and educational packets are available. Call tribal offices for information on dances and the Tribal Fair held in September (800-876-7017).
J, P, Pt

SOUTHERN UTE

Tribal Offices: Ignacio, CO 81137, 24 miles southeast of Durango via Hwy 172, south from US 169, 8 miles from LaPlata County Airport
970-563-0155

The Southern Ute Tribe occupies a beautiful stretch of land between Durango and Pagosa Springs to the north and Aztec and Dulce to the south. The land is rich, nourished by the Animas and La Plata rivers. In the spring the four-day Bear Dance brings residents together in a celebration to waken bear from his winter slumber. Traditional stick and hand games, food, and festivities abound. The four-day Sun Dance is held in late summer.

SELECTED SOUTHERN UTE ARTISTS/CRAFTSPEOPLE

Eddie Box, Sr. (Red Ute of Ignacio), P.O. Box 224, Ignacio, CO 81137, 970-563-4128—Ute love flutes.

UTE MOUNTAIN UTE TRIBE

Tribal Offices: Towaoc, CO 81344, 12 miles south of Cortez, off Hwy 666
970-565-3751
Ute Mountain Tribal Park, Towaoc, CO 81334, 970-565-3751 ext. 282

The Ute Mountain Ute Tribe occupies the land directly west of the Southern Utes, and stretching to border Utah and the Navajo Nation. The Ute Mountain Ute Tribe provided the land for Mesa Verde National Park and currently oversees the 125,000-acre Ute Mountain Tribal Park that protects a large number of Anasazi ruins. The tribe opened the Ute Mountain Casino in 1992. A pottery cooperative selling slipcast pottery was opened in 1970.

SELECTED UTE MOUNTAIN UTE ARTISTS/CRAFTSPEOPLE

Ute Mountain Pottery, P.O. Box 288, Hwy 160 S., Towaoc, CO 81334, 1 mile N. of casino, 12 miles S. of Cortez
970-565-8548
M–Sat 9:00–6:00
Sun (Summer) 12:00–6:00

JICARILLA APACHE
P.O. Box 507, Dulce, NM 87528
505-759-3242 for information
Jicarilla Apache Fair (Go-Jii-Ya Feast
Day), mid-September in Dulce;
Little Beaver Roundup, early July
    The Jicarilla Apache
Reservation's big draws are
hunting, fishing, and camping.
Surrounded by lands filled with
timber, water, and grass, the artists
of this area excel in basketry
because materials are available
everywhere.

JICARILLA APACHE RESERVATION

30. Apache Mesa Gallery and Gifts

Best Western Jicarilla Inn,
P.O. Box 233, Dulce, NM, Hwy 64
and Hawks Dr.
505-759-3663, FAX 505-759-3170
Daily 8:00–9:00
Owner: Thomas Vigil
♦ M, V, D, AE, C, S, HA

Opened in 1984, this gift shop is inside the Best Western Jicarilla Inn. While the selection is small, we found a few unique items. Available are handmade shawls, one case of beaded jewelry, key rings, small silver jewelry, reasonably priced beaded bottles, small paintings of wildlife, and beaded moccasins, pouches, and walking canes. We found a few Apache baskets.
B, C, J, M, Pt, R, Clothing

31. Jicarilla Arts and Crafts Museum

P.O. Box 507, Dulce, NM 87528
505-759-3242, ext. 274
M–F 8:00–5:00
Owner: Jicarilla Apache Tribe
Director: Brenda Julian
♦ T, HA (2 steps)

Jicarilla is Spanish for "small basket." It is interesting that baskets were identified so strongly with the Apache. The great selection of baskets on display in this museum explains why. They come in all shapes and sizes. You can also see fishing creels, beadwork including bridles and headdresses, interesting dolls, paintings, old pottery, and photographs.

You may purchase items from the shop, including multicolored baskets from $150, basket vessels, cases of beaded jewelry, beaded kerosene lamps, hand beaded caps, and other items. The building is an unlikely looking tin structure, so make sure you keep your eyes open for it on the main highway through Dulce.
Б, J, P, **Beadwork**

32. Sweetwater Gallery—Lydia Pesata: Basketweaver

P.O. Box 114, Dulce, NM 87528,
Hwy 64 next to the park at the turn in the road
505-759-3298, before 10:00 am and evenings, answering machine

Lydia Pesata started weaving baskets thirty years ago, teaching herself everything about traditional Jicarilla Apache basketry. She collects sumac and willow, and researches and collects the vegetal dyes made from a dozen or so plants, barks, berries, and roots. Baskets range from a 36" x 18" oval basket in the Cimmaron Museum to a nickel-size coil basket of willow and sumac with twelve to fifteen rounds. Her studio, Sweetwater Gallery in Dulce, is family owned. You may also

Jicarilla Apache, Four Point Star Design with Full Moon, 14" diameter, by Lydia Pesata. Courtesy of the artist

find Lydia working on moccasins, clothing, or pottery. She travels extensively, demonstrating basketry. She teaches workshops at Crow Canyon. In 1988 she received the New Mexico Governor's Award. She traveled to the Museum of the American Indian in New York in 1990, and in 1992 she demonstrated at the Smithsonian Folk Life Festival in Washington D.C.

Lydia sometimes takes orders for her baskets, or you can find her and her family (see below) at the annual Santa Fe Indian Market.

SELECTED JICARILLA APACHE ARTISTS/CRAFTSPEOPLE

Rainey Julian, P.O. Box 315, Dulce, NM 87528, 505-759-3737—Jewelry, a unique combination of silver and beadwork.

Joan Pesata, P.O. Box 935, Dulce, NM 87528—Star quilts.

Melvin Pesata, P.O. Box 114, Dulce, NM 87528 , 505-759-3298—Apache baskets.

Melbourne Pesata—Apache baskets.

Molly Pesata—Micaceous pottery and baskets.

Vida L. Vigil, P.O. Box 227, Dulce, NM 87528 , 505-759-3103— Beadwork, quillwork.

CHACO CANYON AREA

33. Counselor Trading Post
Counselor, NM 87018
505-568-4453
M–F 8:00–6:00, Sat 8:00–12:00
Owners: McDonald Enterprises; managers: Pat and Kelly Aragon
♦ M, V, D, AE, C, S, HA (with some difficulty)

Ask to see the rug vault (50 to 100 rugs, $35–$4,000). They carry Two Grey Hills, Shadowbox, Ganado, *Yei'ii bichai,* and Storm Pattern rugs. They also carry Navajo baskets for ceremonies. Counselor functions as a traditional post, bartering for sheep, wool, mohair, and rugs.

Counselor has a forty-plus-year-old tradition called Navajo Christmas. On the Saturday before Christmas, local customers form long lines in the pre-dawn cold for a thousand bags filled with rock candy, apples, peanuts, choc-olate, and popcorn balls. Those in line are warmed by a continuous supply of coffee, glazed doughnuts, and boiled hot dogs.
B, J, **R**

34. Lybrook Mercantile
HCR 17, P.O. Box 600, Cuba, NM 87013
505-568-4477

M–F 8:00–5:00, Sat 8:00–4:00
Owner: Al and Sandra Chapman
♦ C, S

This store contains general merchandise, a laundry, and one display case of old pawn. Look for the "Spectacular Fireworks" sign.
J

35. Escrito Trading Post
HCR 17, P.O. Box 1000, Cuba, NM 87013-9406
505-568-4478
M–Sat 7:00–6:00
Owner: Al Chapman
♦ M, V, AE, C, S, HA

Escrito carries general merchandise and a few arts and crafts. There is one long case of jewelry with some old pawn, cradleboards, and lariats. They also sell gas and do auto repairs.
J, R

36. Lawrence Jacquez: Woodcarver
P.O. Box 275, Nageezi, NM 87037
505-320-6172

Lawrence Jacquez's early life was turbulent and filled with tragedy. Through it all, he finds the strength and will, with the support of his wife Luann, to create sandpainting sculptures and wood figures of *Yei'ii bichai* dancers, strong Navajo women, and even skinwalkers. Lawrence says, "I draw a lot of inspiration from my grandmother. I am trying to find a place between folk and fine art. I have learned much from looking at Hopi carvers, but what I carve is always Navajo." His wooden sculptures have a powerful presence, with large physical proportions that imply an outer and inner strength. He is an artist of rising reputation to watch for.

Artist Lawrence Jacquez with carved Yei'ii bichai *dancer, Nageezi, New Mexico*

37. Nageezi Trading Post/Chaco Inn

Nageezi, NM 87037
505-632-3646, 800-96CHACO
M–Sat 8:00–5:00
Owners: Don and Carol Batchelor
♦ M, V, C, S, HA

Jim McKuen opened the Nageezi Trading Post in 1939, and Harry Batchelor bought it in 1970. His son, Don, and wife, Carol, took over in 1990, opening an adjoining bed-and-breakfast. The post sells gas, groceries, general merchandise, Anasazi reproductions, and carvings by Robin Wellito, his brother, Harold Willeto, and their mother, Elizabeth Willeto Ignacio. (The brothers spell their names differently to corollate to Navajo Nation mail.) The family's patriarch, Charlie Willeto, was a famous Navajo folk artist. (The Willetos live close to the post.)

> Rug designs sometimes come from strange places. Back in the seventies, a weaver brought in a very unique rug. We liked it and asked her where she got the design. She smiled and ran out to her truck and proudly brought in a Kleenex box that was decorated with a similar design.
> —**DON BATCHELOR**, Nageezi Trading Post/Chaco Inn

Sometimes backroads are casually marked

Sculptures by Lawrence Jacquez are also available. He also lives nearby and has painted a large mural on the red barn north of the post.

Don has a genuinely friendly nature and has developed friendships with all the locals. He has a personal collection of work by the Willetos and Lawrence Jacquez and allows aficionados to visit the Chaco Inn to see the pieces. The Batchelors are very welcoming, and the Chaco Inn is a nice place to stay when visiting Chaco Canyon. If you plan to visit in the summer, be sure to make reservations early. Many people are discovering the Batchelors' hospitality.
B, Bk, J, R, Sv, Folk Art

38. Navajo Brethren in Christ Mission Inc. Crafts Store

HC 63, Box 6000, Bloomfield, NM
87413-9405, off NM 44 on
Hwy 57 to Chaco Canyon
505-632-1212
M–Sat 8:00–5:00
Director: Charlie Byer
♦ M, V, C, S

The craft store is inside the mission compound. The mission was opened in 1947 by two registered nurses from Thomas, Oklahoma, as a tent city. The first building was built out of WWII ammunition boxes. The craft store opened about 1954, originally taking trade for boarding Navajo students or hospital payments. The kindness of these missionaries in an emergency many years ago is remembered by one of the authors.
J, P, Pt, R

39. Blanco Trading Post

Hwy 44, Bloomfield, NM 87413,

Highway 666, south of Shiprock, New Mexico

Nancy Thomas frying bread at Blanco Trading Post, south of Bloomfield, New Mexico

30 miles south of Bloomfield
505-632-1597
Daily 8:00–6:00
Owner: Julie Burch
♦ M, V, C, S, HA

Blanco Trading Post was originally opened in the thirties. Present owner Julie Burch, although young, has the hardworking values of the early traders. The front of the building displays groceries, general merchandise, post office, and gas. The back room has old and new Navajo baskets including unusual pitch baskets, wool, and a good selection of concho belts and jewelry. One of the most impressive aspects of this wholesale/retail business is the large selection (300 to 400) of rugs. Some are old, and they range from $35 to $10,000. Julie buys wool, mohair, piñons, and rugs. She still trades with the locals and extends credit.
B, Bk, D, **J**, **R**, P

40. Carson Trading Post

P.O. Box 490, Bloomfield, NM 87413, 14 miles south of Bloomfield off Hwy 44 on County Rd. 7150, then another 6 miles on County Rd. 7300. Signposts are difficult to read, so watch for the nearby Huerfano Chapter House on this road. The post

Robert Garlinghouse, Carson Trading Post, south of Bloomfield, New Mexico. Hand-tinted photograph

Carson Trading Post. Hand-tinted photograph

is just to the left before you go over a metal bridge.
505-325-3914
M–F and Sun 7:00–9:00,
Closed Saturdays
Owner: Raymond Drolet; manager/leaseholder: Lorraine Garlinghouse
◆ S, HA (with difficulty)

The Carson Trading Post is a stop for travelers interested more in historic posts themselves rather than the arts and crafts. Originally opened in 1918, it was started as a ten-man tent in the wilderness by the Meyer brothers. The current owners took over in 1990 after the post had been closed for four years. Part of the original bullpen counter has been removed, and the rug room has been turned into a game room with pool table.

The trading post compound is still intact, as one might have found it in the active days of Stokes Carson. The site itself is interesting, too, with one of the few rural metal bridges in the area.

The book *Stokes Carson* by Willow Roberts offers a history of the post. We suggest calling before making the trip.
B, P

41. **Delbert Buck: Woodcarver**
P.O. Box 1012, Fruitland, NM 87416

Delbert Buck, born in 1976, is the youngest and one of the most prolific artists in this book. His artwork is often a group project involving his father Wilford and his sister Emma. Delbert began carving at age nine, creating a series of rifles, machine guns, and pistols to use as toys. His work evolved into large figures on horseback and of whimsical subject matter. He uses bits of fabric and found objects and prefers to paint the sculptures with a bright palette.

The Bucks' home is surrounded by a series of small buildings and a seemingly endless supply of wood. The family lives without electricity or

Woman on Horse with Cradleboard and Orange Cat, 28" x 24", by Delbert Buck, Fruitland, New Mexico

42. Tsaya Trading Post

P.O. Box 298, Kirtland, NM 87417 (mailing address), on Hwy 371, in Lake Valley, 55 miles south of Farmington
505-786-7007
Summer: M–F 8:00–7:00,
Winter: M–F 8:00–6:00
Owner: Ashcroft family;
manager: Ross Ashcroft
♦ M, V gas only, C, S, HA

The Tsaya Trading Post is the lifeblood of this area. They sell general merchandise, and their microwavable sandwiches are as close to a restaurant as you will find locally. The post uses an old mail system, with everyone in the area picking up mail here and using the post's address as their own. At this location since 1961, the post is the center of activity for the Lake Valley area. You will find elderly men trading stories as they warm themselves by the large heater.

Ross Ashcroft's family owns Tsaya Trading Post, Lake Valley, New Mexico. He was raised at the old post (now in ruins). Ross will give detailed directions to any artist in the area, which is very important in the web of unmarked dirt roads in the Lake Valley.

running water. Although just out of Bloomfield, their home has a windswept and very isolated feel that the family enjoys. It was difficult locating their home even though Delbert drew an extensive color-coded map and marked the turnoffs with tires. Delbert is very modest about his work. His high school art teacher is unaware that her student is one of the rising stars of Navajo folk art.

Delbert's work is available at the Leslie Muth Gallery and The Rainbow Man in Santa Fe. Delbert accepts special orders.

43. Johnson Antonio: Woodcarver

P.O. Box 298, Kirtland, NM 87417

The New Mexico Veterans' Memorial Highway 371 stretches from Farmington to Thoreau, and ribbons across the silent and austere beauty of the Bisti Wilderness region. Approximately fifty miles south of Farmington is the Lake Valley area and the Tsaya Trading Post.

A couple of miles from the highway on a well-kept dirt road is the Antonio residence. It is nestled in a cluster of four homes surrounded by horses, dogs, sheep, and voracious goats that enjoy eating the exterior of the house. Johnson and Lorena love all these creatures and talk about certain animals with particular affection and enthusiasm.

Behind the main house is a small structure made of discarded wood. It is here that Johnson carves, whittles, and paints his sculptures. His work captures an essence of this area and its people. Johnson and his family endure many hardships so they can live here. Water is transported by truck from fifty miles away, and they have no telephone. However, like many other Navajos, they enjoy the serenity, peace, and everyday poetry this isolation brings.

Johnson does not speak much English, but Lorena, his children, or a neighbor are always around to help translate. He is quite willing to

Woodcarving, 24", by Johnson Antonio, Lake Valley, New Mexico

demonstrate his abilities and answer questions. Using a simple buck knife, he carves his figures from a single piece of cottonwood that can range from six inches to three feet in height. His sculptures have great integrity, and a visit to Lake Valley will make

their inspiration apparent. From a figure of an old Navajo man smoking or a woman being swept off her feet by her husband, to a man carrying a deer over his shoulder—all are in evidence in Lake Valley.

Johnson collects his wood from the river banks around Farmington. He uses only hand tools and his color comes from inexpensive sources or *dleesh*, a local white clay used in ceremonies. From these simple materials he creates art that epitomizes and celebrates the Navajo traditional lifestyle.

Johnson Antonio, Navajo folk artist, Lake Valley, New Mexico

44. **Savage's Trading Company**
P.O. Box 6173, Farmington, NM 87499
505-320-1712
Sun–Th 8:00–6:00
Owners: George and Rena Savage
♦ S, HA

Fifty miles south of Farmington, and 1.5 miles east of Hwy 371, is the Savage Trading Company. It is a surreal experience in the midst of the Bisti Wilderness region. They offer wedding gowns; auto parts; snack items; used merchandise; some small, locally woven rugs; and a few small items by local artists. If you are interested in seeing the ruins of the old Tsaya Trading Post, they will show you its adjacent location, some great horned owl rookeries, or the nearby spring for which Tsaya is named. (Tsaya translates as "water under rock.") The Savages are very hospitable and enjoy talking about the Lake Valley area, its history and its landmarks.
R, Folk Art

NORTHEAST NAVAJO NATION FAIRS

July: Mesa Verde Indian Arts and Crafts Show and Sale, Mesa Verde National Park Morefield campground, 505-327-6296.

September: Totah Festival, Native American Fine Arts Show and Sale, Rug Auction, Powwow, Farmington Civic Center, 800-448-1240.

October: Shiprock Navajo Fair, Shiprock, NM.

SELECTED NORTHEAST NAVAJO NATION ARTISTS/CRAFTSPEOPLE

Bob Beyale, P.O. Box 298, Kirtland, NM 87417—Folk art Navajo dolls.

Harrison and Rena Juan, P.O. Box 298, Kirtland, NM 87417—Folk art Navajo dolls, paintings, and ceramics.

Lucy Leuppe McKelvey and daughters, Cecilia, Celeste, & Celinda, 620 N. Jordan, Bloomfield, NM 87413, 505-632-1686—Pottery.

Wood figures, 14", by Bob Beyale, Lake Valley, New Mexico

Pot, 20" diameter, by Lucy McKelvey, Bloomfield, New Mexico

Rickie Nez, P.O. Box 1193, Kirtland, NM 87417, 505-326-3015—Alabaster sculpture.

Sidney Nez, P.O. Box 1575, Shiprock, NM 87420—Jewelry.

Mark Silversmith, P.O. Box 5295, Farmington, NM 87499, 505-326-6854—Watercolors.

Herb Thompson, P.O. Box 1764, Kirtland, NM 87417, 505-598-6460—Contemporary Navajo jewelry.

Orville and Darlene Tsinnie, P.O. Box 537, Hwy 666, Shiprock, NM 87420, 505-368-5936, -4240—Traditional/contemporary jewelry, silver/gold, turquoise, coral and other gem-quality stones.

Leonard Tso, P.O. Box 461, Fruitland, NM 87416, 505-598-1072—Alabaster sculpture.

Anita Tsosie, 24101 County Rd. E. 5, Cortez, CO—Weaving, specializes in Teec Nos Pos, Sandpainting, and Revival rugs.

Louise White, P.O. Box 279, Teec Nos Pos, AZ 86514—Weaving, specializes in *Yei'ii* rugs.

Robin Wellito and Harold Willeto, P.O. Box 151, Nageezi, NM 87037—Folk art.

Valorie Willie, P.O. Box 2233, Bloomfield, NM 87413—Beadwork.

Rosie Yellowhair, P.O. Box 1104, Fruitland, NM 87416—Navajo sandpainting.

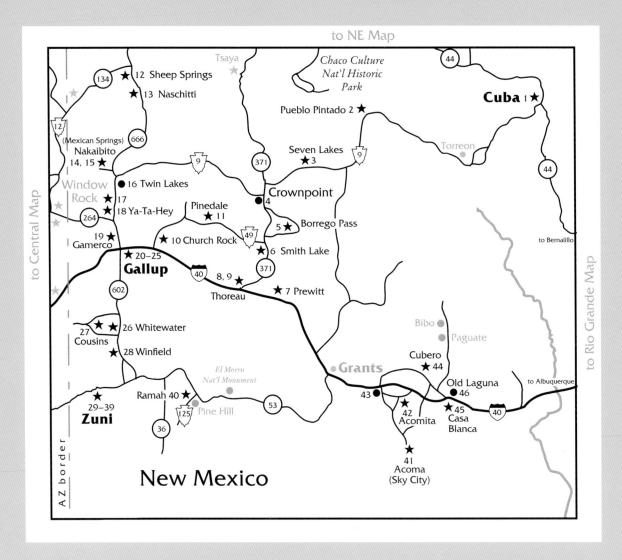

to NE Map

Tsaya

Chaco Culture
Nat'l Historic
Park

44

Cuba 1 ★

★ 12 Sheep Springs

★ 13 Naschitti

134

Pueblo Pintado 2 ★

12

(Mexican Springs)
Nakaibito
14, 15 ★

666

Torreon

Seven Lakes
★ 3

44

9

371

9

Window
Rock

● 16 Twin Lakes

★ 17

264

18 Ya-Ta-Hey

Pinedale
★ 11

Crownpoint
● 4

5 ★ Borrego Pass

to Bernalillo

to Central Map

19 ★
Gamerco

★ 10 Church Rock

49

6 Smith Lake

★ 20–25

Gallup

40

8, 9
★

371

★ 7 Prewitt

Thoreau

602

27 ★ ★ 26 Whitewater
Cousins

★ 28 Winfield

Bibo ●

Paguate ●

El Morro
Nat'l Monument

● Grants

Cubero
★ 44

Old Laguna
● 46

to Albuquerque

29–39 ★
Zuni

Ramah 40 ★

125

Pine Hill

53

36

43 ●

★
42
Acomita

★ 45
Casa
Blanca

40

to Rio Grande Map

★
41
Acoma
(Sky City)

New Mexico

AZ border

LEGEND

★ **Trading Post in this chapter**

★ **Trading Post in other chapter**

● **Other site**

Southeast Navajo Nation, Gallup, Zuni, Acoma, and Laguna

♦ ♦ ♦

Very nice, the great South-West, put on a sombrero

and knot a red kerchief round your neck, to go out in the great free spaces!

D.H. Lawrence, *"New Mexico"*

This region is the heart of jewelry production in the Southwest, and Gallup is its capital. To the south, Zuni stands separate, unique, and proud of its tradition of creative, prolific jewelers, fetish carvers, potters, painters, and artists of other forms. From the rocky terrain east of Zuni rises the spectacular fortress of Acoma, Sky City, alive with its world-renowned potters. Acoma's neighbor, Laguna Pueblo, is blossoming with a newly revived pottery tradition of its own. North of these pueblos, the wind sweeps across the ghostly ruins of Chaco Canyon and Crownpoint, where Navajo weavers of the "checkerboard" area often sell their rugs at auction. Many of the trading posts, such as Borrego Pass, are far enough off the beaten path that they retain the ambiance of another era.

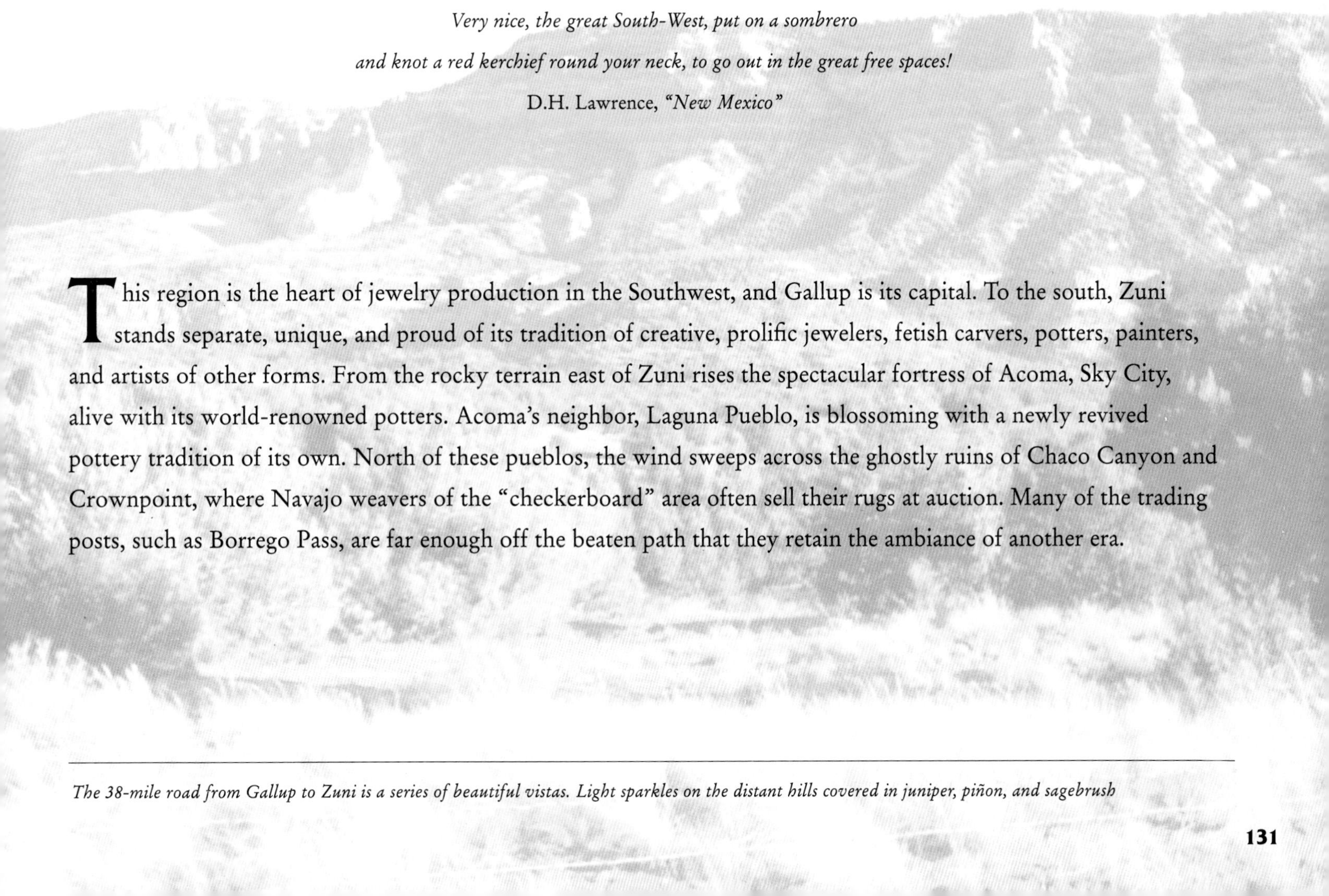

The 38-mile road from Gallup to Zuni is a series of beautiful vistas. Light sparkles on the distant hills covered in juniper, piñon, and sagebrush

CROWNPOINT AND SURROUNDING AREA

1. Richard's (Arts and Crafts)
P.O. Box 97, 6431 Hwy 44, Cuba,
NM 87013
505-289-3284
M–Sat 9:00–3:00
Owner: Richard Velarde
♦ M, V, D, AE, S

This shop is for tourists. The work is usually by local Navajo artists. Some of it has a charming, naive, non-professional quality, for a true one-of-a-kind feeling. A collection of old sandpaintings (over twenty-five years old) and a large collection of paintings and drawings fill the shelves. The drawings by Johnson Charley were particularly impressive. Ask to see the hundred or so scratchboards by Sammy Sandoval and his brothers. It's fun to browse here and see what the local artists are up to.

B, P, **Pt**, R, **Sp**

Richard Velarde, Richard's (Arts and Crafts), Cuba, New Mexico

2. Pueblo Pintado Trading Post
HCR-79, Cuba, NM 87013-9601, 50 miles from Cuba and 50 miles from Crownpoint
505-655-3310
Daily: 8:00–7:00, F 7:00–6:00
Owner: Eugene "Rusty" Vigil
♦ C, S, HA

According to owner "Rusty" Vigil, this trading post was started by the Ford Foundation in 1975 when they realized the need for a post in this isolated area. He sells works by a few favorite local artists such as Hoskie Yazzie, who does shadow work in silver and storyteller bracelets.

B, R, J

3. Seven Lakes Trading Post
Corner of Hwy 9 and Chaco Canyon 57, 16 miles east of Crownpoint
505-786-5954
M–Sat: 8:30–6:00, Sun 9:00–5:00
Owners: Henry and Sue Elkins
♦ M, V, C, S, HA

This store serves visitors to Chaco Canyon. They sell gas, groceries, jackalope heads, and a wide selection of souvenirs. You can call this post to inquire about weather, road conditions, and accessibility to Chaco in the winter.

J, K, P, R, **Sv**

4. Crownpoint Rug Weavers' Association, Inc.

Auction Crownpoint Elementary School on NM 371
Held on the third Friday of each month, Preview 3:00–6:00, Auction starts at 7:00, call to confirm dates
505-786-5302, -7386

♦ T, C (with proper I.D.)

Started in 1968 by trader LaVon Palmer, from the former Palmer's Trading Post in Crownpoint, the auction has become an anticipated event. Manager Ena Chavez says, "We always have about 300 rugs and most of the weavers come to the auction. Recently we sold a Storm Pattern rug by Bessie Tom for $13,000. She worked two and a half years on it. We usually have rugs of all prices, though."

Anne Hedlund, author of *Reflections of a Weavers World,* encourages tourists and collectors to attend the Crownpoint rug auction:

It's a great place for visitors to join in with a Navajo community. It is one of only two cooperatives (the other is Ramah) and is dependable and reliably scheduled. Weavers come from a wide area and are often in attendance. You can expect a diversity of styles. Top-grade rugs usually aren't in the auction, but there is a good selection of mid-range rugs at a great price. Because the weavers get most of the purchase price, they are happy as well. It is a great experience.

If you decide to attend the auction, Anne suggests, "Show up early. I can't stress this enough. Go through the rugs in advance. Handle them, feel the wool and their weight. See if they lay flat and are symmetrical in design. Make your decisions early, look over the rugs carefully, and you'll get a rug you love and have a great time."

At this event you may also find up to thirty booths selling jewelry, pottery, and other arts and crafts. Navajo tacos, chili, and fry bread are sold at the school.

5. Borrego Pass Trading Post

P.O. Box 329, Prewitt, NM 87045, 12 miles east of Crownpoint, 8 miles on Indian Rt. 48, east from Smith Lake
505-786-5396
M–F 8:00–6:00, Sat 8:00–12:00

Owner: Smouse family
managers: Merle and Rosella Moore

♦ D, C, S, HA

The out-of-the-way location of Borrego Pass Trading Post has allowed it to remain unchanged over the years. It is situated in the checkerboard area, so called because alternate sections of land are Navajo Reservation and non-reservation areas. Originally built by Ben Harvey in the late twenties from piñon logs and adobe, the post was then owned by Vernon Bloomfield. In 1939, after Bloomfield was shot in an incident with two teenage boys, the post was sold to Don Smouse, who was at

Rosella and Merle Moore, Borrego Pass Trading Post, Prewitt, New Mexico

> The smell of the post always was the same, desert or mountain: a concentrated essence of very dry dust, of sweet tanned leather and sour sweat and oil and metal, an abrasive lining of spit, tobacco smoke, and kerosene, and sometimes, for charity's sake, a whiff of sagebrush carried through the chinks and cracks of walls and roof.
>
> —FRANK McNITT, *The Indian Traders*

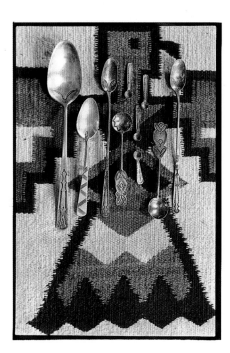

Toadlena Trading Post. He developed a successful silversmithing enterprise at Borrego Pass and at one point worked with more than sixty silversmiths.

The Moores have retained a traditional post atmosphere. They ran the former Mariano Lake Trading Post for ten years before they came here. Merle can usually be found chewing the fat with some of his local Navajo customers.

Ask to see the rugs in the back room. They stock locally made jewelry punches, groceries, and general merchandise. The arts and crafts are not what they were in Smouse's earlier days, but there is an abundance of atmosphere and a beautiful setting. The old arched-roof stone warehouse is full of clothing, appliances, and inventory from the fifties. The carefully groomed hollyhock garden remains a memorial to Fern Smouse's love of gardening. In our travels, people often told us that this was their favorite post. When you drive the eight miles of dirt road to the post, you won't just be reaching a rural post, you will be visiting a quieter moment from the past.

D, J, P, **R**

Rug and silver collection. Courtesy of Borrego Pass Trading Post, Prewitt, New Mexico. Hand-tinted photograph

6. **Chaffin's**
P.O. Box 90, Smith Lake, NM 87365
505-786-5578
M–Sat: 8:00–6:00
Owners: Kenneth and Virginia Chaffin
◆ M, V, D, HA (no ramp, but not difficult)

Ten or twelve local weavers supply the post with rugs. Particularly impressive are the Storm pattern rugs of Bernice Toledo, the *Yei'ii* rugs of Virginia Snyder, and the Two Grey Hills designs of Manual Henderson. Usually there is some jewelry including some dead pawn. They also supply food, gas, and a full post office service. The post buys sheep, cattle, piñons, and mohair, and takes pawn. The new owners plan a gift shop with t-shirts and other Native American crafts.

B, J, P, **R**

7. **Prewitt Trading Post**
P.O. Box 553, Prewitt, NM 87045
505-876-4041
M–F: 8:30–7:00, Sun 10:00–6:00
Owners: Rufus and Marlene Thomas
◆ AE, D, C, S, HA

This post has gas and groceries, buys and sells livestock, and serves the needs of the locals. They occasionally get older Navajo jewelry.

J

8. Rainbow Trading Company

P.O. Box 695, Thoreau, NM 87323,
Hwy 57 and Aspen St.
505-862-7119
M–Sat 8:00–7:00
Owner: David Hayes
♦ M, V, C, S, HA

Rainbow Trading Company does a booming pawn and wholesale business. They carry Pendleton blankets and a selection of jewelry that includes a few Navajo pieces. Most of the jewelry is rodeo influenced, with custom buckles emblazoned with bronco busters, names, and other assorted Western motifs.

B, D, **J**, P, R

9. Zuni Mountain Trading Company

140 Hwy 371, Thoreau, P.O. Box 3610, Milan, NM 87021
505-862-7766
Daily 8:00–8:00
Owner: Wayne Harris
♦ M, V, C, S, HA

Wayne says that most of his business is wholesale. He carries a diverse inventory that includes pipes; Navajo rugs (usually fifty or so); pottery from Jemez, Santa Clara, Acoma, and Navajo potters; and a large selection of jewelry. Wayne also carries many relics of the Old West, such as bear traps, chaps, wagon wheels, and other gear. He also sells silver supplies and stones. Ask to see the antique rugs when you visit. Wayne is especially proud of Gary Yazzie's paintings and Gibson Nez's impressive jewelry. Be sure to see the rare albino buffalo head.

B, D, I, **J**, K, **P**, Pt, **R**, S, Sp, groceries

10. Outlaw Trading Post

P.O. Box 328, Church Rock, NM 87311, in Red Rock State Park, 7 miles east of Gallup
May 1–Sept 1: 7:30–10:00, Sept 1–Oct 1: 7:30–6:00, Oct 1–May 1: 7:30–5:00
Owner: Marshalene Klade
♦ M, V, C, HA

Outlaw Trading Post occupies a building that was built in 1888 and has been used as a trading post for over a century (closing only for intervals in the seventies and eighties). It serves the Church Rock community. The current owner took over in 1992 and carries many items catering to the campers and visitors to Red Rock State Park. The layout is the old trading post bullpen design, and many old counters line the central area.

J, Sv

"Old Trading Post, Thoreau, New Mexico," is the caption on this historic photograph. Courtesy of Museum of New Mexico, Neg. #9123

Outlaw Trading Post, Church Rock, New Mexico

Route 49 to Mariano Lake is a beautiful high-country, scenic drive to Gallup from the Crownpoint area and Route 371. It is a nice detour from the summer heat, with its views of traditional hogans and sheep herds. It bypasses I-40 and can be accessed at Red Rock State Park.

11. Pinedale Trading Post
P.O. Box 800, Gallup, NM 87305, State Road 49, 20 miles west of Smith Lake and Hwy 371
505-786-5270
Daily 7:00–10:00

Manager: Ruby Antonio
♦ M, V, C, HA
This is a grocery, snacks, gas, laundry, showers, and video store.

HIGHWAY 666 FROM SHEEP SPRINGS TO YA-TA-HEY

12. Sheep Springs Trading Post
Sheep Springs, NM 87364, 76 miles south of Shiprock on Hwy 666
505-732-4211

Original owner R.B. Foutz, Sr., opened this store in 1932. The old building is next door to the present shop. R.B. Foutz, Jr., recalls his father having about ten dollars in coin in those early days. He would trade livestock and buy raw wool and rugs by the pound. The only cash flow available was through an old army scout's monthly pension check. R.B. Jr. said that when the check was cashed, his mom and dad would have some spending money and head into town.

13. Naschitti Trading Post
HCR 330, Tohatchi, NM 87335, 200 yards south of Naschitti, west side of Hwy 666
505-732-4208
M–F 8:30–5:30, Sat 8:30–1:00
Owner: Decker Foutz
♦ HA (with difficulty)
The original post, built in 1892, was directly behind the current 1950s-era concrete block structure. The Foutz family has run this post since 1969. The post serves the locals with gas, food, hardware, clothes, and general merchandise. They usually have a good choice of Navajo baskets in the $40–$100 range, and buckskins for ceremonial use. **B**

14. Ernie Franklin: Painter, Illustrator, and Fine Artist
P.O. Box 244, Tohatchi, NM 87325
505-735-2225

Art is second nature to Ernie Franklin. He recalls, "When I was little I'd make mud toys of cowboys and Indians. When I tended sheep I'd draw horses and animals into the sandstone cliffs. In the late forties my grandmother brought home some calendars from the old Powell's Trading Post (Mexican Springs) and they really inspired me." Ernie drew all through school and was encouraged by his teachers, but mainly he is self-taught.

Hannah Smith, weaver. The favorite trading post of her childhood is nearby Mexican Springs, New Mexico.

Mexican Springs Trading Post, Nakaibito, New Mexico, circa 1993

In 1967, while teaching at Fort Wingate High School, he met Ernie Bulow, who taught English. The two have teamed up on numerous book projects and with Tony Hillerman to create unique books and limited editions of Hillerman's classics. The books and a selection of originals are available from Ernie Bulow at Buffalo Medicine Books, 505-722-2904.

Franklin creates illustrations, oils, watercolors, and ink drawings. He draws with the deftness of a Russell or Remington. He says "Watercolor is especially fascinating to me. I don't sketch, I wet the paper, spill colors,

alcohol, and salt, and let it sit. I look at the patterns and find something wonderful and unique. I bring it out with color and brushes, not by drawing." Look for his work at the Gallup Ceremonial, where he is a perennial award winner (see photo page 4).

15. **Mexican Springs Trading Post**
General Delivery, Mexican Springs, NM 87320, 18 miles north of Gallup off 666, at the sign for Nakaibito, then three miles west
M–F 7:00–8:00, Sat and Sun 8:00–7:00, Summer: Daily 8:00–7:00
Owner: Cora Johnson
♦ V, M, HA

You won't find arts and crafts here, but the post is worth a visit. It was built in the early thirties. Its large front porch is often occupied by locals that sit and exchange news of the day. A pot-bellied stove occupies the back of the room, and like the posts of old, replaces the porch as the place to chat during the cold winter months. The old post office, viga ceilings, wood counters, and ceiling fans complete the old country store atmosphere. This post has always had an owner in residence. Mexican Springs is now a convenience store.

16. Clarence and Russell Lee: Silversmiths

P.O. Box 539, Gallup, NM 87305
505-735-2268

Clarence's father, Tom Lee, was the first Navajo Senator. The Twin Lakes Trading Post, started by Tom Lee, closed in 1982, but Clarence continues to live behind the post with his son and protégé, Russell. Clarence recalls, "I learned to make jewelry from some old jewelers that lived nearby, but are now deceased. Most of what I do is self taught. I have a knack for picking things up. Trial and error is a good teacher."

Clarence makes necklaces, belts, bracelets, and pins that start at $20. His large boxes have sold in excess of $40,000. His work reflects his childhood at Twin Lakes. Cowboys, Navajos, roosters, horses, trucks, and people going to town are all captured

in silver. He remembers, "When I was young the kids would meet at the windmill. It was our equivalent of a malt shop. We'd borrow clothes and jewelry to court girls there. I'd wait at the mill and see what young ladies would bring sheep to the water. I try to reflect these memories in my work." Even tradition has a way of evolving. Beside his workbench Clarence has installed a Healthwave Sauna. He says, "I love the sweat house, but this is far more convenient."

Clarence and Russell prefer to sell their work at the Eight Northern Pueblos Artists and Craftsman Show, the Santa Fe Indian Market, and other direct markets. They welcome special orders.

17. Toh-La-Kai Thriftway Pawn

HC 30 Box 2500, Gallup, NM 87301,
9 miles north of Gallup on Hwy 666
505-863-4064
M–Sat: 9:00–9:00, Sun 10:00–7:00
♦ M, V, D, C, S

You will find a good selection of Navajo rugs, Pendletons, saddles, and a nice selection of jewelry. They usually have some dead pawn on hand. They wholesale and are willing to negotiate on prices. Next door is a Partner convenience store that offers gas and groceries and is open twenty-four hours.

B, **J**, **R**

18. Ya-Ta-Hey Trading Company

P.O. Box 4269, Ya-Ta-Hey, NM 87375, located on the west side of Ya-Ta-Hey Jct
505-722-3859
M–F 9:00–5:00, Sat 9:00–12:00
Owners: Mickey and Dolly Vanderwagen
♦ M, V, C, S, HA

This stark, bunkerlike building is well worth a stop. The Vanderwagens stock groceries and general merchandise for their mostly Navajo customers. They take pawn and still conduct trade for merchandise. Mickey's Dutch Reform Missionary grandfather

Clarence Lee, Navajo jeweler, Gallup, New Mexico

Silver pin, 2 3/4", by Clarence Lee, Gallup, New Mexico

developed a thriving trading business from a wagon in Zuni in the 1890s. Look at the 16' x 7' Charles Damrow painting of his grandfather's old post that graces the front wall. Mickey is a great storyteller and can explain wonderful details about the painting. This post also has several paintings by Charles Hicks that interpret various Navajo ceremonies.

If you are interested in older jewelry, be sure to ask to see the vault. Mickey sells wonderful old Navajo and Zuni pieces from his family's collection. He is very knowledgeable about the artists, history, and fabrication of the jewelry and offers the information with enthusiasm and passion for the work.

The stock here varies, but it is not unusual to find an assortment of World War II–vintage brooches, bracelets, buttons, and belt buckles of unusual quality. They also stock

some Pendleton jackets, Navajo pottery, ribbon shirts, and cradleboards. The Vanderwagens also own Gallup Trading Company in Gallup.

B, **J**, K, P, R

⑲ Navajo Shopping Center

P.O. Box 77, Gamerco, NM 87317
505-863-6897
M–Sat 9:00–6:00
Manager: Wade Elkins
♦ M, V, C, S, HA

This sprawling, energized, do-it-all wholesale/retail business opened in 1953 as a limited partnership. It holds more than a million dollars in pawn,

Navajo bracelets, artists unknown. Courtesy of Burch's, Mexican Hat, Utah (top); Ya-Ta-Hey Trading Company (middle) and El Rincon, Taos (bottom).

and a large display of dead pawn is available for sale. If you are interested in Navajo rugs, you must ask to see them. The big attraction here is the jewelry. There is a display area in the front, but a larger area is located at the rear of the store.

It's worth taking a walk around this business. Outside you may see Wade negotiating the price of sheep in the stockyards, locals bringing in piñon nuts, or employees preparing bales of wool for shipment to Scotland. They have saddles, feed, groceries, gas, auto repair, post office, tax service, hardware, and a barber shop under one roof. Stop in and see one of the more unusual shopping centers under the Western skies.

D, **J**, K, P, Pt, **R**

Mickey Vanderwagen, Yah-Ta-Hey Trading Company, Yah-Ta-Hey, New Mexico

GALLUP

Gallup is the capital of Indian arts and crafts. Every other building in this sprawling city offers arts and crafts, making it easy to become confused and indecisive. It is also difficult to decide upon a fair price for items. This is the city of deals and so-called deals. Be wary of half-price claims; they are a common practice here. We find it helpful to compare prices of a few common items at several stores. This practice is not infallible but can be helpful.

Gallup is a regular destination for local Navajos. For the collector, it is also a good place to find older pieces. They are getting rarer and more expensive, but a well-chosen, one-of-a-kind piece becomes an instant heirloom. Good luck in this jewelry wonderland.

20. Richardson Trading Company
222 W. 66, Gallup, NM 87301
505-722-4762
M–Sat 9:00–6:00
Owner: Bill Richardson
♦ M, V, C, S, HA

Richardson Trading Company has been family-owned since 1913, and located here since 1935. It is one of the most famous businesses in the Southwest. The Richardson family was very active across the Navajo Reservation, and many of their efforts

Richardson Trading Company, Gallup, New Mexico. Hand-tinted photograph

have been detailed in *Navajo Trader,* by Gladwell Richardson.

It is hard to imagine a more thriving pawn business. They always have a thousand saddles in pawn, as well as jewelry vaults that go on forever. Old pawn is available, and family items are on display.

Be sure to look up in the rafters. Animal heads, stuffed animals, enormous baskets, beadwork, kachinas, and pottery are spread throughout. We really enjoy the busy atmosphere. Allow time to look at Richardson's gallery of 18" x 24" photographs of Navajo customers. It is a wonderful

collection, and you may see some of the same people shopping. Richardson's is a *must*-stop in Gallup.
B, **J**, K, P

21. Tobe Turpen's Indian Trading Company
1710 S. Second St., Gallup, NM 87301
505-722-3806, 800-545-7958
Web site: http://www. cia-g.com/≈tturpen/turpen.html
Manager: Tobe Turpen III
♦ M, V, AE, D, C, S, HA, I

Tobe Turpen III says that ninety percent of his business is wholesale. He offers a diverse and quality selection of contemporary Native American arts and crafts from across the Southwest. Their main business is Navajo, Hopi, and Zuni jewelry and kachina dolls. We were also impressed with the bead and quill work for sale. As a thriving pawn business, Tobe had over 700 saddles in pawn when we visited. The dead pawn is available for purchase. He stocks a large selection

Jim Turpen, Tobe Turpen's Indian Trading Company, Gallup, New Mexico, 1993

Navajo Indians listening to "The Voice of the Navajo People" at old Turpen's Trading Post, north of Puerco, Gallup, New Mexico. Tobe Turpen, Jr., right. Photograph by George Hight Studio, Courtesy Museum of New Mexico, Neg. #59296

of paintings and drawings (including the Toddy brothers' work).

There is a display of western chaps, photographs, and items from Tobe Turpen's early (1914) wagon-trading days.

This store is a little out of the way but well worth a visit. The staff is helpful and informative.
B, Bk, F, **J**, **K**, P, Pt, R, Sp

22. **Gallup Trading Company**
215 S. Third St., Gallup, NM 87301
505-863-5708
M–Sat 9:00–5:00
Owners: Mickey and Dolly Vanderwagen
◆ M, V, C, S, HA
   Two blocks off Historic Route 66 is this modest-looking business. The owner, Mickey Vanderwagen, also runs the Yah-Ta-Hey Trading Company and has been at this location since 1970. He always has a great selection of old and unique jewelry pieces not found elsewhere.

Nativity scene, carved and painted wood, 10",
by Tom Yazzie, Fort Defiance, Arizona

This store has elaborate hardwood display cases and a variation on the trading post bullpen design. You need to look carefully in the cases. There is so much fine work that selecting pieces can take time. In addition to the jewelry, Mickey stocks occasional old items such as Navajo blouses, silver buttons, and others. If you enjoy older Navajo and Zuni jewelry, this is a great place to look.

B, **J**, K, P, R

23. Tanner Indian Arts
237 W. Coal Ave., Gallup, NM 87301
505-863-6017, home 505-863-6723
by appointment
Owner: Joe Tanner
♦ C, S, HA

Joe Tanner's specialty is southwestern collectables, older estate items, and historic Navajo weavings. He says he carries only natural turquoise, nothing enhanced, stabilized, or artificially altered. When an artist or collector wants that special stone, they come to him. Joe works with many artists and believes that he bridges the understanding between artists, collectors, and materials by forming a network among the three. He also sells prominent estates, and works on projects with contemporary weavers. Almost everything he does is steeped in tradition.

Joe is a fourth-generation trader with a congenial nature. He is proud of his family's trading history and mentions that he is equal part Hunt, McGee, Tanner, and Foutz.

He wholesales to museums and other fine shops. You may have an item sent on approval for ten days with a credit card. Remember that this business is by appointment only, but Joe is happy to receive calls from collectors at home.

F, **J**, **R**

24. Jay Evetts: Trader
P.O. Box 2409, 510 Second St.,
Gallup, NM 87305
505-722-6962
By appointment only

Jay is well known and liked across the Southwest. He buys and sells antique Indian items, pawn jewelry, pottery, and rugs. He's been trading across the Southwest since 1971 and is known to have one of the world's best collections of Navajo silver buttons. He's a great source for that hard-to-find antique Indian item.

25. Shush Yaz Trading Co.
1304 W. Lincoln and 214 W. Aztec,
Gallup, NM 87301
505-722-0130, 800-736-7027,
FAX 505-722-0132

W. Lincoln M–Sat 9:00–6:00
W. Aztec M–Sat 9:00–5:00
Owner: Don Tanner
◆   M, V, AE, D, C, S, HA
Don Tanner is a fourth-generation trader. Both stores carry a similar inventory with a complete line of Native American arts and crafts including jewelry, artifacts, and Navajo rugs. Shush Yaz carries work by painters Jim Abeyta, Robert Becenti, and the Toddy brothers. You will also find a line of clothing from traditional to contemporary styles. The downtown store has a cafe.
B, Bk, I, **J**, K, P, **Pt, R**, S, Folk Art, Clothing

THE INDIAN TRADER
P.O. Box 1421, Gallup, NM 87305
505-722-6694
We recommend this monthly newspaper of Indian arts, crafts, and culture. Editor Martin Link is an expert on Indian culture. He shares his expertise throughout this publication which is widely read by traders, artists, and collectors.

ZUNI AND SURROUNDING AREA

 Joe Milo's Whitewater Trading Company (at Vanderwagen)
P.O. Box 1, Vanderwagen, NM 87326, south of Gallup on Hwy 602
505-778-5531; 800-748-2154
M–F 9:00–6:00, Sat 9:00–4:00
Owner: Joe Milo
◆   M, V, AE, C, S, HA, I
 "Shop where the Indian people trade" is Joe's motto. Joe Milo has been in the business for twenty years. This renovated structure was the original Whitewater Trading Company at Vanderwagen, New Mexico, owned by Rich and Lee Vanderwagen, then bought by Cal and Wanda Foutz. The post is now owned by Joe Milo and remodeled after old trading posts. Joe moved his business from a site four miles north of here. Joe tells us this post is exactly what he has always wanted, with old viga ceilings, wooden floors, benches, and the original 1940s fireplace to serve as a community center where people feel comfortable to sit and chat.
 His wholesale/retail business emphasizes Indian handmade jewelry; silver, turquoise, and jeweler's supplies; and cash pawn. He also carries general merchandise and operates a

INTER-TRIBAL INDIAN CEREMONIAL
Inter-Tribal Indian Ceremonial Association
P.O. Box 1, Church Rock, NM 87311
505-863-3896, 800-233-4528
Native American artists and craftspeople gather to sell their work in an indoor and an outdoor market. There is a rodeo, traditional dances, games, demonstrations, competitions, and a lot of fun activities. The event is held at Red Rock State Park in August. Call for details.

U.S. post office at the post. Dealers are welcome. **J**

 Cousins Bros. Trading Company
P. O. Box 1336, Gallup, NM 87305, 6.6 miles off Hwy 602 near Whitewater
505-778-5662
M–F 9:00–6:00 (Closed 12:15–1:15), Sat 9:00–12:00
Owners: Grant and Grace Wheatley
 Charlie Cousins originally opened in 1909 at Whitewater. In 1925, he followed the Indians away from the development along the highway. He

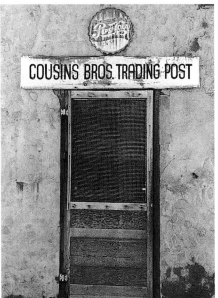

ABOVE AND LEFT: *Cousins Bros. Trading Post near Zuni, New Mexico.* Hand-tinted photograph

SHARON BURCH: NAVAJO
SONGWRITER AND SINGER
Canyon Records
4143 N. 16th St., Phoenix, AZ
85016
707-579-1351 (Agent: Alan
Clarke)

Sharon Burch is a Navajo
singer and composer who grew
up south of Gallup near Cousins
Brothers Trading Company. Her
album *Yazzie Girl* (available from
Canyon Records), sung mainly in
Navajo with a few songs in
English, reflects traditional chants
of her Navajo medicine man
grandfather, Charlie Yazzie, and
lullabies of her childhood. Her
family had a warm relationship
with Bob Cousins of the Cousins
Brothers Trading Company. You
might enjoy listening to *Yazzie
Girl* as you drive the Southwest.

chose the current location in 1930 to protect a stand of large oaks around the post from destruction by road builders. The trees still sway in the wind like elegant guardians. Betty Cousins lives across the road and is a wealth of information on traders in the area.

The post does not offer much in the way of arts and crafts. It sells groceries, general merchandise, and a lot of atmosphere. The beautiful old building's screeching screen door, and frying pans hanging from the rafters, offer the visitor a window into a different era.

28. **Winfield Trading Company**
HCR 331 Box 3, Vanderwagen, NM
87326, Hwy 602 south of Gallup
505-778-5544
M–Sat 9:00–6:00
Owner: Robert Winfield
♦ C, S

Twenty miles south of Gallup is this wholesale-only business, which offers a complete line of traditional and contemporary Zuni and Navajo jewelry.

Robert Winfield's father, M.C. Winfield, started mining turquoise at the Villa Grove Mine in Colorado. The family also owned turquoise mines at Lone Mountain, Smoky Valley, Red Mountain, and Carico Lake, Nevada, and Turquoise Mountain, Arizona.

Growing up in a turquoise mining family, Robert had a unique and varied education.

If you visit Winfield's, be sure to notice the Ernie Franklin watercolor and the Damrow oil painting. **J**

SOUTHEAST FAIRS

July: Eastern Navajo Fair, Crownpoint, NM

SELECTED SOUTHEAST NAVAJO NATION ARTISTS/CRAFTSPEOPLE

George and Frances Begay, P.O. Box 2608, Gallup, NM 87305-2608— Jewelry and weaving.

Gary Custer, P.O. Box 275, Gallup, NM 87305, 505-722-5792— Contemporary/traditional Navajo jewelry.

Norbert Peshlakai, P.O. Box 176, Fort Wingate, NM 87316, 505-488-5649—Contemporary jewelry and metalsmithing; known for silver pots

Fannie Platero, P.O. Box 216, Canoncito, NM 87026—Jewelry.

Felicita P. Sandoval, P.O. Box 417, Canoncito, NM 87026—Jewelry.

Hannah Smith, P.O. Box 473, Gamerco, NM, 505-722-3145 (messages)—Weaving.

Gary Yazzie, P.O. Box 1177, Grants, NM 87020—Navajo paintings.

Virginia Yazzie-Balenger, Gallup, NM, 505-722-6837, 800-377-6837— Native American fashions.

Shop display at Thomas Harley Trading Company, Aztec, New Mexico (closed 1994). Hand-tinted photograph

ZUNI

♦ **GOVERNOR'S OFFICE:**
P. O. Box 339, Zuni, NM 87327 (for general information or a copy of the free visitor guide). Zuni is located 38 miles south of Gallup off NM 53. 505-782-4481, FAX 505-782-2700

♦ **PHOTOGRAPHY:** Permits can be obtained at the Zuni Tribal Building Tourist Office. Hours are 8:00–4:30, M–F. No photography during Shalako ceremony.

♦ **SHALAKO CEREMONY:** late November or early December

♦ **ZUNI MUSEUM PROJECT** is east of the tribal administration building on NM 53, open 9:00–4:00 M–F. Our Lady of Guadalupe Mission is open 1:00–4:00 M–F. Saturday tours call 505-782-4477.

♦ **ZUNI ARTS AND CULTURAL EXPO,** Drawer F, Zuni, NM 87327, 505-782-2869, in August

THE PUEBLO ASKS THAT VISITORS PLEASE RESPECT THE FOLLOWING:

♦ No cameras, sketching or tape recordings are allowed at any religious events.

♦ Visitors should keep a respectful distance from any religious observance and all dancers. Act in a manner befitting a religious occasion.

♦ Ceremonial dances are watched from the roof tops surrounding the plaza, and visitors should follow Zuni etiquette by standing in the back.

♦ Visitors should remember that watching a religious observance is a privilege, as these events have great importance for the well being of the Zunis and for the world in which we all live.

VISITORS TO THE PUEBLO OF ZUNI

Keshi (welcome)

In behalf of the A:Shiwi (Zuni People) we welcome you to the homeland of my people. The A:Shiwi have lived in this area since time immemorial and are the direct descendants of the Anasazi people (old ones). Our homeland is rich in history, culture, arts and crafts, and scenic historical sites. The first Euro-peans made contact in 1539 leading up to centuries of community growth and restoration of our traditional values and customs. A:Shiwi are proud people and they ask only that you respect and honor their unique way of life when visiting Zuni.

Again, welcome to Zuni and may you take home with you, an appreciation and understanding of our Zuni Culture and my Peoples way of life.
—ROBERT E. LEWIS, Governor of Zuni

Zuni is a must for the traveler to the Southwest. Zuni jewelers are famous the world over, working in creative, unique, and exacting styles, including channel, nugget, overlay, inlay, petit point, needlepoint, cobblestone, and mosaic. In addition to jewelry, you will also find beadwork sculptors, world-famous fetish carvers, some of the Southwest's best potters, and many other artists. There has been increased interest in painting and drawing at Zuni in recent years, and a number of artists are creating personal visions of the Zuni religious cycle. The center of this painting phenomenon is Alex Seowtewa's murals at the Old Mission.

Among the 10,000 Zuni an inordinate proportion are talented artists. Zuni is a generous, warm, and hospitable place. Artists and traders seem to be supportive of one another, making it one of our favorite stops in the Southwest. The pueblo allows visitors in the village when kachina dances are being performed, a privilege not allowed at many pueblos.

Zuni Pueblo Church, July 1969. The Mission dates back to 1629. It was built by Zunis under the supervision and force of Franciscan Friars. The church was finished in 1632. It was damaged and fell into ruin. A massive restoration began in 1966. Photograph by Crampton, courtesy of Special Collections, University of Utah Library

29. Alex Seowtewa's Murals at the Old Mission in Zuni

Alex and Odelle Seowtewa
P.O. Box 203, Zuni, NM 87327
505-782-2258
M–F 10:00–12:00, 1:00–4:30

The word masterpiece is overused, but it definitely applies to the mural project of Zuni artist Alex Seowtewa. These fantastic paintings on the walls inside the Old Mission Church may be one of the most ambitious artistic works in all the Southwest. He began the murals in 1970, and they are a true labor of love. Seowtewa has created the four seasons and documented the beauty and grace of the Zuni religious cycle. Alex continues to work on the murals with his sons, Kenneth and Edwin. Kit South of Running Bear Trading Post said, "Alex Seowtewa is the greatest ambassador Zuni has ever had." We concur with his assessment. Alex speaks with insight and eloquence equally with words or a brush. Alex's wife Odelle creates petit point earrings, bracelets, pins, pendants, and squash blossom necklaces. Her work is available in Zuni at Running Bear and Turquoise Village. She sells wholesale, retail, and welcomes special orders.

30. Running Bear—Zuni Trading Post

P. O. Box 489, Zuni, NM 87327
505-782-5505
M–Sat 10:00–6:00
Owner: Jerry Elkins;
manager: Kit South
♦ M, V, AE, C, S, HA

Running Bear is one of the first businesses you see when entering Zuni from Gallup. Kit South has collected a fine array of Zuni jewelry. He does a large wholesale business and has a back room/vault devoted to that aspect of the business. You will find a good selection of fetishes, Zuni and Hopi pottery, and kachinas carved by

Kit South, Running Bear Trading Company, Zuni, New Mexico

Hopi carvers living in Zuni (including some fine work by Wilmer Kaye). They also carry jewelry supplies. Kit has a collection of paintings and drawings by the Seowtewa family, famous for the Zuni mission mural project. When we visited, he did not want to sell them, but he does offer them for sale from time to time.

F, **J**, K, P, Pt

31. The Old Pueblo Trading Post

P. O. Box 1115, Zuni, NM 87327
505-782-2296
M–Sat 10:00–7:00, Sun 9:00–5:00
Owner: Chet Jones
♦ M, V, D, AE, C, Diners, S, HA

The Old Pueblo Trading Post has a large selection of jewelry. Its immense circular display cases offer the best of Zuni. They also carry Navajo, Hopi, and Tohono O'odham baskets, and paintings by Duane Dishta. They sell a little dead pawn that is bought elsewhere, and they offer jewelry repair.

This was originally the C.G. Wallace Trading Post, the first licensed trader at Zuni. Wallace, and those who came after him, opened new markets to Zuni craftspeople, enabling many jewelers to make a living at their craft. These early efforts grew into the successful arts and crafts businesses that thrive today at Zuni.

B, F, I, **J**, Pt, R

32. Randy Nahohai and Rowena Him: Potters

P.O. Box 1303, Zuni, NM 87327
505-782-4763

Zuni has a tradition of creating some of the finest pottery in the Southwest. The *Mast'a:Kya* work of the sixteenth century can sweep your breath away with its complicated, integrated patterns. Randy and and his wife Rowena have studied these early pots and incorporated many of their features into their work. Randy's mother, Josephine, was given the Katherine H. Lamont Fellowship Grant to study this pottery in 1984. After studying pottery with his mother at the School of American Research, Randy began to think about pottery more and more. That year he began to create pots with Rowena. In 1986, the family traveled to the Smithsonian Folklife Festival, where they studied the Zuni pots in the Smithsonian collection.

Randy and Rowena do not simply copy old designs. They epitomize artists who are aware of history but continue to add new ideas to the cultural pool.

Randy has continued to pursue painting and design as well as pottery. These two artists are willing to labor long and hard to create work that is creative, well crafted, ambitious, and traditional. They welcome special orders.

Vessel, 12", by Randy Nahohai. Courtesy of Pueblo of Zuni Arts and Crafts, Zuni, New Mexico

Left to right: Rose Gasper, Josephine Nahohai, Elouise Westika at the School of American Research, Santa Fe. In 1984, Josephine Nahohai and family studied old Zuni pottery at the School. While looking at pots in the basement, the three Zuni women each placed an old Zuni pot upon her head as is the tradition at Zuni Pueblo. The museum director, when seeing the irrepaceable pots on the women's heads, was visibly shaken. "Don't worry," said son Randy Nahohai, "They are professionals." Photograph courtesy of the collection of Randy Nahohai

No reconstituted or stabilized material is used here. The management has stringent guidelines in selecting work for its inventory. Zuni's finest artists are represented: fetishes by Lena Boone; the Quandelacy, Cheama, Quam, and Sheche families; needlepoint, channel, cluster, and inlay jewelry by Edith Tsabetsaye, Alice Quam, Rolanda Haloo, Andrew Dewa, Don Dewa, and Waatson Bryant; beadwork by the Cellicion family, Winifred Caweyuka, and Silas and Mabel Ghahate; and pottery by Marjorie Esalio, Chris Nastacio, Carlos Laate, Eileen Yatsattie, Marjorie Chavez, and the Peynetsa, Kalestewa, and Chopito families. Manager Milford Nahohai is a

Coral Cluster work pin, 2 1/2", by Lorraine Waasta, Pueblo of Zuni Arts and Crafts, Zuni, New Mexico

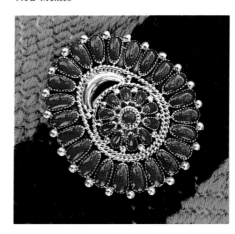

33. Pueblo of Zuni Arts and Crafts

P. O. Box 425, Zuni, NM 87327
505-782-5531, FAX 505-782-2136
M–F 8:00–5:00, Summer: Sat
9:00–4:00, Closed for tribal holidays
Owner: Zuni Tribe; manager:
Lorencita Mahkee
- ♦ M, V, D, AE, C, S, HA, I

The Zuni tribe opened this business in 1984. It is the ideal stop to acquaint yourself with the wide variety of artistic activity at Zuni. The staff is knowledgeable and generous with information. You will find items offered here that are not available elsewhere. The new building was finished in 1993, but the design was based on old architecture. The result is a wonderful space in which to view work and learn about Zuni arts and crafts.

Necklace, Lena Leki Boone, Zuni Pueblo

The Pueblo of Zuni Arts and Crafts also carries and markets work from the Zuni furniture factory, a line of ceramic dinnerware, and a book of remarkable cartoon drawings by artist Filbert Hughte. They welcome phone and mail orders.

Bk, **F**, **J**, **P**, Furniture, Textiles

34. Lena Leki Boone: Zuni Fetish Carver

18-B Harker Circle, P. O. Box 217, Zuni, NM 87327

505-782-2715

When you see one of Lena's fetish necklaces, it is easy to see how she has won top honors at Indian Market. She

is one of Zuni's finest carvers. Lena's grandfather, Teddy Weahkee, was a silversmith, painter, and one of the first to carve fetishes as an art form. When he passed away in 1965, Lena's mother, Edna, began to carve full time. Lena never thought of doing anything else. She continues to use the motorized grinding wheel as did her mother and grandfather. She attends all the large markets, including Eight Northern Pueblos and Indian Market. She creates all the directional animals

Fetish carver Edna Leki in her studio, Zuni, New Mexico

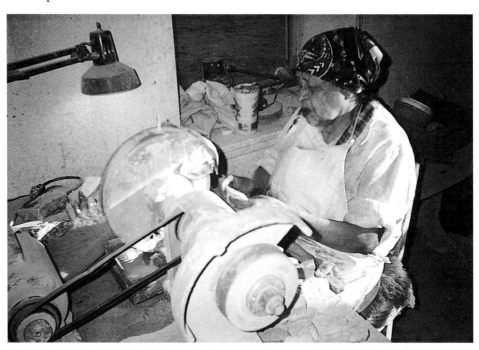

member of the famous Nahohai family of Zuni potters. The best of their work is also available here. Milford's background allows him to be especially helpful in explaining Zuni pottery.

The stated mission here is to revitalize traditional crafts. The textiles echo this by offering white rain belts and sashes woven on an upright loom by the Cooeyate family and Leander Booqua. Embroidered dance kilts by Vivian Kaskalla, Jaunette Nahohai, and Priscilla Tsethlikai are also available.

and beautiful fetish jewelry pieces, specializing in amber hummingbirds.

When we visited the family, on a day of 100 plus degrees, we found everyone hard at work at the grinding wheels. Lena's mother simply looked up, gave us a warm smile, and attended to the stone frog at hand.

Lena and her mother welcome special orders.

35. Turquoise Village

P. O. Box 429, Zuni, NM 87327,
Hwy 53
505-782-5521, 800-748-2405,
FAX 505-782-2846
M–Sat 10:30–6:00
Owner: Greg Hofmann
♦ M, V, AE, C, S, HA (difficult)

Opened in 1978, this business always seems to be crowded with Zuni artisans and visitors seeking their work. The front room supplies the

Coyote fetish, 1" x 4", by Lance Cheama,
Zuni Pueblo. Courtesy of Turquoise Village

artists, and at the counter you can usually find Greg and his staff purchasing work from several Zuni artists. The back room is for arts and crafts and has an ever-changing inventory. This business clearly moves a large number of items in a day, and we suggest that you do not postpone purchases here, as chances are what you want will be gone before you return.

Turquoise Village has trays of fetishes sorted by animal. The selection is enormous so we suggest that you allow sufficient time to make a choice.

They offer jewelry by many of Zuni's finest jewelers, including Alice Quam, Lorraine Waatsan, Dennis and Nancy Edaakie, Harlan Coonsis, Nancy and Ruddell Laconsello, Edith Tsabetsaye, Velma and Don Dewa, Virgil and Shirley Benn, Vincent Johnson, Fred Natachu, Mildred Unkestine, Amy Westley, Ed Beyuka, and many others.

Zuni Fetish carvers Lorendina and Thelma
Sheche with Greg Hofmann of Turquoise
Village

Pottery is made by Noreen Simplicio, Marcus Homer, Quanita Kalestewa, Eileen Yatsattie, Randy Nahohai, Edna Leki, and the Peynetsa family.

Paintings include work by Duane Dishta, Anthony Sanchez, Ronnie Cachini, and Phil Hughte.

Fetishes are by a group of artists far too large to list. Ask Greg about particular requests.

Greg offers many Hopi items and is licensed as a Zuni and Hopi dealer. He also has a nice selection of Acoma pottery and beadwork by the Cellicion family. He takes phone and mail orders.
B, **F**, **J**, K, **P**, Pt, R

36. Claudia Cellicion: Beadwork Figures

P. O. Box 332, Zuni, NM 87327

Claudia's mother made the small Zuni beaded dolls that filled souvenir shops for generations. These early dolls were never more than a few inches high and are still readily available throughout the Southwest. They were built over a frame of cloth, watermelon seeds, and sticks. Claudia discovered that if she carved a wooden structure, she could create more elaborate and ambitious dolls. Her husband, a fetish carver, carves these wooden structures for her.

Her figures include a vast array of Native American dancers. She creates Hopi snake dancers, hoop dancers, eagle dancers, and various other figures. Her figures range from two to twelve inches in height. The large figures take Claudia two days to make. These are the finest beaded sculptures being made today. She does not have a telephone but will take mail orders.

Claudia's sister also creates wonderful beaded sculptures. Using a similar technique, she creates storytellers, horses, and unusual figures. She can be reached at the same address.

37. Zuni Village Trading Post and Tribal Treasures

1207-B Hwy 53, P. O. Box 1307, Zuni, NM 87327;
Tribal Treasures: 1202-B Hwy 53

Zuni beaded sculpture, 6", by Claudia Cellicion, Zuni, New Mexico

Zuni Village: 505-782-4545,
Daily 9:00–6:00
Owners: Lisa and Fawzi Abu
♦ M, V, D, AE, C, S, HA

Both stores have a similar inventory and the same owners. Stone inlaid pocket knives were particularly attractive.

D, F, **J**, K, P, S, Sp

38. Zuni Craftsmen Cooperative

1177 Hwy 53, P. O. Box 426, Zuni, NM 87327
505-782-4521
M–Sat 9:00–6:00, Sun 11:00–2:00
Owners: Member Zuni craftspersons
♦ M, V, AE, C, S, HA (ask to have ramp placed on steps)

The cooperative opened in 1967. The front of the building has jewelry supplies, equipment, and stones to supply artists. The small back room is lined with display cases. Cellicion family beaded sculptures, a large selection of fetishes, and jewelry are available.

The jewelry supply department has its own phone, 505-782-4605. Mail and phone orders are accepted and a catalog is available.

F, J, P

39. Shiwi Trading Post

1173 W. Hwy 53, Zuni, NM 87327
505-782-5501, 800-628-3831
Daily 9:00–6:00
Owner: Nassar
♦ M, V, D, AE, C, S, HA

This post does a large wholesale business and has produced a twenty-page, color catalog that showcases its jewelry.

B, Bk, F, **J**, K, P, R, Sp

SELECTED ZUNI ARTISTS/CRAFTSPEOPLE

Carolyn Bobelu, 731 Kevin Court, Gallup, NM 87301, 505-722-4939—Zuni jewelry.

Phil Hughte, P.O. Box 151, Zuni, NM 87327—Painting, drawing, illustration.

Carlton and Julie Jamon, Drawer F, Zuni, NM 87327, 505-782-2869—Jewelry, Two Grey Hills weaving.

Loren Panteh and Yolanda Laate, P.O. Box 682, Zuni, NM 87327, 505-782-2454—Jewelry.

Agnes Peynetsa, P.O. Box 252, Zuni, NM 87327, 505-782-2981—Pottery.

Veronica Poblano, P.O. Box 1087, Zuni, NM 87327, 505-782-2156—Raised inlay jewelry.

Lynn and Jayne Quam, P.O. Box 583, #76 Main St., Blackrock, Zuni, NM 87327-0583—Fetishes and jewelry.

Andres Quandelacy, P.O. Box 266, Zuni, NM 87327—Fetishes.

Ellen Quandelacy, P.O. Box 266, Zuni, NM 87327—Jewelry.

Noreen Simplicio, P.O. Box 324, Zuni, NM 87327, 505-782-2543—Pottery.

Edith Tsabetsaye, P.O. Box 285, Zuni, NM 87327, 505-782-4295—Cluster, needlepoint jewelry.

40. Ramah Navajo Weavers Association

P.O. Box 153, Pine Hill, NM 87357
505-775-3253 by appt.

The Navajo community of Ramah New Mexico, formed after the "Long Walk" in 1868, is a rural reservation settlment south of the larger Navajo Reservation. The Ramah Navajo Weavers Association is a grassroots cooperative of over 40 weavers. Their stated goals are to increase family self reliance from indigenous resources and native skills, and to strengthen important and distinctive land-based traditions, values, and spirituality for future generations of Ramah Navajos. Each weaver raises her own sheep, spins her own yarn, dyes the yarn with vegetal dyes from local plants, creates her own designs, and weaves in the traditional Navajo manner.

Rugs range from miniatures of five inches to ones of six feet. They sell raw or washed and carded fine Rambouillet and Navajo-Churro wool. Two-ply knitting yarn and Navajo-Churro breeding stock are also available.

Special orders are welcome, and a small pamphlet about the association is available on request.

Old Arbuckle's coffee crate, Thomas Harley Trading Company, Aztec, New Mexico (closed 1994). Hand-tinted photograph

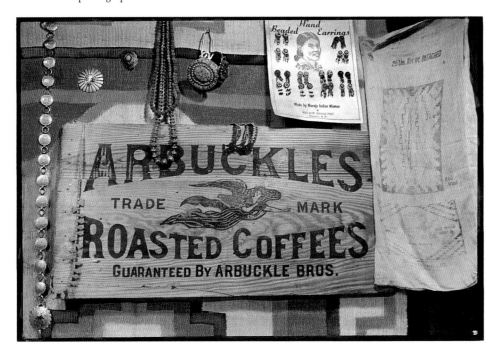

ACOMA PUEBLO

Tribal Office: P.O. Box 309, Acoma, NM 87034, I-40, exits 89, 96, 102, or 108
505-552-6606

♦ Still camera fee (no photography on feast days), no video.

♦ Stay within the plaza and street area. No hiking, camping, climbing on rock formations. Check with visitor center for complete visitor's etiquette. Admission fee for tour of Sky City (otherwise not accessible)

♦ San Estévan Feast Day: September 2

♦ Acoma Arts and Crafts Fair: mid July at the visitor center

♦ Language: Keres

Sky City at Acoma Pueblo is one of the most spectacular settings in the Southwest. After the twelve- or so mile drive off I-40 (there are various exits), your first stop is the Acoma Visitor's Center. The center has a museum that clearly outlines the history of the pueblo and houses a large collection of artifacts. The many booths usually found in the parking lot offer a variety of locally made items. Acoma is internationally known for its pottery. After viewing the pottery in the museum, you may find it interesting to see the newly created work that shows an interplay of tradition and innovation. When purchasing pottery at Acoma make sure you are aware of the differences in slipcast and traditional pottery. (This is covered in the introduction to this book.)

The visitor center sits below the 365-foot mesa upon which Sky City perches. To visit Sky City you must take a guided walking tour of the mesa top village. A bus takes you to the village where a guide explains historical, cultural, and architectural aspects of the ancient village and its spectacular church. There are a few brief opportunities to look at pottery in this wonderful setting, but time restraints prevent any serious shopping. You are given the option of climbing down the mesa using well-worn hand and footholds or returning to the visitor center by bus.

ACOMA/SKY CITY, LAGUNA, AND SURROUNDING AREA

41. Acoma Visitor's Center and Museum

P.O. Box 309, Acoma, NM 87034
505-470-4966, 800-747-0181
Daily: Nov–March 8:00– 4:30, April–Oct 8:00–7:00, except July 10–13 and Oct first or second weekend
No admission fee for the museum

42. Pueblo Pottery

P.O. Box 366, San Fidel, NM 87049, exit 102, 4 miles south of I-40, Acomita area
505-552-6748, 800-933-5771
Web site: http://www.collectorsguide.com/pueblopottery
Daily 9:00–6:00
Owners: Arthur and Carol Cruz
♦ M, V, C, S, HA, I
The Cruz family started selling

Acoma Pueblo, New Mexico, July 1971.
Photograph by Crampton, courtesy of Special Collections, University of Utah Library

Acoma woman with water jar. Photograph courtesy of Rowena Martinez, El Rincon, Taos, New Mexico

and are moving up." Excellent pottery from all the pueblos is available in addition to paintings by Zuni artists Duane Dishta, San Juan/Sandia artist Robert Montoya, Cochiti artist Manuel Chavez, and Hopi artists Anthony Honahnie and Neil David, Sr.

Arthur offers return customers a 10 percent discount on purchases. He is concerned with the artists' prosperity and is developing creative outlets for the work through corporate incentive projects.

F, I, J, K, **P**, Pt, R

43. Barbara and Joseph Cerno: Potters

109 Star Rt. 1, Grants, NM 87020, residence in McCartys; call ahead and they will meet you at exit W. 96 on I-40
505-552-6857

Joseph and Barbara Cerno are from families of potters. They create large vessels that have become increasingly rare at Acoma. Their designs are traditional, and at times include Hopi and Zuni motifs that are borrowed from Joseph's childhood in Zuni and Barbara's Hopi family background. Joseph is proud of the craftsmanship of his pottery, particularly the thin walls.

Joseph has studied Acoma pottery at the School of American Research in Santa Fe and enjoys the task of trying to "remake the old ways of painting." A visit to the Cernos educates one

Large Mimbres seed pot, approximately 16" diameter, by Barbara and Joe Cerno, Acoma Pueblo

The parrot design has become a traditional motif at Acoma. Like many other potters, Joseph Cerno considers his pots to be alive. He states, "I talk to the parrots as I paint them. The last thing we paint is their eyes. As we paint their eyes, we tell them to wake up and see the beautiful world. I like to wash their heads and bodies and sing to them. They really are alive."

pottery from a van in 1989. The present building went up in 1990. Arthur was born in San Juan Pueblo and Carol was born at Acoma into a family of potters. They can teach you about quality and the differences between traditional and slip-cast pottery, the various pueblo styles, and how to tell whether a pot has a hairline crack.

Arthur has served as a judge at the Eight Northern Pueblos Artist and Craftsman Show and he states, "I carry the artists that are actively doing shows

to true artistry and traditional techniques. "If people let us know when they are coming, we will try to plan a firing, so they can see pottery fired in the traditional way." The Cernos welcome visitors and their questions and feel comfortable with cameras and camcorders.

The Cernos enjoy selling from their home and offer pottery seminars. They welcome commissions and mail orders. Their work can be seen at Robert Nichols in Santa Fe and Gallery 10 in Scottsdale.

SELECTED ACOMA ARTISTS/CRAFTSPEOPLE

Carolyn Concho, P.O. Box 284, Acoma, NM 87034—Pottery.

Anne Lewis Hansen, 8239 Pinefield Dr., Antelope, CA 95843, 916-332-0356—Pottery.

Marilyn Henderson, P.O. Box 504, San Fidel, NM 87049—Storytellers.

Diane M. Lewis, P.O. Box 431, Acoma, NM 87034, 505-552-7329—Pottery.

Suiumi Lewis, P.O. Box 1422, Paguate, NM 87040—Pottery.

LAGUNA PUEBLO

Governor's Office: P.O. Box 194, Laguna Pueblo, NM 87026, 46 miles west of Albuquerque off I-40 505-552-6654, FAX 505-552-6941

◆ Obtain permission from tribal governor's office for cameras, recorders, or sketching. Photographing ceremonies is prohibited.

◆ FEAST OF ST. JOSEPH: September 19 at Old Laguna

◆ CHRISTMAS AND HARVEST DANCES: December 24–28, at Old Laguna and all six villages

◆ ARTS AND CRAFTS FAIRS: Early December and Mother's Day at Old Laguna

◆ LANGUAGE: Keres

The old pueblo of Laguna seems to hold the San José Mission upon its shoulders. It is clearly visible from I-40. Completed in 1701, its interesting interior artwork combines Spanish influence and traditional Indian symbolism.

Arts and crafts of the pueblo include some simple basketry, sashes, gourd rattles, and pottery. Laguna's pottery tradition shares many aspects with Acoma. By the sixties, Laguna pottery appeared extinct. Evelyn Cheromiah and Gladys Paquin have worked rigorously and are devoted to reestablishing the art form at the pueblo. Through their pottery and teaching, Laguna pottery is alive and well.

Laguna Pueblo consists of six villages. These include Old Laguna, Mesita, Seama, Encinal, Paguate, and Paraje. The villages, though under the umbrella title of Laguna Pueblo, are independent and celebrate their own feast days. They pull together to celebrate special days at Old Laguna.

Old Laguna Pueblo Church, Laguna Pueblo, New Mexico. Hand-tinted photograph

44. Villa de Cubero

P.O. Box 67, Cubero, NM 87014, on old Route 66, take I-40, exit 104. This business is located 0.75 mile north of I-40 between exits 102 and 104
505- 552-9511
M–Sat 7:00–8:00, Sun 8:00–5:00
Owner: Keith Gottlieb;
manager: Betty DeSoto
◆ M, V, D, AE, C (local), S, HA

This family business, originally known as the Cubero Trading Company, was opened by Solomon Bibo around 1876. It was taken over by Sidney Gottlieb in 1918. The original building is now used as a studio by sculptor Frederico Armijo. The Villa de Cubero opened on the Route 66 site in 1938 as a trading post, motel, and cabins. Present owner Keith Gottlieb sells groceries, hardware, liquor, gas, diesel, and Acoma pottery. The artists vary and you find both traditional and slipcast pottery here.
P

45. Casa Blanca

P.O. Box 400, New Laguna, NM 87038, I-40, exit 108
505-552-9030
M–Sat 7:00–10:00 Sun 7:00–9:00
Winter: M–Sat 7:00–9:00,
Sun 7:00–8:00

Casa Blanca is a large general merchandise/grocery store. In the back they have a small arts and crafts area. Casa Blanca operates a post office, gas station, and snack bar. In the plaza outside, The Blue Eyed Indian Bookshop offers a selection of books on the Southwest and a gallery of photographs and posters with southwestern themes.
Bk, F, J, P

46. Evelyn Cheromiah, LeeAnn Cheromiah: Potters

P.O. Box 45, Old Laguna, NM 87026
505-552-9528

Evelyn is proud that her daughters, LeeAnn and Mary Cheromiah Victorino, and her grandson, Wendell Kowemy, have all followed her into pottery. Evelyn remembers helping her mother paint pots. She says:

Back then everyone made small souvenir pots, no large pottery. In 1972 I got into pottery. I went to see an old lady to ask her about temper in the clay and how to get air pockets out of the walls of the pots. Temper is really important. You must grind up sherds and add it to the clay. We'd go to old places and pick up the sherds to use for temper. When I look at old sherds, the designs are so neat, straight, bold, streamlined. I like to think about who made them, what they were like and if they were my family.

Skulls are available at a number of roadside stands in the Santa Fe/Taos area

In the early seventies Evelyn began a search for a pottery style that incorporated the old designs. She explains:

I was instructing a group of women from the pueblo and we went to the museum in Santa Fe. We began to use the traditional Laguna designs. Laguna and Acoma are a lot alike, but different. They paint a parrot, but our bird is more like a pigeon with only two tails. Acoma likes to use lots of lines, parrots and thunderbirds that run on into a continuous design. We could do that here, but we like to stick to our own traditional designs. My family likes to use brushes, but I like using the yucca. It goes faster and the lines lay down like I want. The old folks used to chew them, but I like to pound it until it is soft and the fiber threads show. I decide how thick a line I want and cut away some threads until it is the right thickness.

Evelyn and her family take commissions and mail orders. Their work ranges from inexpensive miniatures to ambitious large museum pieces.

> When I started pottery no one made large pots at Laguna. The Acoma potters didn't want to show us the way, but we learned by our own determination.
> —EVELYN CHEROMIAH

SELECTED LAGUNA ARTISTS/CRAFTSPEOPLE

Sue Dailey, Paguate, NM 87040—Weaving.

Max Early, Paguate, NM 87040—Pottery.

Andrew Padilla, P.O. Box 826, Laguna, NM 87026, 505-552-6794—Pottery.

Glenn and Opal Paquin, P.O. Box 123, New Laguna, NM 87038, 505-552-7164—Jewelry.

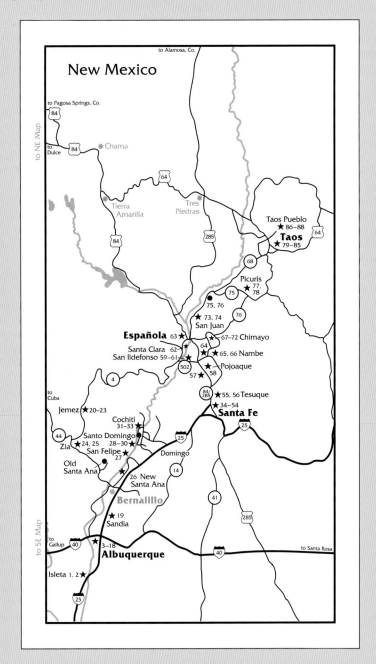

New Mexico

to Alamosa, Co.

to Pagosa Springs, Co.

84

to Dulce 84 ● Chama

64

Tierra Amarilla

Tres Piedras

84

285

Taos Pueblo ★ 86–88

Taos ★ 79–85

64

68

Picuris ★ 77, 78

75

● 75, 76

76

★ 73, 74 San Juan

Española 63 ★

★ 67–72 Chimayo

Santa Clara 62 ★
San Ildefonso 59–61 ★

64 ★

★ 65, 66 Nambe

502

57 ★ 58 ★ Pojoaque

to Cuba

4

84 285

★ 55, 56 Tesuque

★ 34–54

Jemez ★ 20–23

Cochiti 31–33 ★

Santa Fe

44

Santo Domingo ●

25

Zia ★ 24, 25

28–30 ★

San Felipe ★ 27

Domingo

14

Old Santa Ana ●

★ 26 New Santa Ana

41

Bernalillo

285

to SE Map

★ 19 Sandia

to Gallup 40 ★ 3–18

40

Albuquerque

to Santa Rosa

Isleta 1, 2 ★

25

LEGEND

★ **Trading Post in this chapter**

★ **Trading Post in other chapter**

● **Other site**

Rio Grande Pueblos, Albuquerque, Santa Fe, and Taos

◆ ◆ ◆

I think New Mexico was the greatest experience from the outside world
that I ever had. It certainly changed me for ever.

D.H. LAWRENCE, *"New Mexico"*

The Indian Pueblo Cultural Center in Albuquerque is a good introduction to the Rio Grande Pueblos. Here, visitors can learn of the artistic differences among the pueblos, highlighting the unique strengths, ceremonies, and traditions of each pueblo. The center also can answer questions and provide a calendar for dances, ceremonies, and special events.

Each pueblo is autonomous. Rules are established at each pueblo and *enforced*. You should check in at the governor's office, and be advised of all rules before visiting any pueblo. Some pueblos charge entry fees, others charge a fee for photography or sketching, or prohibit these activities. If they are prohibited, keep your camera in your car and out of sight. We have seen visitors' cameras confiscated, and their plight does not stir much sympathy.

Remember, people live here. You are a guest. Be sure you act in accordance. If photos are permitted, never photograph individuals without their permission. In most cases, a small donation is expected. Stay away from kivas,

Sunflowers, Santa Fe

Cornmeal holder, 8", by Louis and Virginia Naranjo, Cochiti Pueblo. Wall plaques containing cornmeal are usually hung by a front door. The meal is scattered to the four directions while a prayer is offered.

ceremonial rooms, cemeteries, and private residences without a welcome. Do not climb on any structures, no matter how insignificant they look. Try not to interfere with the normal life at the pueblo. Do not look into doors or windows or otherwise draw attention to yourself.

If you attend dances at the pueblos, remember that these are religious ceremonies. Be silent, respectful, and do not ask questions or talk to participants in the ceremonies while they are dancing or resting. Do not applaud, walk across the plaza, or obstruct anyone's view. The pueblo dances are prayers for the entire world. The pueblo people's spirit is generous. On feast days the families' hospitality is extended to many, and you may be invited into a home to share a meal. Keep your visit brief.

The pueblos, their dances, and arts and crafts have had a profound effect on visitors for centuries. Today, the artists produce works that rival those in museums. On your visit, be aware of the pueblos' stylistic differences and expose yourself to the full range of artistic expression before selecting your purchases.

ISLETA

1. Teller Pottery

P.O. Box 411, Isleta, NM 87022
505-869-3118, -3506

Stella Teller's great-grandparents made utilitarian pottery, and they, along with her mother, taught her their pottery techniques. Stella quickly adds that her work is not "Isleta" pottery in the traditional sense. She states, "I've been working with the clay for over thirty years and as an artist, I just wanted to change. So I began to make

my own designs." Although her designs are innovative, her techniques remain rooted in tradition. She collects her own clay, vegetable dyes, and minerals around the Isleta area. (She buys only the cobalt used to create the beautiful blues in her work.) She fires in the traditional outdoor dung firing, and says that it is required because kilns distort the clay and colors.

Stella is proud that daughters Robin, Chris, Mona, and Lynette and granddaughter Leslie are all following in her footsteps and creating pottery of their own. The family takes special orders, and they welcome visitors. They ask that you call in advance for an appointment. Their work can be seen at the Agape Southwest Pueblo Pottery and the Adobe Gallery in Albuquerque's Old Town. In Santa Fe you can find their work at the Museum of Indian Arts and Culture and the Case Trading Post at the Wheelwright Museum. They also participate in the Santa Fe Indian Market and the Eight Northern Pueblos Artist and Craftsmen Show. Stella finished our conversation by promising, "My daughters and I will always do our very best on each and every piece we create. That is our way in the Teller family."

Storyteller, 9", by the Teller family, Isleta Pueblo, New Mexico

ISLETA PUEBLO

Governor's Office: P.O. Box 1270, Isleta Pueblo, NM 87022
505-869-3111, FAX 505-869-4236
Language: Tiwa

Isleta Pueblo is about twelve miles south of Albuquerque. Pueblo residents are proud of their church, St. Augustine Mission, the oldest in New Mexico. Most tourists head north to Santa Fe and never visit this southernmost pueblo, making it difficult for arts and crafts businesses to survive. Artists and craftsmen do sell from their homes, however. The governor's office is helpful in locating artists. The jewelry is usually influenced by Navajo turquoise. There is wonderful clothing sold here. Belts, skirts, blouses, shawls, and a wide variety of embroidery are available. The pottery includes polychrome in white, red, and black that is influenced by Laguna Pueblo, and there is also utilitarian ware. The best known Isleta pottery is from members of the Teller family, who create storytellers and a diverse group of pottery designs.

Isleta Pueblo is known for its wonderful bread. Early in the morning, there are several bakers who pull the loaves from their *hornos* (domed adobe ovens).

2. **Jessie Overstreet: Native Pueblo Clothier**

33 Tribal Rd. 76, Albuquerque, NM 87105

505-869-3881

(Jessie lives at Isleta Pueblo although she has an Albuquerque address.)

Jessie recalls growing up at Isleta with her friend, Stella Teller. She remembers, "Fifty years ago I would help Grandma sell her pottery to tourists for five or ten cents a pot. I never thought pottery would sell for what it does today. So it never attracted me." Interested in a means of support, at age thirteen she became attracted to the home economics sewing program at the Albuquerque Indian School. Not long ago she went into business for herself and wishes that she had done so sooner.

Jessie machine-embroiders pow-wow shawls with flowers and sun designs, Isleta-style pullover blouses, gingham blouses and aprons with cross-stitched Indian designs, sashes, and some of the most beautiful mantas we have ever seen. Jessie says, "People come from all nineteen pueblos for my clothing. Some come all the way from Hopi. Sometimes, collectors will purchase mantas or traditional clothing for display, but it would be improper for them to wear a manta and I make sure they understand this."

Jessie does take special orders and welcomes visitors by appointment. In a gracious voice she invites, "Come visit my little shop. I'm not a factory and don't make lots and lots, but I always have plenty to look at."

SELECTED ISLETA ARTISTS/CRAFTSPEOPLE

Caroline Carpio, P.O. Box 1222, Peralta, NM 87042, 505-869-0827—Traditional pottery.

Anthony Jojola, P.O. Box 166, Isleta, NM 87022—Hot glass.

Deborah Jojola-Sanch, P.O. Box 430, Isleta, NM 87022—Painting.

Andy Lee Kirk, P.O. Box 460, Isleta, NM 87022, 505-869-6098—Jewelry.

Michael Kirk, Tribal Rd. 10, #374, Isleta, NM 87022, 505-869-3317—Contemporary jewelry, silver and gold inlay, one-of-a-kind specialty.

Sherman Paquin, 1534 State, Albuquerque, NM 87105—Jewelry.

Christine Teller, P.O. Box 9, Isleta, NM 87022—Pottery.

Lynette Teller, P.O. Box 135, Isleta, NM 87022—Pottery.

Ramona Teller, P.O. Box 81, Isleta, NM 87022—Pottery.

ALBUQUERQUE

Albuquerque was once the center of the Indian arts wholesale market. It now shares the market with Gallup. We enjoy the businesses in Old Town, and our suggestions center around this area. If you are spending much time in the area, we suggest picking up a copy of:

The Wingspread Collectors Guide, **Albuquerque Edition, P.O. Box 13566-M, Albuquerque, NM 87192, 800-873-4278.**

You will find this guide free in many businesses in the city, or you can order it by phone or mail. It is published annually.

3. **Adobe Gallery**

413 Romero NW, Albuquerque, NM 87104

505-243-8485, 800-821-5221

M–Sat 10:00–6:00, Sun 1:00–4:00

Owner: Alexander Anthony, Jr.; director: Kenneth W. Zintak

♦ M, V, D, AE, C, S, HA (a few small bumps)

This beautiful gallery specializes in museum-quality, one-of-a-kind items. You will find the storytellers of Helen Cordero and Louis

Naranjo. Neal David, Sr., and Cecil Calnimptewa kachina dolls look out over J.B. Moore rugs. Paintings by J.D. Roybal, Tony Abeyta, Helen Hardin, Raymond Naha, and many others grace the walls. The collection of miniatures offered is especially attractive.

The Adobe also offers fine arts and crafts furniture and an impressive selection of books. The gallery publishes about two books a year on southwestern topics under the imprint of Avanyu Publishing.

Alexander and Kenneth have a playful energy that comes from doing what they love to do.

Bk, J, **K**, P, Pt, **R, Furniture**

4. Hanging Tree Gallery

416 Romero Rd., Albuquerque, NM 87104
505-842-1420
M–Sat 10:00–6:00, Sun 12:00–6:00
Owners: Reggie and Kay Sawyer
♦ M, V, AE, C, S

Reggie and his wife Kay sell old pawn, old Pueblo pots, old Navajo weavings, cowboy items, antique New Mexican furniture, and an impressive array of mostly old Santa Fe and Taos artists' paintings. Reggie lights up when he talks about the various artists.

He has a personal collection of early Isleta tin work and Santo Domingo depression necklaces from the early twenties to the forties (not for sale). The necklaces are made from bakelite, Edison records, battery cases, toothbrushes, combs, and whatever else was available. He offers a 10 percent discount to senior citizens.

B, J, P, Pt, R, Antiques, Furniture

5. Agape Southwest Pueblo Pottery

414 Romero Rd., Albuquerque, NM 87104
505-243-2366
M–Sat 10:00–6:00, Sun 12:00–6:00
Owner: Richard Myers

Old Santo Domingo Depression jewelry, personal collection R. Sawyer, Hanging Tree Gallery

♦ M, V, D, AE, C, S

Richard Myers has collected pottery since the late sixties. After collecting 600 pots, he decided it was time to open a business. This is an ideal place to learn about the various pueblo styles. Richard clearly understands that a love of pottery begins with knowledge. Don't be afraid to ask him questions. You can see examples of the most impressive potters and work from all nineteen pueblos.

Richard suggests Stephen Trimble's book, *Talking with the Clay,* for the beginning pottery collector.   **P**

6. Tanner Chaney

410 Romero Rd. NW, (Old Town)
Albuquerque, NM 87104
505-247-2242, 800-444-2242
M–Sat 10:00–6:00, Sun 12:00–6:00
Owned by a group of investors: the
Tanner, Chaney, and Baker families
◆ M, V, D, AE, C, S, HA

To the south is a room lined with
cases of jewelry, both contemporary
and antique. To the north is a gallery
with a large selection of pottery, textiles, kachinas, and baskets. The historic textiles are impressive. If you
have certain pieces you are looking
for, be sure to ask. Tom Baker enjoys
discussing weaving with visitors and
answering questions. The shop often
has weaving demonstrations. The
work here is of the highest quality. Be
sure to look also at their expanded
collection of pre-1940 old pawn.

In 1994, the owners opened Native
Gold (400 Romero, Suite B), devoted
to special 14K and 18K gold by the
Southwest's leading Native American
craftsmen.
B, Bk, **J**, K, **R**, P

7. Santo Domingo Indian Trading Post

401 San Felipe NW, Albuquerque,
NM 87104

505-764-0129
Daily 8:00–7:00
Owner: Lita Wagner
◆ M, V, AE, C, S, HA (one step)

Indian-owned and operated, this
post offers a wide selection of jewelry.
All nineteen pueblos are represented.
Navajo work is also available. The in-
house silversmith can do special orders.
Santo Domingo potter Juanita Peters
also works on site.
J, P, Pt

8. Palms Trading Company

1504 Lomas, Albuquerque, NM 87104
505-247-8504, 800-748-1656
M–Sat 9:00–5:30, Sun 11:00–4:00
Owners: Guy Berger and Jim
Franchini
◆ M, V, D, AE, C, S, HA

The prices are the great attraction
at the Palms. It is not unusual to hear
"fifty percent off the marked price,"
but at the Palms it seems to be true.
The shelves are usually overcrowded
with items. It is easy to overlook
tremendous buys because of this.
Museum-quality work sits next to
souvenirs. The pottery is often shrink-
wrapped to prevent problems with
rubbing and chipping. There is a large
selection of pots from most of the
pueblos. Ask to see old items. The
jewelry counters often carry items
ranging from inexpensive to the
expensive, museum-quality work of
top-name artists. If you like a piece,
buy it, because you will be pleased
with the price and it will probably be
gone if you come back later.

Owner Guy Berger and Sergio Vigna, Palms Trading Company, Albuquerque

It is hard to imagine any business selling more pottery than the Palms. Guy said he didn't know how many he sold in a year, but it was well into six figures. The Palms is in the same building as Las Palmas Import Company, which offers a line of products from Mexico that fits easily into a Southwestern decor.

B, Bk, **J**, K, **P**, Pt, R, S, Sp, Beadwork

9. Indian Pueblo Cultural Center

2401 12th St. NW, Albuquerque, NM 87104

505-843-7270, 800-766-4405

Daily Museum & shops: 9:00–5:30, Restaurant: 7:30–3:30

Admission fee

This center is an ideal introduction to Pueblo culture. It has a variety of displays, guest artists, archives, demonstrations, and traditional Indian dances on weekends. Call or write for a calendar of special events.

Within the building is a series of retail shops. Offering a full range of arts and crafts, everything is Indian made except for books, t-shirts, and curios. There is also a wholesale division.

The center has a series of murals by some of the Southwest's finest painters, including Pablita Velarde, Dennis Silva, Charles Lovato, Philbert Hughte, Helen Hardin, Jose Rey Toledo, Bob Chavez, Francis Tafoya, Robert Montoya, Encarnacion Pena, J.D. Medina, and Tommy Montoya. The murals are reason enough to visit. The work is ambitious and beautiful.

B, Bk, D, I, J, K, M, P, Pt, R, Sv, Clothing

10. Penfield Gallery of Indian Arts

2043 S. Plaza NW, Albuquerque, NM 87104

505-242-9696

Daily 10:00–6:00

Owners: Julia and Ruth Reidy

♦ M, V, AE, C, S, HA (with 5" step)

The family once ran Penfield Mercantile Company in Lincoln, New Mexico, which Ruth's great-grandfather opened in 1877. If you are a believer in the old saying "Good things come in small packages," you will like this store. They specialize in miniatures: small intricate pots, horsehair baskets, and an extensive collection of miniature wooden dolls. The wooden dolls are made by Hopi artist Yvonne Louis. They also carry miniature dolls by Acoma artists Steve Cerno, brother of the famous potter Joseph Cerno, and Adrian Leon, who also sells to the Smithsonian and other museums.

The Reidys also have an outstanding inventory of pottery of all sizes, and Zuni fetishes. Ruth states, "We probably buy more than we should, but we love them." The owners' enthusiasm and amiable nature make visiting this retail-only business a joy. (Mail orders are welcome.)

B, **F**, J, **K**, **P**, Sp

11. Cowboys and Indians Antiques

4000 Central Ave. SE, Albuquerque, NM 87108

Mural, 9' 6" x 22', by Jose Rey Toledo, Indian Pueblo Cultural Center, Albuquerque

505-255-4054
Daily 10:00–6:00
Owner: Terry Schurmeier, Manager: Mary Mackie

- ◆ M, V, AE, D, C, T, S, HA, ATADA member

Cowboys and Indians Antiques is the only cooperative in New Mexico to carry antique Native American, Hispanic, and cowboy memorabilia. Opened by Terry in 1995 in a renovated Route 66 building, the shop sells quality material from traders throughout the west. There is a different focus each month with inventory changing accordingly. The shop contains mostly pre-1940s items with a limited number of pieces by contemporary artists. They have one of the largest selections of older jewelry in Albuquerque. Terry and Mary have a combined twenty years' experience in the Native American art business. They are enthusiastic and fun to talk to. Terry's specialties are baskets, jewelry, and antique Plains Indian beadwork; Mary's is Pueblo pottery, Navajo weaving, and books. This is one of our favorite businesses in Albuquerque, and always provides us with a surprise.
B, Bk, F, **J**, K, M, **P, R, Antiques**

⑫ Nizhoni Moses Ltd.
326 San Felipe NW, Albuquerque, NM 87104
505-842-1808
Daily Summer: 9:00–9:00,

Winter: 10:00–8:00
Owner: Tom Moses

- ◆ M, V, D, AE, C, S, HA

Tom Moses' family has been involved with Native American arts and crafts for many years. Tom's father, Horace, was one of the founders of the Gallup Ceremonial and his step-mother, Margaret Winnips Moses, was a courier for the Fred Harvey Company.

Daughter Margaret Moses Branch began this business with her mother, the late Penny Moses, in 1984. Tom now runs the store, which is known particularly for its pottery. The inventory includes pots by Maria Martinez, an extensive collection of Navajo pottery, and clay sculpture by Dennis Andrew Rodriguez, who worked under Allan Houser.

Tom also carries Navajo, Hopi, and Zuni jewelry, old and contemporary weavings, fetishes, Hopi kachina dolls, Navajo folk art, a select group of books for children and books about the Southwest.
Bk, F, **J**, K, M, **P**, R

⑬ Antiques on Rio
400 Rio Grande Blvd., Albuquerque, NM 87104, (Old Town)
505-244-1533
M–Sat 10:00–5:00
Owner: Eric Phillips

- ◆ M, V, AE, C, S

Eric has been a dealer for twenty-

five years, and opened this shop in 1996. His emphasis is on antique Native American art. He carries approximately 85 rugs (1870–1940), historic Pueblo pottery (1880–1950s); Hopi-, Zuni-, and Pueblo-related items; Southwest baskets including Apache and Pima, from 1900 through the 1930s; Plains Indian beadwork, and some old pawn.
B, Bk, F, **J, K**, P, Pt, Rugs, Antiques

⑭ Andrews Pueblo Pottery and Art Gallery
303 Romero NW, Ste. 116N., Albuquerque, NM 87104
505-243-0414
Daily 10:00–6:00
Owners: Helen and Robert Andrews

- ◆ M, V, D, AE, C, S, HA

The Andrews moved into their new contemporary space in 1994. Their inventory includes Paiute, Hopi wicker and coiled baskets, miniature baskets by Madeline Lamson, and pottery by Virgil Ortiz, Blue Corn, Christine McHorse, Lonnie Vigil, and other of the Southwest's best potters. They sell Zuni fetishes, the Cellicion family's Zuni beadwork, paintings by Harrison Begay, and some contemporary serigraphs by Anglo artist Doug West. They are a retail-only business, will accept mail orders, and will work on special requests.
B, F, P, Pt, Beadwork

15. Skip Maisel

510 Central SW, Albuquerque, NM 87102
505-242-6526
M–F 9:00–5:30, Sat 9:00–5:00
Owner: Skip Maisel
♦ M, V, D, AE, C, S, HA

Skip's grandfather Maurice built this "Pueblo Deco" style building in downtown Albuquerque in 1937 and hired students just out of high school and college to paint murals on the front of the building. Today, visitors will recognize many of these now-famous names (Pablita Velarde, Harrison Begay, Olive Rush, Tony Martinez, Theodore Suina, Ha-So-de, Awa Tsireh, and Joe Herrera). Starting as a wholesale-only business, the shop now depends on thousands of Native American craftsmen working out of their own homes, for its brisk wholesale (open to the public) and retail inventory. This shop and the revitalized KiMo Theater across the street are two excellent reasons for a stroll down historic Central Avenue (part of old Route 66).
B, Bk, D, F, J, K, M, P, Pt, R, S, Sp, Sv

16. Allison Lee: Silversmith

3332 Stanford Dr. NE, Albuquerque, NM 87107
505-884-2090

Born in 1958, Allison Lee learned silversmithing from his mother and uncle in Mexican Springs, New

Allison Lee, silversmith, Albuquerque

Mexico. He worked in shops around Gallup and moved to Albuquerque, starting his own business, Allison Snowhawk Inc., in 1988. His designs range from contemporary to traditional. He says, "I make every type of quality jewelry." His prices range from $20 to $8,000 and his work is available at the Heard Museum (Phoenix), Southwest Trading Company, St. Charles, Illinois, and Naja (Sedona, AZ).

17. Kennedy Indian Arts and Crafts

P.O. Box 6526, 602 Montano Rd. NW, Albuquerque, NM 87107
505-344-7538

John W. Kennedy wholesales by appointment, specializing in Pueblo pottery. He is a second-generation trader. His father, George E. Kennedy, built the Salina Springs Trading Post and traded at the post known today as the Thunderbird at Canyon de Chelly. John is a virtual encyclopedia of trading post history. Born in 1912, he still travels the entire Southwest buying, trading, and wholesaling.

John's daughter, Georgiana, owns Kennedy Indian Arts in Bluff, Utah. His son, John D. Kennedy, started the Indian Arts and Crafts Association in the late seventies and continues to trade in Albuquerque.

18. Wright's Collection of Indian Art

Park Square, 6600 Indian School Rd. NE (at Louisiana), Albuquerque, NM 87110
505-883-6122
M–F 10:00–6:00, Sat 10:00–5:00
Owner: Marguerite Chernoff
Manager: Wayne Bobrick
♦ all credit cards, C, T, S, HA

Wright's opened in 1907. Owned originally by Charles and Katherine Wright, it was bought by Mrs. Chernoff in the early fifties. Wright's sells anything Native American as long as it is hand-made by one artist, and well made. They buy directly from the artists who come to the shop. Wright's, originally a trading

INDIAN ARTS AND CRAFTS ASSOCIATION (IACA)

122 LaVeta NE, Albuquerque, NM 87108

505-265-9149

http://www.atiin.com/iaca

The IACA is an association of museums, traders, dealers, collectors, scholars, artists-craftspeople, and tribal enterprises. Members adhere to a code of ethics, and the association has been a positive influence in the marketplace. They produce a directory of all members, available for purchase through their office.

SELECTED ALBUQUERQUE ARTISTS/CRAFTSPEOPLE

R.C. Gorman, 323 Romero NW, Albuquerque, NM 87104, 505-843-7666—Paintings and prints.

Louis Montoya, Albuquerque, NM 87108, 505-265-0876—Jewelry.

Paul Thompson, P.O. Box 837, Albuquerque, NM 87103, 505-275-8466—Flutes.

SANDIA

19. Bien Mur Indian Art Center

P.O. Box 91148, Albuquerque, NM 87199, I-25, Tramway exit 234, East 505-821-5400, 800-365-5400 http://www.bienmur.com M–Sat 9:00–5:30, Sun 11:00–5:00 General Manager: Robert Van Caster

- ♦ M, V, D, AE, C, S, HA (main floor), I

The Bien Mur Indian Art Center was bought by Sandia Pueblo in 1989. The Center carries strictly Indian arts and crafts, including Siri from Mexico and Canadian crafts.

There is a large inventory of art and crafts including antique items for sale. When we visited, they had old Navajo blouses with silver ornaments, old medicine pouches, and a good selection of Fred Harvey vintage jewelry. There is

SANDIA PUEBLO

Governor's Office: P.O. Box 6008, Bernalillo, NM 87004, 13 miles north of Albuquerque, east of NM 313

505-867-3317

- ♦ No photography, recording, or sketching; however, visits to the pueblo are not encouraged. Visitors are invited to visit Sandia Indian Bingo and Sandia Lakes Recreation Area as well as the Bien Mur Indian Market Center.
- ♦ St. Anthony Feast Day: June 13
- ♦ Language: Tiwa

Sandia is not known for its arts and crafts. A few artists make baskets, pottery, and paintings. These can be found at the Bien Mur Indian Art Center or at the Pueblo Indian Cultural Center in nearby Albuquerque.

post, now has a gallery setting. Included in their vast inventory you will find ledger type paintings by teenager Benjamin Nelson, and the work of elder Santo Domingo jeweler Leo Coriz. Also represented is Navajo potter Alice Cling, many of the great Zuni fetish families, and hot blown glass artist, Tony Jojola. B, D, F, **J**, K, **P**, Pt, R, S, Sp, hot blown glass

also a smoke shop on the premises. (No tax is charged on purchases.)

They welcome phone and mail inquiries and are eager to photograph jewelry, weavings, and other items for your consideration. Promotional events include performances, cooking, and artist demonstrations. Call for more information. B, Bk, C, F, I, J, K, M, P, R, Sp, Sv

SELECTED SANDIA
ARTISTS/CRAFTSPEOPLE

Robert Montoya, 5741 Osuna, Albuquerque, NM 87109—Painting.

JEMEZ

20. **Walatowa Visitor Center**
Dept. of Tourism, P.O. Box 100, Jemez Pueblo, NM 87024
Take I-25 to Bernalillo, exit 242.

Take Hwy 44 going NW. At San Ysidro take NM 4, 5 miles north to the pueblo. Look for signs. 505-834-7235, FAX 505-834-7331 M–F 10:00–5:00, Weekends: 10:00–4:00

With advance arrangements, the visitor center will set up a tour. They will alert you to all rules and help you locate various artists at the pueblo. Their display of work for sale includes pottery by Delia Gachupin, Geraldine Sandia, Juanita Seonia, and Tomasita Tosa; melon bowls and wedding vases by Erna Chosa, who works at the center; and storytellers by Lyda Toya, Delores Toya, and Bessie Yepa. There is jewelry by Patricia Valencia that incorporates a variety of stones and silver. Paintings by Malcolm Yepa include eagles, buffalo, and traditional dancers as subject matter. Sometimes the center carries Corina Wauie's traditional Towan willow baskets. The center sponsors artist demonstrations and the annual Memorial Day week-

---

JEMEZ PUEBLO

Pueblo Offices: P.O. Box 100, Jemez Pueblo, NM 87024, take I-25 to Bernalillo, exit 242. Take Hwy 44 to San Ysidro, then NM 4, 5 miles north to the pueblo. Look for signs.
505-834-7359

♦ Photography, audio recording, and sketching are prohibited at the pueblo, but encouraged at Red Rock Scenic Area, three miles north of the pueblo on NM 4.

♦ WALATOWA VISITOR CENTER is open to the public; the village itself is open to visitors only on feast days. No tours of village.

♦ No unauthorized publication of information regarding pueblo activities.

♦ No climbing on walls or other structures. Do not pick up or remove artifacts or objects.

♦ Pueblo kivas and graveyards are not to be entered by non-pueblo people.

♦ No alcohol, weapons, drugs, or pets.

♦ Obey all traffic, parking, speed limit signs.

♦ The Pueblo of Jemez is not responsible for injuries, theft, or damages incurred by visitors.

♦ FEAST DAYS: St. Persingula, August 2 and San Diego, November 12

♦ EVENTS: Open Air Market, April–October; Annual Jemez Red Rocks Arts and Crafts Show, second week in June; December Arts and Crafts Show

♦ LANGUAGE: Towa

*The Pueblo of Jemez wishes to welcome you to our beautiful village of Walatowa. We invite you to our Visitor Center to experience attractions we have to offer.
—Pueblo of Jemez Department of Tourism*

Jemez is the only culture that speaks the Towa dialect, and a traditional law forbids that the language be translated into writing. Jemez is usually pronounced *Hay-mez.* The Walatowa Visitor Center should be the first stop at the pueblo. Check in here; do not wander around the village.

end "Jemez Red Rocks Arts and Crafts Show," which includes arts and crafts, traditional dances, artist demonstrations, storytelling, Sunrise Ceremony, and performances by Native American musicians.
B, **J**, **P**, Pt

21. Jemez Trading Post

P.O. Box 68, Jemez Pueblo, NM 87024, Hwy 4 near Jemez Pueblo entrance
505-834-7404
Daily 8–5:30 (closed for lunch)
Owner: Toya family;
manager: William Toya
♦ C, HA (east side of porch has 2 steps)

This trading post opened in the mid-thirties. The building has been remodeled but still has square dark vigas. When Jack Toya opened, he did a brisk business in pawn and handled an extensive arts and crafts selection. Today they sell groceries, a small selection of pottery, some woven belts, and Indian dolls.
D, P

22. Juanita C. Fragua: Potter

P.O. Box 389, Jemez Pueblo, NM 87024
505-834-7556

Juanita's melon bowls and wedding vases have an elegant grace that makes you think they evolved over generations of fine-tuning, but they are her

Jemez potter Juanita Fragua, Santa Fe Indian Market

own designs. When asked how she started doing them, she modestly states, "When you're doing pottery you just feel like doing something different sometimes. So I did." Juanita made her first pot in the forties. She says, "Grandma (Benina Medina) learned to make pottery when she grew up at Zia. She taught Mom and the aunties and they were the first to make them here at Jemez. I didn't know Grandma because she died before I was born, but I learned many of her techniques from watching Mom make her wedding vases."

Juanita uses volcanic ash for temper, as do the artists of Zia. She says that it

is collected from a dangerous cave. She also collects the clay and other minerals needed from the Jemez–Cuba area. Potters who use volcanic ash temper always note the difficulty of grinding the ash but claim that it makes the pots more durable.

Jemez has a pottery tradition that has sputtered and had periods of disruption. When you hold one of Juanita's melon bowls, you can feel a new Jemez tradition taking form.

Juanita welcomes visitors and commissions.

Storyteller, 9", by Reyes Panana, Jemez Pueblo, New Mexico

23. Reyes Panana: Potter

P.O Box 165, Jemez Pueblo, NM 87024

Reyes' Koshare figures, with their personal style and flawless technique, are sculptures of visual impact. She started making the Koshares around 1984. She grew up in Jemez and digs her clay and slips from the hills around the pueblo, except the red slip, which comes from Santo Domingo Pueblo. Her work can be seen at the Agape Gallery and Palms Trading Company in Albuquerque. She welcomes commissions and special orders.

SELECTED JEMEZ ARTISTS/CRAFTSPEOPLE

Joe and Esther Cajero, P.O. Box 377, Jemez Pueblo, NM 87024, 505-834-7533—Joe: Traditional bows and arrows; Esther: Storytellers and figurines.

Glendora Daubs, 207 Summer Winds Dr., Rio Rancho, NM 87124, 505-891-8703—Pottery.

Henrietta Gauchipin, P.O. Box 252, Jemez Pueblo, NM 87024—Pottery.

Joseph Gauchipin, P.O. Box 358, Jemez Pueblo, NM 87024—Pottery.

Laura Gauchipin, P.O. Box 433, Jemez Pueblo, NM 87024—Pottery.

ZIA PUEBLO

Pueblo Offices: 135 Capitol Square Dr., Zia Pueblo, NM 87053-6013

505-867-3304, FAX 505-867-3308

♦ No photography, tape, or video-recording or sketching of the pueblo or dances.

♦ The pueblo is open only during daylight hours.

♦ Language: Keres

Dear Visitors:

Welcome to the Pueblo of Zia. Zia is a Keresan speaking Pueblo and is one of the nineteen pueblos. Archaeological findings credit the People of Zia as being direct descendants of the Chaco Canyon, and Anasazi civilization. The present site of Zia was settled and has been occupied continuously since 1250 A.D.

Zia Pueblo celebrates the following events, which are open to the public. January 6, Buffalo dances celebrating Three Kings Day; Easter Celebration; August 15, Annual Fiesta Corn Dances celebrating Our Lady of Assumption Patron Saint; December 25–26, Buffalo dances celebrating Christmas.

The Pueblo of Zia has a small Cultural Center/Museum which exhibits local arts and crafts. The Zia's are known for their fine potterymaking.

We hope you have a pleasant stay and we invite you to come again.

—Henry Shije, Governor of Zia

Zia potters are particularly proud of their pottery tradition and the hard durability of their pots, which comes from mixing the ground black basalt, which the pueblo is built upon, into the clay. Zia pottery is difficult to find in galleries because the potters tend to sell their work directly through arts and crafts shows. The beautiful polychrome pots with their typical black, brown, and red or white designs have always been highly sought after. The prancing Zia bird beneath its flat rainbow band is one of the most recognizable motifs in the Southwest. The sun design of the New Mexico State flag is a Zia motif.

Helen Henderson, P.O. Box 618, Jemez Pueblo, NM 87024, 505-834-7053—Pottery.

Mary Rose, Norma, and Eloise Toya, P.O. Box 142, Jemez Pueblo, NM 87024, 505-834-7704—Pottery.

Alvina Yepa, P.O. Box 164, Jemez Pueblo, NM 87024—Pottery.

Lawrence Yepa, P.O. Box 339, Jemez Pueblo, NM 87024—Pottery.

ZIA

24. **Zia Cultural Center**

162 B Zia Blvd. (Tribal Office Complex), Zia Pueblo, NM 87053-6002, 17 miles northwest of Bernalillo on Hwy 44
505-867-3304 (Tribal Office)
M–F 9:00–5:00 (closed 12:00–1:00 for lunch)

The cultural center sits within the Tribal Office Complex. The museum offers a glimpse of Zia's history and outlines the development of Zia pottery. A display of artwork by Zia residents is on hand complete with the artists' names and phone numbers. Maps of the pueblo showing artists' homes are also available.

Sophia Medina, potter, Zia Pueblo, New Mexico

25. **Sofia and Lois Medina: Potters**

089 Northeast Dr., Zia Pueblo, NM 87053
505-867-5273

Sofia made her first pot in 1958. She didn't get involved full time until returning to Zia in 1964. Children Rachel, Herman, Marcellus, and Lois have all become artists.

Sofia Medina's pottery has set the standard for contemporary Zia pottery. Her pots are large, ambitious, and crafted with great care and skill. It is important to understand the work involved in pottery production to understand the pricing. Sofia explains:

People think we charge too much, but they don't understand the work we go through.

We grind volcanic ash for a week to fill one sixteen-pound shortening can so we can add it to the clay. We dig our own clay and slip and I must drive out to Torreon to get four- or five-inch pieces of sheep manure, then dry it. Only sheep manure fires are hot enough to cook our clay through. Sometimes you make a beautiful sixteen-inch pot and it cracks in the firing. It is a heart aching feeling. Your heart cries especially when you have a debt. It makes you feel like not working. You must go through it to see how much time it takes. Pottery makes your back and arms ache.

Sofia welcomes commissions, mail orders, and visitors. She says that people have come out to help with firing, but they always give up because

it's too hot. She has sold pots for $5,000 but laughingly says she'll make one for $15, adding that it will be like a button. Sofia says she has safely used her pottery in a microwave.

SELECTED ZIA ARTISTS/CRAFTSPEOPLE

Ralph Aragon, P.O. Box 013, Zia Pueblo, NM 87053—Painting.

Gloria Gauchipin, P.O. Box 104, San Ysidro, NM 87053—Pottery.

Katherine and Reyes Pino, 015 Plaza Alley, Zia, NM 84053, 505-867-4583 —Traditional pottery.

Diana Lucero and Vincentita Pino, P.O. Box 105, San Ysidro, NM , 505-834-7338—Pottery.

SANTA ANA

 Ta-Ma-Ya Arts and Crafts Co-op

2 Dove Rd., Bernalillo, NM 87004, New Santa Ana: NM 44 to NM 313,

north 2 miles on left
T, Th, Sat 10:00–4:30
President: Clara Paquin, Vice President: Lena Garcia
♦ C, HA

This friendly little cooperative is located in the Governor's Office Complex. Clara Paquin, Lena Garcia, and their friends have collected an interesting assortment of items. Homemade cookies and baked goods are available while you look through an impressive inventory of dance paraphernalia. Rattles, shoulder shells, fox furs, dance kilts, woven belts, ribbon shirts, leggings for the deer and antelope dances, skunk skin leggings, gourd dance shawls, textiles, and Santa Ana black crosses with straw inlay are available here.

We can't imagine a friendlier business than this. The women seem to love running the enterprise. They sit and embroider dance kilts as they tell stories. (When you leave the co-op you feel as though you have visited some long-lost aunts.) The co-op maintains a booth in the Santa Fe Indian Market.

P, **Dance paraphernalia**, **Textiles**

Lena Garcia and Clara Paquin, Ta-Ma-Ya Arts and Crafts Co-op, New Santa Ana Pueblo, New Mexico

SELECTED SANTA ANA ARTISTS/CRAFTSPEOPLE

Elmer Leon, P.O. Box 1284, Bernalillo, NM, 87004—Straw crosses.

Arthur Menchego, P.O. Box 68, Bernalillo, NM 87004—Painting.

Steven Sanchez, P.O. Box 1273, Pena Blanca, NM 87041—Pottery.

SANTA ANA PUEBLO

GOVERNOR'S OFFICE:

2 Dove Rd., Bernalillo, NM 87004. The old village is 8 miles northwest of Bernalillo on NM 44. The new village is 2 miles north of NM 44 off NM 313.

505-867-3301, FAX 505-867-3395

◆ No photography, recording, or sketching

◆ The old village is open to the public January 1, 6, Easter, June 24, 29, and Feast days: July 25, 26, and December 25–28.

◆ LANGUAGE: Keres

The old pueblo, Tamaya, is open to non-pueblo visitors on feast days only. If you plan to visit on a feast day, it is advisable to call in advance. The government offices and cooperative are in the new village in Ranchitos, a rich farming area purchased from Spanish colonists in the eighteenth century by Santa Ana Pueblo. The new village is open to the public.

SAN FELIPE PUEBLO

GOVERNOR'S OFFICE:

P.O. Box 4339, San Felipe Pueblo, NM 87001, located off I-25, 10 miles north of Bernalillo

505-867-3381, FAX 505-867-3383

◆ No photography, recording, or sketching

◆ Visitors are welcome on Feast Day, May 1

◆ CRAFTS FAIR: The first week of October, off I-25 near the old baseball field

◆ LANGUAGE: Keres

The conservative leadership at San Felipe has little interest in attracting tourism. We suggest stopping at the Governor's Office as soon as you enter the pueblo to register, and to obtain a current list of regulations.

San Felipe is not known for its arts and crafts. A small amount of pottery is made, but there is not a pottery tradition here. Recently Joe Latoma and his family have been creating jewelry, which they sell from their house.

The plaza and the San Felipe Mission are beautiful. Non-Indians, however, are not permitted to enter the church. The lack of interest in visitors has made the pueblo less than inviting to tourists, but a couple of shops do exist at the pueblo.

SAN FELIPE

 Bob and Dora Garcia's Blanket Shop

P.O. Box 361, Algodones, NM 87001
505-867-5797
Daily 9:00–9:00

This little shop is located 3/4 mile from I-25, exit 252. They carry silver and turquoise jewelry made by their relatives Geraldine and Virgil Valencia; Jemez and Acoma pottery; prints by Dora's nephew, Fernando Padilla; and of course, blankets. Pendletons have always been close to the Pueblo people's hearts, and the Garcias have a great selection to choose from. Baby blankets, shawls, jackets, and blankets come in diverse array of colors and patterns.

J, M, **Blankets**

SELECTED SAN FELIPE
ARTISTS/CRAFTSPEOPLE

Daryl Candelaria, P.O. Box 4046, San Felipe, NM 87001, 505-867-0653—Pottery.

Santo Domingo Trading Post, Domingo, New Mexico, was a stop for the old Atcheson, Topeka, and Santa Fe Railroad (closed 1994).

Hubert Candelario, P.O. Box 602, Algodones, NM 87001, 505-867-0673—Pottery.

Richard Chavez, P.O. Box 336, Algodones, NM 87001—Jewelry.

SANTO DOMINGO

 Santo Domingo Cultural Center Gift Shop
P.O. Box 159, Santo Domingo, NM 87052, just west of the I-25 Santo Domingo exit
Closed winters
Owner: Santo Domingo Business Enterprise

♦ M, V, C, S, HA

The Santo Domingo Cultural Center Gift Shop occupies a small building near the Santo Domingo Pueblo exit off Hwy 25. The center doubles as a gas station and is surrounded by artists' tables where jewelry and Native American food are sold Thursdays through Sundays. The cultural center has some historical information, displays of older Santo Domingo jewelry (including heishi, inlaid shell, and Santo Domingo depression jewelry), and a small gift shop.
J, M, P

29. **Robert Tenorio: Potter**
P.O. Box 62, Santo Domingo Pueblo, NM 87052
505-465-2609

With their beautiful bold designs, Robert's pots are among the finest produced in the Southwest. His modest, amiable personality makes a visit even more memorable. Robert's great respect for his religion and Santo Domingo traditions is evident in his pottery. The level of craftsmanship and deft handling of beeweed, the plant that produces permanent black paint, may be taking Santo Domingo pottery to a new standard of excellence.

While studying at the Institute of American Arts, Robert began making pottery with the encouragement of Otellie Loloma. He remembers, "The early days were frustrating. I had lots of cracking and exploding in the firing." Through these many accidents he refined his technique and reduced the number of problems. Robert still echoes his grandmother's warning when he says, "You can't count on

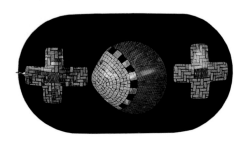

Heishi (shell) mosaic jewelry, center piece approximately 6" diameter, by Angie Reano Owen, Santo Domingo Pueblo

your pots while you are working. The final judgment is in the firing."

A visit to Robert Tenorio's beautiful home in Santo Domingo is an opportunity to see and buy some of the finest pots created in the Southwest. Of his own collection of pottery, Robert says, "I enjoy showing the older pottery to visitors. We have the collection because of my grandmother and mother. Santo Domingo is known for its trading and

Mother would trade her jewelry for pottery after dances and we continue doing so." His sister Mary also makes beautiful pottery. Be sure to see her work, too. Santo Domingo tradition does not allow for figurative pottery or decoration, so she came up with the creative solution of a miniature hearth and beautiful interior from clay. These are the Santo Domingo versions of storyteller sculpture. They are unique and usually are painted by Robert.

SANTO DOMINGO PUEBLO

GOVERNOR'S OFFICE:
P.O. Box 99, Santo Domingo Pueblo, NM 87052, Santo Domingo exit off I-25
505-465-2214, FAX 505-465-2688

♦ No photography, recording, or sketching

♦ FEAST DAY: August 4

♦ SANTO DOMINGO PUEBLO ANNUAL ARTS AND CRAFTS MARKET: Labor Day Weekend, 505-465-0406 or write P.O. Box 369

♦ LANGUAGE: Keres

The Santo Domingo Business Enterprise is very helpful in locating the pueblo's numerous artists. The pueblo is beautiful and its arts and crafts are renowned. Many of the home-based shops are willing to negotiate on prices.

In 1925 author Charles Lummis called Santo Domingo the most stiff-necked of the pueblos in clinging to the ways of the old." Santo Domingo still holds tightly to the "old ways." The pueblo's dances are famous for the enthusiasm and complete participation of the citizens. This tenacity to maintain tradition is also found in the pueblo's arts and crafts.

Jewelry at the pueblo includes every configuration of beadwork and mosaic. Necklaces of liquid silver, turquoise, and stones of every kind, and heishi (shell) in every color imaginable are created in profusion. The mosaic jewelry combines colors in vibrant juxtapositions with precise technique and design. There is also a strong tradition of silverwork at the pueblo. Older jewelers Vidal Aragon and Leo Coriz serve as inspirations for younger silversmiths.

Santo Domingo pottery does not include storytellers as does its neighbor Cochiti. It is forbidden to create figurative pottery or use human figures as decorative motifs. You will find the pottery decorated with a tulip motif, birds, floral patterns, and a diverse group of geometric designs. We suggest that you do not purchase a Santo Domingo pot until you have seen the pottery of the Tenorio family.

Santo Domingo potter Robert Tenorio at Eight Northern Indian Pueblos Artist and Craftsmen Show, San Juan Pueblo, New Mexico

SELECTED SANTO DOMINGO ARTISTS/CRAFTSPEOPLE

Vidal Aragon, P.O. Box 28, Santo Domingo, NM 87052, 505-465-2702—Jewelry.

Lorraine Cate, P.O. Box 203, Santo Domingo, NM 87052, 505-465-0140—Silver jewelry, heishi.

Arthur and Hilda Coriz, P.O. Box 549, Santo Domingo, NM 87052, 505-465-1504—Pottery.

Joseph D. Coriz, P.O. Box 133, Santo Domingo, NM 87052, 505-465-2732—Jewelry.

Viola Coriz, P.O. Box 37, Santo Domingo, NM 87052—Jewelry.

Marvin and Lillian Lovato, P.O. Box 395, Santo Domingo Pueblo, NM 87052—Heishi jewelry and pottery.

You can find Robert's pottery at Robert F. Nichols in Santa Fe and the Adobe Gallery in Albuquerque. He does not like special orders, commissions, or mail orders, preferring to sell the work after it is completed.

30. Leo Coriz: Silversmith

P.O. Box 241, Santo Domingo, NM 87052 ♦ 505-465-2902

Born in 1913, Leo originally shoed horses and taught himself to make jewelry. He says, "I didn't sell my work in the early days. I traded with Navajos and Hopis for weavings and buckskins. I still make my jewelry the old way. I design it so it can't be duplicated with machines. My designs keep to the old traditions." Mark Arrowsmith of Arrowsmith's Relics of the Old West in Santa Fe, adds, "Leo is bright, articulate, and a living encyclopedia of Santo Domingo culture. His work retains the flavor of another era." Leo especially enjoys talking about the history of pueblo crosses. He has taught his children and grandchildren to silversmith. Dressing in traditional Santo Domingo style, Leo is not just a tremendously talented artist, he is also a living reminder not to settle for less than excellence.

Tufacast silver pendant, 3", and pin, 2", by Leo Coriz, Santo Domingo Pueblo. Courtesy of Arrowsmith's, Santa Fe, New Mexico

Paulita, Gilbert, and Andrew Pacheco, P.O. Box 411, Santo Domingo, NM 87052, 505-465-2456—Pottery.

Frank Poolheco, P.O. Box 250, Santo Domingo, NM 87052, 505-892-7146—Beaded gun holsters.

Percy and Charlotte Reano, P.O. Box 315, Santo Domingo, NM 87052, 505-465-2668—Jewelry.

COCHITI

31. **Virginia and Louis Naranjo: Potters**

P.O. Box 24, Cochiti Pueblo, NM 87072

505-465-2320

When Louis talks about his pottery, it becomes obvious that his heart goes into each and every piece. He learned how to work the clay from his mother, Frances Suina, and when she grew older he helped her by painting

some of her figures. Virginia learned from working with her aunt, Juanita Arquero. Both Louis and Virginia make finely crafted antelope, deer, and buffalo dance figures, human and animal storytellers, nativities, and cornmeal wall plaques with dancer or animal heads protruding. Louis is very proud of the snowflake design on his storytellers, a design his mother created and was very fond of.

The Naranjos work with care and reverence for the clay. Louis said, "We try to never waste. Nature provides us what we need. When pieces break in the firing, I collect them and we return them to the river. We let them flow into the water with a prayer."

The Naranjos welcome special orders and commissions. It is well worth a visit to their home to share their wonderful stories, good hearts, and humor. If you can't make it to

Clay figures of Rivermen, center figure 8", by Pablo Quintana, Cochiti Pueblo. Cochiti celebrates the Rivermen every May 3. The Pueblo Rivermen come out of the river and capture all the children. Mothers bake bread crucifixes and exchange them with the Rivermen for their children's freedom. Afterwards, a celebration ensues before the Rivermen return to their watery homes.

Storyteller artists Virginia and Louis Naranjo, Cochiti Pueblo

COCHITI PUEBLO

GOVERNOR'S OFFICE:

P.O. Box 70, Cochiti Pueblo, NM
87072, west of I-25, 45 miles north of
Albuquerque and 25 miles south of
Santa Fe
505-465-2244, FAX 505-465-1135

◆ No photography, recording, or
sketching

◆ FEAST DAY: July 14

◆ LANGUAGE: Keres

Cochiti has been nestled in this beautiful river valley since the thirteenth century. When you drive to the pueblo, you will see the immense Cochiti Dam that creates Cochiti Lake, a popular recreation area for fishing, camping, boating, and picnicking.

At the pueblo, many artists sell from their homes. Don't be surprised if children bicycle up to your car and ask if you are looking for storytellers. They will gladly direct you to a family artisan. Many homes also post signs offering pottery and storytellers.

Cochiti is the home of the storyteller. There is some dissension about who created the first storyteller, but it was in the 1960s. Alexander Girard, whose collection is housed at the International Museum of Folk Art in Santa Fe, collected more than 600 of Helen Cordero's storytellers. It was an idea that found a large audience, and today storytellers are created throughout the pueblos and actively collected. Many Cochiti potters create them, and you might find choosing one a difficult task.

Cochiti is also famous for its drums. Cochiti Ray's enormous drums vary in size from six inches to a hundred inches in diameter and serve as beautiful tables. Guadalupe Ortiz's fanciful drums seem dreamlike with their multiple animal heads.

Cochiti turquoise and silver jewelry are also well respected. The most notable jeweler is Cippy Crazy Horse. His work has a clarity of vision and precision of technique that sets him apart. This pueblo stamps everything it touches with its unique personality.

The Governor's Office is very helpful in locating various pueblo artists.

Cochiti, you can find their work at Packards, Storyteller, and the Rainbow Man in Santa Fe, and at Agape Gallery and Adobe Gallery in Albuquerque's Old Town.

 32. Seferina, Virgil, and Guadalupe Ortiz: Potters and Drummakers

P.O. Box 146, Cochiti Pueblo, NM
87072
505-465-2939

Seferina began making small animals and bowls in 1959. Her mother and grandmother were also potters. She is currently making bears, canteens, storytellers, cornmeal holders, bathing beauties, and "whatever comes to mind." When asked about changes over the years she says, "The biggest changes have been in the prices, and now many potters use commercial paints, but I like the old ways and only use the traditional red and white slip and my beeweed for the black."

A unique feature of Guadalupe's drums is his whimsical use of knots and eccentricities in the wood. He makes these imperfections into singing animal heads and humorous beasts, and suggests that this is his contribution to the Cochiti storytelling tradition.

Of their six children, four are currently working with clay. The most ambitious of the four is Virgil, who has been studying older Cochiti figures of carnival sideshow characters

Virgil, Seferina, and Guadalupe Ortiz, potters and drummakers, Cochiti Pueblo

and, at times, strange and bizarre figures. He is meticulously reviving this forgotten aspect of the Cochiti figurative tradition while bringing to it his own unique vision and fine craftsmanship to his work.

The Ortiz family enjoys visitors to their shop in Cochiti and welcome

Figure (business card holder), 6", Seferina Ortiz, Cochiti Pueblo

commissions and mail orders. Call ahead to be certain someone will be around. Seferina adds, "There are no special hours, just come on by."

33. Cochiti Ray's Drums

P.O. Box 327, Algodones, NM 87001
505-867-3802

Ray Gallegos' drums vary in size from six inches to a hundred inches in diameter. The large drums are usually used as coffee or end tables. Ray says you can specify the shape and size and he can make it. His drums can be seen in shops across the Southwest. He obtains his wood from the city of Albuquerque when they clear the old cottonwoods for a new building.

Ray's grandpa ran a trading post close to the San Buenaventura Mission in Cochiti. Ray says, "He carried everything Cochiti and the neighboring villages needed. It was the only place you could get gasoline for the few cars in the villages. My dad bought the house and store and family still lives there today. As time went on it was hard to earn a living at the store. My father learned the art of drum making from an old drummaker named Diego. He taught me this art at a young age."

Ray takes commissions and special orders and is willing to ship his drums. He also does a brisk wholesale business.

SELECTED COCHITI ARTISTS/CRAFTSPEOPLE

Cippy Crazyhorse, P.O. Box 94, Cochiti Pueblo, NM 87072—Jewelry.

Ivan Lewis, P.O. Box 14, Cochiti Pueblo, NM 87072—Storyteller pottery.

Pablo Quintana, P.O. Box 80, Cochiti Pueblo, NM 87072, 505-465-2341—Pottery.

Ada Suina, P.O. Box 56, Cochiti Pueblo, NM 87072—Storyteller pottery.

SANTA FE

Santa Fe, the third largest art market in the United States behind New York and Los Angeles, has become an international center for art, fashion, and design.

The business community changes monthly. There are two annual free publications that list the various galleries and artists showing in the Santa Fe-Taos vicinity. They are:

The Wingspread Collectors Guide
P.O. Box 13566
Albuquerque, NM 87192
(800) 873-4278

Santa Fe and Taos Arts
c/o The Book of Santa Fe
Publications
535 Cordova Rd., Suite 241,
Santa Fe, NM 87501
505-471-5475

These are available at many locations in town, or they can be ordered by mail or telephone.

34. Institute of American Indian Arts Museum Gift Shop

108 Cathedral Place, Santa Fe, NM 87501
505-988-6212
M–Sat 10:00–5:00, Sun 12:00–5:00, Closed on Mondays
Manager: Marguerite Wood
♦ M, V, D, AE, S, HA

The shop is inside this beautiful new museum, which opened in June 1992. The shop showcases contemporary art created by many Native American groups in the U.S. and Canada, including the Northwest, Northern Plains, Onondogan, Mohawk, and Aliute.

The Museum of American Indian Arts houses the national collection of contemporary Indian art.
Bk, C, **J**, **P**, Pt, S, t-shirts, cards

35. La Fonda Indian Shop and Gallery

100 E. San Francisco, Santa Fe, NM 87501, inside La Fonda Hotel
505-988-2488

M–Sat 9:00–9:00, Sun 9:00–6:00
Owners: Rick Smith and Rich Edelman
♦ M, V, D, AE, C, S, HA (except downstairs; will take work upstairs)

The downstairs gallery, somewhat hidden, exhibits work in a less crowded manner than its upstairs counterpart. Jewelry by Charles Supplee, Watson Honanie, and Richard Chavez can be found here among work by many other fine artisans. You'll find Tohono O'odham horsehair baskets and pottery from all the pueblos.

Pottery by Lucy McKelvey, Tina Garcia, Anita Suazo, Sylvia Naha, Frogwoman, James Nampeyo, and Steve Lucas is available. They also carry a selection of Casas Grandes pottery from Mexico.
B, Bk, **J**, **P**, R, Beadwork

36. Packard's

61 Old Santa Fe Trail, Santa Fe, NM 87501
505-983-9241
M–Sat 9:30–6:00, Sun 9:30–5:00 (hours can vary)
Owners: Richard and Carolyn Canon; manager: Ramona Brainard
♦ M, V, AE, C, S, HA, I

Packard's feels like a series of small stores under one roof. Here you will

Painter, printmaker Dan Lomahaftewa, Santa Fe

find pottery by Louis and Virginia Naranjo; Ivan Lewis; the Tenorio, Tafoya, Lewis, and the Coriz families; and fine jewelry including unusual sterling items like letter openers, ash trays, magnifiers, and hat bands. Packard's is a Santa Fe institution.

B, F, **J**, K, **M**, **P**, **R**, Belts

37. **The Rainbow Man**

107 E. Palace Ave., Santa Fe, NM 87501

505-982-8706

Daily 9:00–6:00

Owners: Bob and Marianne Kapoun

◆ M, V, AE, C, S, HA (through courtyard)

Our favorite stops have always been those rare enterprises that feel like they could not exist anywhere else. Rainbow Man is one that is the essence of Santa Fe. It offers the eccentric, romantic, traditional, and historic. The work here must appeal to the owners to be added to the inventory. The result is a mixture of Navajo folk art, old jewelry, Huichol pieces, Navajo weavings, old Mexico collectibles, Leroy Archuletta's sculptures, pottery by the Ortiz family and Louis and Virginia Naranjo, and one of the finest collections of Edward Curtis photographs. Bob Kapoun authored a book on Indian blankets and offers the best selection of them that we have seen.

This business appears modest from the exterior. The rooms connect like train cars to create a unique collection of items evocative of old Santa Fe. In the forties, the last two rooms served as a clearing house for the Los Alamos Laboratory. Anyone visiting Los Alamos had to obtain security clearance from this office.

J, **P**, S, **Blankets**, **Folk Art**, Photographs

38. **Simply Santa Fe**

72 E. San Francisco, Santa Fe, NM 87501

505-988-3100

M–Sat 9:30–6:00,

Sun 10:00–5:00,

Owners: Sarah Wilson and Armand Ortega

◆ M, V, D, AE, C, S, HA elevator

This multilevel store sits on the plaza. The basement is completely western and evokes an old trading post atmosphere. Old display cases, advertising, and sundry cowboy gear are contained within the stone walls.

Bk, J, Antiques, Furniture, Home accessories, Clothing

Concha belts, Dewey Galleries Ltd., on the Santa Fe Plaza

39. Dewey Galleries Ltd.
76 E. San Francisco, Santa Fe, NM
87501, on the plaza, upstairs
505-982-8632,
FAX 505-982-4803
M–Sat 10:00–5:00 or by appt.
Owners: Ray and Judy Dewey
♦ M, V, AE, C, S, HA (gallery)

For those who love old Navajo and Hispanic textiles, Dewey's offers some of the finest available. Beaded gauntlets, strike-a-light bags, rattles, Matachine dance wands, old pawn, Native American antiquities, and pottery by famous artists are available here.

They welcome mail and phone orders.
B, **J**, K,P, **R, Antiques**

40. Cristof's
106 W. San Francisco, Santa Fe, NM
87501
505-988-9881
Daily Winter: 9:30–5:00,
Summer: 9:30–5:30
Owners: Buzz and Pam Nicosin-Trevathan
♦ M, V, AE, C, S, HA, I

Cristof's carries a variety of items, but its main focus is contemporary Navajo weaving. This is a great location to educate yourself to the various styles and levels of quality. At Cristof's, you'll find rugs from $195 to $26,000. Buzz and Pam are wildly enthusiastic

about Navajo weaving. They also carry Vangie Suina's storytellers, Navajo pottery, and some work by Anglo artists.

They have free brochures on Navajo weaving and welcome mail and phone orders.
P, **R**, S

41. Andrea Fisher Fine Pottery
221 W. San Francisco, Santa Fe, NM
87501
505-986-1234
Summer: M–Sat 10:00–6:00, Sun
12:00–6:00, Winter M–Sat 10:00–5:00
Owner: Andrea Fisher
♦ M, V, D, C, S, HA

Andrea Fisher opened this shop in 1993, coming from the Case Trading Post at the Wheelwright Museum. This small contemporary space is filled with pottery ranging from $6 to $50,000. Most pueblos and the Navajo Nation are well represented. She always has Maria Martinez pottery available, in addition to other mainstays of Southwestern pottery. The staff enjoys establishing or embellishing collections and is willing to locate specific requests.
P

42. The Original Trading Post
201 W. San Francisco, Santa Fe, NM
87501
505-984-0759
Daily Summer: 9:00–9:00,

Winter: M–Th 9:30–5:30,
F–Sun 9:30–6:30
Owner: Lynn Atkinson;
manager: Dennis Baca
♦ M, V, D, AE, C, S, HA

An Indian trading post at this location appears on a map of Santa Fe in 1766. This shop has sold curiosities and Native American arts and crafts to generations of visitors; at one time it was the Old Original Curio Shop, boasting such famous customers as Sinclair Lewis and William Jennings Bryan. The building is said to date to 1603, earlier than most of Santa Fe. Today's shop sells an assortment of goods from the inexpensive to the collectible. Their focus is the pueblos of the Southwest and includes a selection of Southwestern clothing.
B, J, K, P, Sp, Sv, Clothing

43. Keshi, The Zuni Connection
227 Don Gaspar, Santa Fe, NM 87501
505-989-8728
Daily 10:00–5:00
Owner: Robin Dunlap
♦ M, V, AE, D, C, T, S, HA

Keshi was started by Zunis as a direct outlet cooperative for Zunis and other Pueblo artists in 1981. This store with its "down home feel" specializes in all aspects of Zuni fetishes. They also carry old-style fetishes by Cochiti Pueblo artists Salvadore and Wilson Romero, who carve the rocks they

Old Original Curio Store, Santa Fe, circa 1940

find on the land. Keshi offers an opportunity to purchase traditional and contemporary Zuni inlay, petit point, medicine bags, and Zuni fetish necklaces. They do repairs and enjoy teaching people about Pueblo art and culture.

F, J

44. The Storyteller
228 Old Santa Fe Trail, Santa Fe, NM 87501
505-982-6819
Sun 10:00–5:00
Summer: M–Th 9:30–5:30; F & Sat, and Dec 9:30–9:00

Winter: M–Th 9:30–5:00,
F & Sat 9:30–6:00
Owner: Sunwest Silver
Manager: Dolores Romero
♦ M, V, D, AE, C, S, HA (with a small bump at the door)

Storytellers have become some of the most collected items in the Southwest. Storytellers were first made in Cochiti and are now made throughout the pueblos. You will find good examples by Helen Cordero, Louis and Virginia Naranjo, Linda Fragua, and artists from Jemez, Taos, Acoma, and Santo Domingo.

J, **P,** t-shirts

45. Arrowsmith's Relics of the Old West
402 Old Santa Fe Trail, Santa Fe, NM 87501
505-989-7663
M–Sat 10:00–5:00 (varies seasonally)
Owner: Mark Arrowsmith
♦ M, V, C, S, HA (will assist with 2 steps)

Rex Arrowsmith opened this establishment in 1959. The building dates to the 1600s, and the objects inside seem very much at home here. A large buffalo head stands watch

Navajo jeweler Ray Tracey, Santa Fe

over three rooms bulging with American Indian arts, artifacts, pawn jewelry, santos, and a wide array of Western Americana. You might find early work by Louis Naranjo, an old Navajo blouse with stamped silver ornament, Winchester rifles, saddlebags, chaps, spurs, or a timeworn Acoma clay pipe.

The Arrowsmiths have a good eye. In the sixties, Rex Arrowsmith bought almost the entire life work of Navajo woodcarver Charlie Willeto. Two large pieces that are now in The Smithsonian once adorned the front porch. Today, any of Willeto's work is

Mark Arrowsmith, Jeri Ah-be-hill, and Billy Valenzuela in the rug room of Arrowsmith's Relics of the Old West, Santa Fe

Leslie Muth and Navajo folk art, Leslie Muth Gallery, Santa Fe

highly sought after by museums and collectors.

J, R, Antiques

46. **Leslie Muth Gallery**
131 W. Palace, Santa Fe, NM 87501
505-989-4620
Winter: T–Sat 10:00–5:00
Summer: daily 10:00–5:00
Owner: Leslie Muth
♦ M, V, AE, C, S, HA

Leslie's selection of folk art from across the United States is probably the best you will find anywhere. She handles work by thirty-eight Navajo folk artists, including Johnson Antonio, Mamie Deschillie, Robin

Wellito, Alice Cling, Faye Tso, Wilford Yazzie, Bob Beyale, Dennis Pioche, Silas Claw, Homer Warren, the Hathale family, baskets by the Black family, and many others. Leslie knows the artists and can provide background on each. She conducts an annual Navajo folk art exhibit and often has artists demonstrating in the gallery.

In addition to the Navajo work, she carries exceptional pieces by the Archuletta family and other folk artists.

Folk Art

47. Spanish and Indian Trading Company

924 Paseo de Peralta, Ste. 1, Santa Fe, NM 87501
505-983-6106
10:30–5:00, closed Sun and Wed
Owners: John Molloy, Eric Erdoes
♦ M, V, C, S, HA

This company specializes in nineteenth-century Plains Indian art. They also handle Indian jewelry from the early twentieth century and have a nice selection of silver Navajo buttons and topical vintage postcards. They have special gallery displays on specific areas of interest, are willing to help collectors locate items, and welcome telephone and mail orders.

Bk, **J**, K, P, **Antiques,** Vintage textiles

48. Silver Sun/Helen Hardin Estate Gallery

656 Canyon Rd, Santa Fe, NM 87501
505-983-8743, Fax 505-983-0553
M–Sat 10:00–5:00, Sun 11:00–4:00
Owners: Deanna Olson and Cheryl Ingram
♦ M, V, AE, D, C, T, S, HA (with some difficulty)

This business carries lots of Navajo and Pueblo jewelry; Pueblo, Navajo, Casas Grandes, and Winnebago pottery; and contemporary Navajo rugs ($650–$5,000). The gallery sells from the Helen Hardin estate, and work by her daughter, Margarete Bagshaw-Tindel.

Bk, **J**, K, P, **Pt**, R, S

49. Robert F. Nichols

419 Canyon Rd., Santa Fe, NM 87501
505-982-2145
Summer: Daily 10:00–5:00,
Winter: M–Sat: 11:00–5:00
Owner: Robert F. Nichols
♦ HA (with one step on porch, one inside)

Here you will find antique Americana, tramp art, unique folk art, country furnishings, and a most impressive collection of Pueblo pottery. Robert carries the work of a surprisingly large number of potters including Diego Romero, Ida Sahmie, Barbara and Joseph Cerno, Les Namingha, Forrest Naranjo, Dolores Curran, Paulita Pacheco, Delores Aragon, Elizabeth and Marcellus Medina, Virginia Garcia, Nampeyo family, Nathan Begaye, Gladys Paquin, Robert and Mary Tenorio, Arthur and Hilda Coriz, and many others. You will not find any poor examples of the artists' work. Robert is one of Santa Fe's most knowledgeable pottery experts.

Robert does exhibits of individual artists' work and sponsors artist demonstrations. Contact him about his schedule.

P, Pt, **Antiques**

50. Morning Star Gallery

513 Canyon Rd., Santa Fe, NM 87501
505-982-8187, FAX 505-984-2368
M–Sat 9:00–5:00
Owners: Masco Corp., Taylor, Michigan;
Directors: Joe Rivera and Richard Pohrt, Jr.
♦ M, V, AE, C, S, HA (with a small bump)

The Morning Star is a consistent source of museum-quality antique American Indian art, and they somehow continue to outdo themselves. The building's L-shape leads the visitor on a tour of beautiful old Plains Indian beadwork, Navajo textiles, Pueblo pottery, Southwest basketry

Robert Nichols of Robert F. Nichols, Santa Fe, holding an Ida Sahmie pot

and jewelry, and material from the Great Lakes and Northwest coast. Allow time to sort through their amazing collection of textiles. They provide parking for customers.

Bk, J, K, P, **R**, **Antiques**, Furniture

51. East West Trading Company

727 Canyon Rd., Santa Fe, NM 87501
505-986-3489
Daily 9:30–5:30
Owners: Jimmy Luman and Bo Icelar

♦ M, V, D, AE, C, S, no HA

East West Trading is no place for

those suffering from claustrophobia. Every inch of your visual field is filled with an eclectic array of Western treasures. The first room is full of old cases filled with an impressive collection of jewelry. Racks of blankets and serapes lean against displays of old cowboy bookends and Indian kitsch salt shakers. You will discover antiques, spurs, beaded moccasins, and jackalopes tucked away in the corners. The second room has a good collection of Western items, clothing, and some wonderful cowboy china.

Jimmy and Bo keep their store fun to visit, adding new inventory

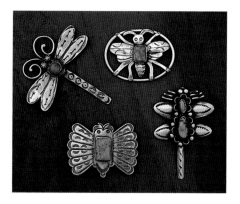

Turquoise and silver jewelry; clockwise from upper left, 2 1/2", 2", 2 1/2", 2". Courtesy of East West Trading Company, Santa Fe

all the time, and they provide parking for customers.

Bk, **J**, Antiques, Clothing, Folk Art

52. Case Trading Post: Wheelwright Museum of the American Indian

P.O. Box 5153, 704 Camino Lejo, Santa Fe, NM 87502
505-982-4636, 800-607-4636,
FAX 505-989-7386
M–Sat: 10:00–5:00, Sun 1:00–5:00
Manager: Robb Lucas

♦ M, V, T, C, S, HA (at side door)

The Case Trading Post tries to create the atmosphere of a turn-of-the-century post crowded with a large selection of new and old items. While carrying traditional work, manager

Morning Star Gallery, Santa Fe

189

Robb Lucas is actively promoting younger jewelers who are innovative and have an individual style. Some of the jewelers he mentioned were Jan Loco (Apache), Norbert Peshlakai (Navajo), Eugene Nelson (Navajo), Jolene Eustace (Cochiti/Zuni), and Jerry Begay (Navajo). We enjoyed the selection of Fred Harvey Company jewelry and old pawn jewelry.

The trading post carries work by some great potters, including the Nampeyo and Maria Martinez families (including great-great-grandson Cavan Gonzalez). We found work by Gladys Paquin, who is reviving Old Laguna–style storage jars. Alvin Curran does precise San Juan pots, and Dolores Curran, originally from Santa Clara, does miniatures. Effie and Orville

Garcia of Santa Clara produce highly polished and deeply carved pottery.

The post also carries the large older Navajo rugs (Germantown, transitional, regional) that make quite an impression, but Robb is also committed to carrying examples of the contemporary rugs, specializing in pictorials.

J, K, **P**, **R**

 53. Museum of Indian Arts and Culture
710 Camino Lejo, P.O. Box 2065, Santa Fe, NM 87504
505-827-6344, 982-5057 (books and gifts)
Daily 10:00–5:00 except major holidays, closed Mon
Owned by Museum of New Mexico

Every morning Native American artists pick numbers for a space under the Portal of the Palace of the Governors, Santa Fe

Foundation, a non-profit organization. All profits go to fund Museum programs.
Admission Fee, gift shop
Prehistoric, Historic and Contemporary Indian Arts

The New Mexico Foundation has been buying work directly from artists for more than twenty years. The museum carries an impressive list of artists, and stocks antique and estate items. It has a large inventory of old and new Navajo rugs, and their jewelry list is a who's who of southwestern jewelers. You will find pottery by Angela Baca, Ada Suina, Christine

Santa Fe Indian Market

SANTA FE INDIAN MARKET
Southwestern Association for Indian Arts, Inc. (SWAIA)
509 Camino de los Marquez, Ste. 1, Santa Fe, NM 87501-4137
505- 983-5220
President: Paul D. Gonzales
The most visible program established by SWAIA is the annual Indian Market. A hundred thousand visitors jam into the Santa Fe Plaza to see work by more than 1100 to 1200 of the finest Native American artists. This two-day event (on the weekend following the third Thursday in August) has the reputation for attracting collectors, dealers, and museums worldwide. This is the place to see and buy the best work by the established and emerging Indian artists.

This is a membership organization whose mission is "to develop, sponsor, and promote educational programs and events that encourage cultural preservation, intercultural understanding, and economic opportunities for American Indians through excellence in the arts."

McHorse, Louis and Virginia Naranjo, Russell Sanchez, Robert Tenorio, the Nampeyo family, Joseph Lonewolf, Florence Naranjo, and Maria Martinez. Also available are children's books and a wide range of videos, tapes, and CDs.
Bk, F, I, **J**, K, M, **P, R,** Antiques

54. **Palace of the Governors**
914 Palace Ave., Santa Fe, NM 87501
505-827-6476, 982-3016 (books)
Daily 9:30–5:00 except major holidays, museum is closed Mon, but shop is open
Admission fee, gift shop
   The Palace of the Governors gift shop contains books and items that reflect its collections, namely Southwestern, Native American, and Hispanic cultures.
Bk, F, I, **J**, K, M, **P, R**

SELECTED SANTA FE ARTISTS/CRAFTSPEOPLE

Clifford Brycelea, 1721 Montano St., Santa Fe, NM 87501, 505-984-8632—Watercolors and acrylic paintings.

Carol Duwyenie, 2500 Sawmill Rd., Apt. 513, Santa Fe, NM 87505-5687—Pottery and jewelry.

Craig Goseyun, Rt. 2, Box 305 A, Santa Fe, NM 87505, 505-471-9218—San Carlos Apache sculpture.

Roderick and Lela Kaskalla, Rt. 1, P.O. Box 120F, Santa Fe, NM 87501, 505-455-3578—Jewelry.

Dan Lomahaftewa, c/o El Cerro Graphics, 26 Airport Rd., Los Lunas, NM 87031, 505-865-5602—Painting, printmaking.

Christine McHorse, P.O. Box 8638, Santa Fe, NM 87504, 505-989-7716—Pottery.

Ray Tracey Ltd., Ray Tracey Gallery, 66 E. San Francisco, Santa Fe, NM 87501, 505-989-7570; manufacturing: 800-458-2500—Jewelry.

Nelson Tsosie, P.O. Box 23285, Santa Fe, NM 87502, 505-474-4480—Stone/bronze sculpture and pastels.

TESUQUE

55. Camelrock RV

Rt. 5, Box 360-H, Santa Fe, NM
87501, Hwy 84-285, north of Santa Fe
by Camel Rock
505-455-2661, 1-800-TRY-RVPARK,
FAX 505-455-3815
Manager: Ramos Romero

The office of the campground serves
as a store. They offer a variety of food
supplies and hot coffee. If you are interested in the ceremonial dress of the
pueblo be sure to see the inventory
Ramos keeps in the back room. Handmade Tucson-based Desert Sun brand
moccasins sit alongside parrot feathers,
rattles, fox pelts, shoulder shells, sashes,
hand-embroidered kilts, and mantas.
I, J, **M**, P, Dance Paraphernalia,
Pendleton blankets

56. Ignacio Duran: Potter

P.O. Box 339, Tesuque, NM 87594
505-983-7078

Ignacio Duran taught herself to
work the clay and made her first pot
when she was five. Her daughter, Reyes
Duran Herrera, is also an accomplished
potter. Their methods are traditional.
They dig their own clay in Tesuque
and travel to the mountains to dig
micaceous clay. They find most of
the slips, but the red slip comes from
Santo Domingo.

In addition to traditional pottery,
Ignacio makes the Tesuque rain gods

Ignacio Duran and daughter Reyes Herrera,
Tesuque Pueblo, north of Santa Fe

that were so popular as souvenirs in
the forties and fifties. She says, "A
Santa Fe trader, John Candalario of
the Original Curio Store in Santa Fe,
gave them the rain god title. At Tesuque
they are called *monas*, which means
'funny man.' When I'm here and not
too busy," says Ignacio, "I don't mind
demonstrating. People call up and I
tell them if I can do it." She doesn't
make much pottery in the winter
months. Ignacio sells almost exclusively from her home and welcomes
commissions and special orders.

> Of course I sing to the clay!
> Sometimes, I jump up and dance
> too. I'm here alone a lot. I have
> fun when I work on the pottery.
> —IGNACIO DURAN

TESUQUE PUEBLO

GOVERNOR'S OFFICE: Rt. 5, Box
360-T, Santa Fe, NM 87501, Hwy
84-285, north of Santa Fe
505-983-2667, FAX 505-982-2331

◆ **PHOTOGRAPHY:** Check with
Governor's Office for fees

◆ **FEAST DAY:** November 12

◆ **LANGUAGE:** Tewa

Tesuque was originally called
Taysoongay, meaning "Cottonwood
Tree Place." Artists at Tesuque create pottery that is usually small,
with a combination of black, red,
tan, and white colors. Decades ago
Tesuque potters were famous for
their small rain god figures that
were sold in tourist shops across
the Southwest. In the early seventies, pottery production began to
wane, but now a few families are
revitalizing pottery at the pueblo.

Tesuque is not known for its
jewelry, but a few jewelers are
active at the pueblo. Some of the
most impressive work at Tesuque
are the kilts, mantas, and other
objects associated with the dances.
The people of Tesuque Pueblo are
proud of their traditions, which is
evident in the elaborate labor of
love that is their ceremonial dress.

SELECTED TESUQUE
ARTISTS/CRAFTSPEOPLE

Teresa Tapia, Rt. 11, Box 1, Santa Fe, NM 87501, 505-983-7075—Traditional Tesuque micaceous pottery.

 57. Cowboys and Indians

P. O. Box 3339, Fairview, NM 87533, 12 miles north of Santa Fe on Hwy 84-285
Daily 9:00–6:30
Owner: Tommy Elkins
♦ M, V, AE, C, S, HA

This is a nostalgic Route 66-type roadside attraction. You can find both

Mona, by Ignacio Duran, Tesuque Pueblo

souvenirs and antiques here, including arrowheads, bone drills, saddles, spurs, concho belts, and coonskin caps. Some beautiful Fred Harvey Company bracelets were available.
Bk, **J,** P, Sp, Sv

POJOAQUE

 58. Pojoaque Tourist Center: "A Native American Art Gallery" and Poeh Museum

Rt. 11, Box 21, Santa Fe, NM 87501, Hwy 84-285, 12 miles north of Santa Fe
505-455-3460, FAX 505-455-7128
Daily 8:30–5:30
Owner: Pueblo of Pojoaque; manager: Geri Luhan
Museum: 505-455-2489,
T–Sat 8:00–4:30

The Native American Art Gallery's modern display cases are filled with a diverse collection of belt buckles, bracelets, rings, and necklaces. On the wall behind the cases are 200 bola ties and hat bands with silver conchos. The pottery varies in quality and includes Navajo and most pueblos. They have fine miniature pottery at reasonable prices.

The tourist center offers information and the usual array of souvenir items to keep the kids occupied while you look through the gallery.

Try the fresh-baked Indian bread from San Juan, and try to catch

POJOAQUE PUEBLO
GOVERNOR'S OFFICE: Rt. 11, Box 21, Santa Fe, NM 87501, near the junction of Hwy 84-285 and NM 502, 16 miles north of Santa Fe 505-455-3901, FAX 505-455-3363

♦ **PHOTOGRAPHY:** Check with Governor's Office for fees

♦ **DANCES IN HONOR OF OUR LADY OF GUADALUPE:** December 12

♦ **ALL KINGS DAY:** January 6

♦ **POJOAQUE PLAZA FIESTA:** first Saturday in August

♦ **INDIAN MARKET AT POJOAQUE,** the end of May

♦ **LANGUAGE:** Tewa

Pojoaque Pueblo suffered a catastrophic smallpox epidemic in 1890 and the pueblo was deserted by 1915. In 1933, descendants returned to rebuild the pueblo and revitalize their traditions. This break in habitation and maintenance of the pueblo and its traditions can still be felt at Pojoaque today.

The pueblo has developed a number of pueblo-owned businesses and gaming operations along Hwy 84. The development of the ambitious Poeh Center should help the pueblo revitalize its art forms, traditions, and link it with the other Tewa pueblos.

the summer dances 11:00–1:00 on weekends.

The Poeh Museum celebrates the arts and traditions of the Tewa Pueblos. The museum has a small but impressive collection of pottery, sculpture, jewelry, and photographs depicting pueblo life. Be sure to look at Teresa Taia's turkey pottery and Maria Martinez' beautiful pottery. The new cultural center is scheduled for completion in 1999. The model and work to date reveal an ambitious and visionary project.

F, I, **J**, K, M, N, P, Sp, Sv

SELECTED POJOAQUE ARTISTS/CRAFTSPEOPLE

Cordie Gomez, Rt. 11, Box 71 CC, Santa Fe, NM 87501 — Pottery.

Linda Gutierrez, P.O. Box 3225, Santa Fe, NM 87501, 505-455-7483 — Pottery.

Lois Gutierrez Lujan, P.O. Box 3225, Santa Fe, NM 87501, 505-455-3262 — Pottery.

Lu Ann Tafoya, P.O. Box 1763, Española, NM 87532 — Pottery.

Lucy Year Flower Tafoya, Rt. 11, Box 1037, Española, NM 87532 — Pottery.

Joe and Thelma Talachy, P.O. Box 3504, Santa Fe, NM 87501 — Pottery.

Charlie Tapia, P.O. Box 3573, Pojoaque, NM 87501 — Painting.

Richard Tapia, Rt. 11, Box 71, Santa Fe, NM 87501 — Jewelry.

SAN ILDEFONSO

 59. **San Ildefonso Pueblo Visitor Center and Museum**
Rt. 5, Box 315-A, Santa Fe, NM 87501, San Ildefonso exit is 8 miles west of Jct 285-502, just off the Los Alamos Hwy 502, follow signs to pueblo
505-455-3549
Daily 8:00–5:00
Museum: M–F 8:00–4:00

SAN ILDEFONSO PUEBLO
GOVERNOR'S OFFICE: Rt. 5, Box 315 A, Santa Fe, NM 87501, 22 miles northwest of Santa Fe on NM 502
505-455-2273, FAX 505-455-7351

♦ Photography and sketching are allowed by paid permit with restrictions.

♦ All visitors must register at the visitor center before entering the plaza area. Be sure to read all of the rules and regulations. There are specific rules pertaining to where a visitor may wander. The pueblo map clearly defines much of this information and shows locations of individual artists' homes.

♦ FEAST DAY: January 23

♦ LANGUAGE: Tewa

San Ildefonso was the home of Julian and Maria Martinez. Around 1920 they developed a technique of painting matte black designs on highly burnished black pottery. Their elegant work helped create the worldwide recognition that pueblo pottery has achieved.

Potters at San Ildefonso continue to be influenced by Maria, Julian, and their son, Popovi Da. Da created two-tone pottery and added pieces of turquoise as accents on the lustrous surfaces of his pots. When you visit shops here, it is enjoyable to see the influence of these earlier innovators' work on potters today. Most shops are open 10:00–5:00.

(closed 12:00–1:00)

Admission fee

The museum explains the pottery-making process and has an exhibit of the pueblo's arts and crafts. Excellent examples of pottery, embroidery, and displays of photographs and pueblo history make this a logical first stop before shopping for pottery.

60. **Aguilar Indian Arts**

Rt. 5, Box 318 C, Santa Fe, NM 87501

505-455-3530

Summer 8:00–5:00

Winter: 9:00–5:00

Owner: Alfred Aguilar

Serpent design, black-on-black plate, 12" diameter, by Maria Martinez and Popovi Da, San Ildefonso Pueblo, near Santa Fe. Permanent collection, Utah museum of Fine Arts, Universty of Utah

Michael Aguilar holds the work of his father, Alfred, at their shop, Aguilar Indian Arts, San Ildefonso Pueblo

Alfred Aguilar's shop is the first stop after registering at the visitor center. If the visitor center is closed (on weekends in the winter), you can register and get information about visiting the pueblo here.

In the sixties this was a grocery store. The building's large front porch is inviting. Inside you will find Mr. Aguilar, who specializes in distinctive, highly polished, black-and-etched-red pottery. He also features sculpture and nativity scenes, clay figure storytellers, paintings, and hand-designed notecards. He also carries fine Zuni and Santo Domingo jewelry and Zuni fetishes.

F, J, **P**, Pt, S

SELECTED SAN ILDEFONSO ARTISTS/CRAFTSPEOPLE

Blue Corn Pottery, Rt. 5, Box 316-AA, Santa Fe, NM 87501—Contemporary and traditional pottery.

Popovi Da Studio of Indian Arts, c/o Anita Da, R.F.D. 5, Box 309, Santa Fe, NM 87501, on the plaza, 505-455-3332—Pueblo pottery, paintings, jewelry, and museum work by Maria Martinez and her family.

John Gonzales, Rt. 5, Box 316, Santa Fe, NM 87505, 505-455-3432—Pottery.

Robert and Reycita Pena, Rt. 5, Box 318-A, Santa Fe, NM 87501, 505-455-3758—San Ildefonso pottery.

Juan Tafoya Pottery, Rt. 5, Box 306-A, San Ildefonso Pueblo, NM 87501, on the plaza, 505-455-2649—Black-on-black and red sienna pottery.

Elvis "Tsee-Pin Torres," Rt. 5, Box 312, San Ildefonso, NM 87501, 505-455-7547—Traditional black-on-black and buff-on-red pottery.

Dora Tse-Pe, P.O. Box 3679, Santa Fe, NM 87501—Pottery.

61. **Babbitt's Cottonwood Trading Post**

Rt. 5, Box 320, Santa Fe, NM 87501, San Ildefonso Pueblo Reservation exit, 8 miles west of Jct 285-502, (Pojoaque) just off the Los Alamos Hwy 502
505-455-7596, 800-766-6864
M–Sat 9:00–5:30
Owners: Joe and Judith Babbitt
♦ M, V, C, S, HA

Babbitt's Cottonwood Trading Post is nestled among the giant cottonwood trees within the San Ildefonso Pueblo Reservation. In this rural, idyllic setting, Babbitt blends the needs of the local Indians with the interests

Trader Joe Babbitt, Cottonwood Trading Post, San Ildefonso Pueblo. When you talk to Joe, his passion for pottery becomes obvious.

of Pueblo visitors. Enamelware, tubs for baking bread, moccasins, ribbon shirts, fox pelts, and Pendleton blankets fill half the store. Across the room, over one thousand pieces of Pueblo pottery line the shelves and cases.

Joe Babbitt, a third generation Indian trader from Flagstaff, Arizona, always has a few nice historic pieces by the famed potter Maria Martinez and her sisters Maximilliana and Desidera, and daughter-in-law Santana

on hand. Local potters who trace their heritage to Maria and Rose Gonzales work at the trading post and are genuinely interested in helping you make informed purchases.

Joe has put together a remarkable inventory of San Ildefonso pottery by Dora Tse-Pe and her daughter Candace Martinez; Albert and Josephine Vigil; Carmelita Dunlap and daughters; Adelphia Martinez, and over thirty five other San Ildefonso potters.

In addition, there is a good selection of pottery from other Pueblos: Santa Clara, San Juan, Hopi, Jemez, San Felipe, and Santo Domingo. Zuni fetishes, Navajo rugs; Southwest books and Indian music CDs; and jewelry round out the offerings here. We highly recommend a visit.
Bk, F, J, M, **P**, **R**, Sp

SANTA CLARA

62. **Green Leaves Studio and Gallery**

P.O. Box 171, Española, NM 87532, just off NM 30 on Lower Santa Clara Canyon Road. The entrance to the studio property is clearly marked with a sign stating "Toni Roller Indian Pottery."
505-753-3003
Daily: Summer: 9:00–5:00,
Winter: 10:00–5:00
Owner: Toni Roller

Potters Toni and Cliff Roller, Greenleaves Studio and Gallery, Santa Clara Pueblo

Burnished, incised-design jar, 20", by Margaret Tafoya, Santa Clara Pueblo. Collection of James and Susan Ferguson, Salt Lake City, Utah. Courtesy of Utah Museum of Fine Arts

♦ M, V, C, S, HA

You can visit the Green Leaves Studio and Gallery without paying admission to the pueblo. Toni Roller is the daughter of Margaret Tafoya and "Green Leaves" is Toni's Indian name. The Roller branch of the Tafoya family is abundant with talented potters. Many live away from the pueblo, but still close enough to work at the studio on a regular basis.

Toni is concerned with the number of potters that have incorporated nontraditional techniques in past years. She does not cut corners and creates work in a time-intensive, traditional manner. She has produced a free informative pamphlet explaining the process and outlining the history of Santa Clara pottery.

The family has an open studio reception and exhibition on the Friday before Santa Fe Indian Market. It is an opportunity to meet the entire family, view and purchase some of the Southwest's finest pottery, and enjoy these peoples' gracious hospitality.

SELECTED SANTA CLARA ARTISTS/CRAFTSPEOPLE

Angela Baca, P.O. Box 4, Española, NM 87532—Pottery.

Annie Baca, P.O. Box 1522, Española, NM 87532—Pottery.

Jane Baca, P.O. Box 1041, Española, NM 87532—Pottery.

Reycita Cosen, P.O. Box 554, Fort Apache, AZ 85926—Santa Clara/Apache pottery.

Dolores Curran, P.O. Box 1218, San Juan Pueblo, NM 87566—Pottery.

Effie Garcia, P.O. Box 1647, Española, NM 87532—Pottery.

Tammy Garcia, P.O. Box 4791, Taos, NM 87571—Carved red pottery.

RoseMary and Travis Lewis, P.O. Box 621, Española, NM 87532, 505-753-5121—Pottery.

Joseph Lonewolf, P.O. Box 98, Española, NM 87532, 505-753-2434—Pottery.

Betty and Robert Naranjo, P.O. Box 2039, Española, NM 87532, 505-753-3341—Pottery.

Joyce Sisneros, P.O. Box 40242, Albuquerque, NM 87196—Pottery.

63. **Chimayo Trading Post**
110 Sandia Dr., Española, NM 87532
505-753-9414
Daily 9:00–5:00
Owners: Leo Polo-Trujillo and Beryl Stuart
♦ M, V, AE, C, S, HA

The Chimayo Trading Post is a New Mexican landmark. It is included

SANTA CLARA PUEBLO

TOURISM OFFICE: P.O. Box 580, Española, NM 87532, 2 miles south-west of Española on NM 30
505-753-7326, FAX 505-753-8988
Office hours: M–F 8:00–4:30
Weekends: Visitors are requested not to disturb residents
Director of Tourism: Rose Gutierrez

♦ **PHOTOGRAPHY:** Fee, ask permission before photographing residents

♦ **FEAST DAYS:** June 13 and August 12

♦ **GUIDED AND SELF-GUIDED TOURS** of Puye Cliffs Dwellings daily except Christmas and Feast Days

♦ **LANGUAGE:** Tewa

Santa Clara Pueblo is internationally famous for its pottery. The tourism office will help you locate specific artists. Houses throughout the pueblo display hand-crafted "Pottery" signs, and if you are adventurous and have time you can visit the various homes and shops.

Margaret Tafoya's elegant pottery has captured the world's attention. The carved pottery she developed with her mother, Sara Fina Tafoya, is now made by many of the pueblo's artists. The twisting water serpent, known as Avanyu, and a bear paw are common motifs. The red and black pottery is actually the same clay, with the colors controlled during the firing.

The pueblo also produces beautiful polychrome pottery, ribbed melon bowls, and an assortment of small figurines of animals and people. Many artists create miniature pottery with intricate scraffito designs meandering on the surface. The artists clearly enjoy the amazement on visitors' faces when they see this work for the first time.

Beryl Stuart and Leo Polo Trujillo, Chimayo Trading Post, Española, New Mexico

in numerous articles, books, and even in American Express advertisements. This family business was founded on integrity, tradition, and New Mexican hospitality.

The building's interior matches its exterior beauty. Natural light floods the antique cases displaying fine old and new jewelry, Navajo and Chimayo weavings, curious wooden crucifixes, and an assortment of items epitomizing the artistic Southwest.

We were particularly impressed with the pottery. Grandma Cora and Anthony Durand from Picuris, Margaret Tafoya, Mida Tafoya, and Mary Cain from Santa Clara, Domenguita Naranjo, and Norman and Ronita de Herrera from San Juan

One of the many shops at Santa Clara Pueblo. near Española, New Mexico

are just a few of the outstanding artists represented.

Leo's grandfather, Gavino Trujillo, originally opened Chimayo Trading Post in Chimayo at the turn of the century. Esquipula Trujillo, Leo's father, moved the post to its current location in the thirties. The Trujillo family has always extended their friendship to artists and visitors alike. Leo and Beryl have maintained this same level of integrity and hospitality. They offer visitors free coffee, doughnuts, candy, and accurate information to just about anywhere. Their desk is cluttered with small cans collecting money for the Chimayo Dog Lady, the local Penitente chapel, and other worthwhile community causes. Beryl and Leo are the type of people you hope you will meet when you travel, and will remember long after you have returned home.

B, Bk, J, K, **P**, R, **Santos**, Antiques, Clothing

THE HIGH ROAD TO TAOS

When traveling from Santa Fe to Taos, you have two options (of course, you can travel on one and return on the other). Each route offers unique experiences. Hwy 68 is the quickest route and offers an efficient highway for the

Esquipula Trujillo, father of Leo Polo-Trujillo of Chimayo Trading Post wearing one of his creations, the original Chimayo jacket. Photograph courtesy of Leo Polo-Trujillo.

entire stretch. The "high road" to Taos (Hwys 76 and 518) is slower but offers a look into some of New Mexico's most beautiful landscapes. This route takes you through the areas where Robert Redford filmed *The Milagro Beanfield War*, past the old church at Las Trampas with some of the finest santos in New Mexico, and through Chimayo, where you can visit the Sanctuario de Chimayo and various weavers.

64. House of Old Things

Rt. 1, Box 186-F, Santa Fe, NM 87501
505-455-2506
Daily 9:00–5:00
Owners: Valerie and Allen McNown
♦ T, C, S, no HA

The House of Old Things is about one and a half miles off Hwy 84-285 on Hwy 503 in Pojoaque before you reach Nambe. Two small "antique" plaques are its only signage. The House of Old Things is truly a wonderful, and somewhat surreal, experience.

Allen and Valerie McNown have assembled an enormous labyrinth of antique furniture, Native American baskets, historic pottery, santos, retablos, ex-voto paintings, beadwork, whimsies, purses, salt and pepper shakers, folk art, lamps, movie posters, and just about anything you can think of.

Valerie's love of santos, retablos, and ex-voto paintings started in Mexico in 1948. Allen loves baskets. He bought his first one when he was in the Boy Scouts, and it blossomed into a life-long affection for this art form.

The McNowns live on the premises and will greet you when you ring the buzzer. They give a short tour of the premises and then allow you to discover treasures on your own. They make a cup of tea and talk to their bird as customers stare wide-eyed at the many treasures around them. They love to talk about the objects, so don't be afraid to ask questions.

It is easy to be overwhelmed at the sheer quantity of objects here. If you look carefully, you might find Allan Houser serigraphs or a Pablita Velarde painting just out of sight.

When we left House of Old Things, we looked at each other with astonishment asking, "Was that real or a dream?" The McNowns have created an antique shop that is usually reserved for the pages of fiction. It is a wonderful, magical, personal place you will return to again and again.

B, J, P, Pt, Folk Art, **Antiques**

NAMBE

65. Nambe Trading Post

20A County Rd. 113A, Santa Fe, NM 87501, Hwy 503, turn at Sacred Heart Church
505-455-2819, 505-455-2513
Daily Summer 8:00–6:00,
Winter 9:00–5:00
Manager: Mel Rivera
♦ M, V, C, S, HA (with a gravel parking lot and a small bump at the entrance)

Owners Delfino and Ruth Romero opened for business in 1979. The trading post sits beside a beautifully manicured garden. Above the door is a humorous ram skull that Delfino has equipped with lights to welcome visitors.

Valerie McNown, House of Old Things, near Nambe, New Mexico

The shop has a beautiful selection of Navajo weavings from $50 to $5,000 and pottery from Nambe, Pojoaque, Santa Clara, San Juan, Cochiti, Jemez, San Ildefonso, and Taos. Ceremonial sashes by Margaret Vigil of Nambe and those woven by the Navajos, Growler family animals, peyote wands, and rattles sit alongside an assortment of elk, ram, and deer skulls.

The manager, Mel Rivera, can usually be found making beautiful

traditional straw applique crosses that are available for purchase. Everyone here is knowledgeable about Nambe, its history, and its artists.

B, I, K, P, **R**, Sp

66. Lonnie Vigil: Potter

Rt 1, Box 121 C, Santa Fe, NM 87501
505-455-2871

Lonnie Vigil is an eloquent spokesperson and ambassador for pueblo pottery. At times his words hang in the air with a poetic magic. Since the early eighties he has been creating a bridge with his ancestors through his micaceous pottery. Before that time Lonnie had established a successful career in the world of economics, eventually leading him to Washington, D.C. It was there that he began to hear the whispering of the clay calling him to return to his mountain home to pursue his true "vocation," a life with the clay.

Upon arriving home, he made a commitment to devote his life to the clay mother. He states, "All I asked from her was to take me to places I've never been and to bring wonderful people into my life." This commitment was complicated by the fact that none of the Vigil family had been working with the clay since the fifties. His great-aunt and great-grandmother had passed away, so his only course was to teach himself. Three years of prayer, meditation, and discipline found Lonnie producing beautiful, shimmering pottery. He created shapes and forms intuitively, but later found that his shapes closely resemble those of his great-aunt's and great-grandmother's pots.

When looking at the limited collection of Nambe pottery in a Santa Fe institution, he said,

I placed a small bowl in my hand and it began to quiver. I began to weep and knew the bowl had been my great-grandmother's. I told the curator, and after checking documentation, he found it had indeed been hers. I have seen other people begin to weep when they hold a pot of mine. This strong emotion is caused by the spirit of the clay ancestors speaking to them. The pots are alive. I know this is difficult for the Western mind to understand.

Lonnie sells work through a few galleries nationally, but he prefers to sell his pottery from his home at Nambe. He feels that when people come to Nambe for the pots they can get a greater sense of what the pottery is really about and begin to sense the pot's origin. The souls of the pots call specific people. When you pick up a Vigil pot and turn it slowly in your hands, it is easy to be dazzled by its perfection and grace. Don't be startled if you hear a faint whispering. Lonnie's pots do indeed have a voice of their own.

NAMBE PUEBLO

OFFICE OF THE GOVERNOR:
Rt. 1, Box 117-BB, Santa Fe, NM 87501, 22 miles northeast of Santa Fe off NM 503
505-455-2036, FAX 505-455-2038

♦ **PHOTOGRAPHY:** Fee

♦ **ST. FRANCIS OF ASSISI FEAST DAY:** October 4, Nambe Falls

♦ **CELEBRATION:** July 4

♦ **LANGUAGE:** Tewa

♦ **PUEBLOS DEL NORTE NAMBE TOURS:** Rt. 1, Box 117-BB, Santa Fe NM 87501, 505-455-3046 for a list of Nambe artists

Welcome to Nambe Pueblo. Whether on Tour, or on Feast Day, you are expected to respect and honor our rules and regulations and our Tribal Officials, as well as any posted signs.

On Feast Day, you may be invited into our homes to share in our traditional food. We ask that you please make your visit brief so that your host may accommodate others. While viewing the dances, please be considerate of elders who may be sitting at the front.

Photography is strictly prohibited at the Pueblo on Feast Day. Violators will be subjected to forfeiture of film and/or camera. Photography at other times is permitted by obtaining a permit at the Governor's Office.

Your visit to Nambe should be interesting and enjoyable, if you will abide by these simple rules. Thank you.
—Office of the Governor

The Governor's Office can help you locate various artists at the pueblo. Nambe arts and crafts include woven belts, beaded items, and traditional polychrome, red, and blackware pottery. There are also some small storytellers being made at the pueblo. Nambe has always used micaceous pottery for utilitarian purposes. This tradition has soared to new heights in the gifted hands of Lonnie Vigil.

SELECTED NAMBE ARTISTS/CRAFTSPEOPLE

Roderick and Lela Kaskella, Rt. 1, Box 120-F, Santa Fe , NM 87501, 505-455-3578—Contemporary channel inlay jewelry.

Dennis and Barbara Nieto, Rt. 1, Box 85-C, Santa Fe, NM 87501, 505-455-2194—Jewelry, beadwork, pottery.

Angie Pena, Rt. 1, Box 120-C, Santa Fe, NM 87501 —Weaving.

Tony A. Perez, Rt. 1, Box 11-A Cundiyo Rd., Santa Fe, NM 87501, 505-455-7275—Animal figures and micaceous pottery.

Pearl Talachy, Rt. 1, Box 114-M, Santa Fe, NM 87501, 505-455-3429—Micaceous pottery.

 Santuario de Chimayo
Off Hwy 76 and Rt 502 about 25 miles northeast of Santa Fe
Daily Summer: 9:00–6:00,
Winter: 9:00–4:00
505-351-4889
Gift shop

We never consider our trip to New Mexico complete unless we visit the Santuario. Bernardo Abeyta had a vision and mystical experience that led to building the chapel in 1816. It is considered one of the finest examples of Spanish Colonial architecture in the Southwest. Its interior is adorned with beautiful santos and painted decor. In the rear of the chapel is a hole with holy dirt. The dirt is believed to have curative properties, and discarded crutches and notes of entreaty and thanks litter the hall as a confirmation to these claims. A statue of the Santo Niño also sits in this area of the Santuario. You will notice newly made baby shoes sitting next to the statue. Many people believe that the Santo Niño walks the community at night, answering prayers and performing miracles. He of course wears out his shoes in the process. Thus, the new shoes are provided.

 El Potrero Trading Post
P. O. Box 706, Chimayo, NM 87522
505-351-4112
Daily 9:00–6:00
Owner: Raymond Bal
◆ M, V, C, S, HA

Located next to the Santuario de Chimayo, this is a great place to grab a drink or a popsicle. Opened in 1949 by Raymond's grandparents, the business handles a variety of religious antiques and artifacts. Serious collectors should talk to Raymond about items that are not on public display, including wonderful retablos and ex-voto paintings. Don't forget to see the work of the better contemporary northern new Mexican santeros, also available at the post.
Sv, Santos

 Centinela Traditional Arts
HCR 64, Box 4, Chimayo, NM 87522,
On NM 76, 1 mile east of NM98
505-351-2180
M–S 9:00–6:00, Sun 10:00–5:00
Owners: Irvin and Lisa Trujillo
◆ M, V, C, S, HA (ramp in back)

The Trujillos are both weavers and sell excellent examples of ten other Chimayo weavers as well. The weaving here is traditional in design and uses natural dyes. You will find purses, coats, bomber jackets, vests, pillows, and cushions. They do custom orders and upholstery as well. Visitors can watch Lisa at work on her loom and ask questions.
R, Clothing

 Ortega's Weaving Shop
P.O. Box 325, Chimayo, NM 87522
505-351-4215
M–Sat 8:30–5:00, Sun 11:00–5:00 during daylight savings with seasonal variations
Owner: Robert Ortega

Five looms occupy the premises and visitors are welcome to watch weavers at work. The Ortegas have practiced weaving for eight generations and are descendants of Gabriel

El Potrero Trading Post at the Santuario de Chimayo, northeast of Santa Fe. Hand-tinted photograph

Ortega, an eighteenth-century Chimayo weaver. The great attractions here are the wool blankets, rugs, coats, vests, purses, and just about anything else woven in the Chimayo style. They also carry Santa Clara pottery and Indian jewelry.

J, P, **R, Clothing**

71. **Chimayo Trading and Mercantile**
P.O. Box 460, Chimayo, NM 87522, NM 76
505-351-4566, 800-248-7859
Daily Summer: 9:00–6:30,

Las Trampas Church on the Old Taos Highway. Hand-tinted photograph

Penitente cross along the Old Taos Highway

Winter: 9:00–5:00
Owner: John Abrums
♦ M, V, D, C, S, HA

John Abrums has a good selection of Native American arts, antiques, furniture, and books. In inventory are 200 to 300 pots by Mary Cain, Tina Diaz, many artists of Santa Clara and San Juan pueblos (including Rosita de Herrera), San Ildefonso artists Cynthia Starflower and Carmelita Dunlap, and artists from Jemez pueblo. Kachina dolls are by Chester Polestewa, Gary Honawa, and Eddie Komalestewa. You will find works by Alice Cling

and Harrison Begay. Bronze sculptures and paintings are also available.
B, J, K, **P**, Pt, S, Antiques

72. **Galeria Ortega**
P. O. Box 434, Chimayo, NM 87522, NM 520 and 76
505-351-2288
M–Sat 9:00–5:30, Sun 11:00–5:00
Owners: Andrew and Evita Ortega
♦ M, V, D, AE, C, S, HA (main showroom)

Andrew Ortega weaves at the Galeria amid a great selection of traditional santos, tin work, kachina dolls, folk art carvings, straw inlay crosses, Native American and Hispanic music, and a selection of some 400 books on the Southwest. A line of locally made souvenirs, t-shirts, snack bar, and patio make this a natural place to stop and appreciate the work of local artisans.

Bk, K, S, Sv, Folk Art

HIGHWAY 68 TO TAOS

The Hwy 68 route to Taos from Santa Fe is not as spectacular or historic as the high road, but it is the quickest journey. There are a multitude of roadside stands along the way, but the Old Sheepherder Horn and Trading Company and Herman Valdez fruit stand are particularly noteworthy.

SAN JUAN PUEBLO

 Oke Oweenge Crafts Cooperative

P.O. Box 1095, San Juan Pueblo, NM 87566, in San Juan Pueblo, 5 miles north of Española on Hwy 85

505-852-2372

M–Sat 9:00–5:00

Manager: April Star

♦ C, S, HA

This cooperative was opened in 1968 by pueblo artisans. There is a

---

SAN JUAN PUEBLO
GOVERNOR'S OFFICE:
P.O. Box 1099,
San Juan Pueblo, NM 87566,
5 miles north of Española
off NM 68
505-852-4400,
FAX 505-852-4820

♦ **PHOTOGRAPHY: Inquire about permits**

♦ **FEAST DAY: June 23–24**

♦ **LANGUAGE: Tewa**

San Juan, the largest of the Tewa Pueblos, has taken great efforts to maintain its traditions. The pueblo has nearly a hundred buildings that are more than 700 years old. San Juan has always played an important role in pueblo leadership. The leader of the 1680 pueblo revolt was Popé, a San Juan religious leader. Today San Juan is the home office for the Eight Northern Indian Pueblos Council.

---

good chance that the pot or jewelry you are admiring was made by one of the friendly people assisting you.

Modern displays and lighting create a gallery atmosphere. Approximately one hundred members sell pottery, jewelry, beadwork, ribbon

---

shirts, sashes, kilts, shawls, and dresses. When we visited, hundreds of different corn and seed necklaces were laid out on the tables. It was amazing to see the creative approaches the artists have taken with the simple materials.

Part of the cooperative mission is education and training. Don't be afraid to ask questions. The staff seems to enjoy educating visitors.

C, **J**, **P**, Pt, S, Dance Paraphernalia

Linda Maestas with her impressive micaceous pot at Oke Oweenge Crafts Cooperative, San Juan Pueblo, New Mexico

74. **Tewa Indian Restaurant**
P.O. Box 1035, San Juan Pueblo, NM 87566
M–F 9:00–2:30 (closed holidays)
Manager: Rosarita Kidd

As you drive into San Juan Pueblo, you can't miss the restaurant's large, white, hand-painted sign and horno. The hours are limited but it's worth the effort to try this establishment's traditional Indian foods, including fry bread, oven bread, Indian fruit pies (try the prune pie), Indian bread pudding, Indian tacos, red and green stews, blue corn maiden, posole, Indian delight, and Indian teas.

SELECTED SAN JUAN ARTISTS/CRAFTSPEOPLE

Jeff Aguino, P.O. Box 1295, San Juan Pueblo, NM 87566, 505-753-9168—Paintings, woodcarving.

Reycita Garcia, P.O. Box 934, San Juan, NM 87566—Pottery.

Carnation Lockwood, 6110 Academy, Albuquerque, NM, 87109—San Juan seed beads.

Linda Maestas, P.O. Box 1033, San Juan Pueblo, NM 87566—Micaceous pottery.

Laurencita A. Bird and Evelyn Quintana, 3616 Shepard Rd. NE, Albuquerque, NM 87110, 505-881-6179—Embroidery.

Bobbie Tewa, P.O. Box 35, San Juan Pueblo, NM 87566, 505-753-6027—Overlay jewelry, with or without stones.

EIGHT NORTHERN INDIAN PUEBLOS ARTIST AND CRAFTSMAN SHOW
Eight Northern Indian Pueblos Council
P.O. Box 969, San Juan Pueblo, NM 87566
505-852-4261
Entrance fee, free parking

Begun in 1972, the show is always on the third Saturday and Sunday in July. This popular show is hosted by different pueblos every year, with more than 500 North American Indian artists' work for sale. There are also traditional dances, musicians, and wonderful food in an outdoor, festival atmosphere. We suggest that you arrive early to enjoy the cool morning air. Write or call for a free visitors' guide.

75. **The Old Sheepherder Horn and Trading Company**
P. O. Box 356, Velarde, NM 87582
Skulls are the mainstay in this giant open-air market.

76. **Herman Valdez Fruit Stand**
P. O. Box 218, No. 1 RA County Rd. 60, Velarde, NM 87582-0218
505-852-2129
Daily 9:00–6:00, closed New Year's, Thanksgiving, Christmas
Owners: Herman and Loretta Valdez

They offer fresh fruit, red chili ristras, and piñons, but they also offer a selection of wreaths and arrangements unlike anything we have ever seen. Loretta creates a wreath titled "Ramona's Love Letter" in which she interprets a novel. She also works with local santeros to produce unique creations. Loretta produces a catalog and sponsors a wreath show and open house the last weekend of October.

PICURIS

77. **Picuris Pueblo Museum and Hidden Valley Restaurant**
P.O. Box 487, Peñasco, NM 87553, near Peñasco on Hwy 75
505-587-2957
Daily 9–6:00
Restaurant: Daily 11:30–6:30
Gift shop with Picuris pottery
Displays show a kiva, pottery,

beadwork, weaving, and other local crafts. The Hidden Valley Restaurant serves northern New Mexican, native Picuris, and American cuisine. The "Picuris Feast" is guaranteed to satisfy the biggest appetite. It includes a blue corn enchilada, red or green chili, salad, beans, posole, Indian fry bread, and Indian bread pudding.

 Anthony Durand: Micaceous Potter

P.O. Box 254, Peñasco, NM 87553, at Picuris Pueblo, west side. Look for the "Pottery for Sale" sign. 505-587-0010

Anthony's pottery is an extension of the micaceous pottery tradition that Picuris shares with Taos Pueblo. His pots may be the most golden micaceous pots ever created. They seem to have an inner light, and the forms he creates seem timeless.

Anthony was born in 1956. As a child, he made pots with his grandmother Cora, but he wasn't serious until 1977. He states, "I noticed that the craft was slowly disappearing. The elders said it would die out if it wasn't kept up and others get involved. It was then that I decided to get steady with pottery." He learned the basic coil and scrape methods from his grandmother, who was born in 1902, and still creates pottery.

Mining destroyed the traditional clay pits, so Anthony and the other

PICURIS PUEBLO

Governor's Office: P.O. Box 127, Peñasco, NM 87553, Hwy 75, known as San Lorenzo on maps, 65 miles north of Santa Fe off NM 68 via NM 518 or NM 75, or north of Española by NM 76

505-587-2519, FAX 505-587-1071

♦ **PHOTOGRAPHY: Pay fee at visitor center**

♦ **SAN LORENZO FEAST DAY: August 10**

♦ **High Country Tricultural Arts and Crafts Fair, first weekend of July**

♦ **LANGUAGE: Tiwa**

Guided and self-guided tours of San Lorenzo Mission, archeological ruins, museum, camping, fishing.

Make the museum your first stop. They will help you locate artists, issue photo permits, answer questions, and give you an overview of the pueblo and its history. Picuris artists sell at the museum gift shop, the Picuris Pueblo-owned Hotel Santa Fe in Santa Fe, and from their homes. You will find leather work, beadwork, and beautiful micaceous pottery.

The original Indian name for Picuris was *Piwwetha*, meaning "Pass in the Mountains," a description equally applicable today. This is the most remote of the Rio Grande pueblos. It shares a strong heritage with Taos Pueblo, whose governor gave Picuris a buffalo years ago. That buffalo was the beginning of the Picuris buffalo herd which continues to grow.

At one time, Picuris was an enormous pueblo with dwellings as large as six stories in height. You can visit the ruins of the original pueblo by registering for a permit at the museum. The citizens of Picuris are proud of their traditions, history, and art. They have just finished a long restoration of their 200-year-old church.

If you attend Picuris on feast day, you may have the opportunity to try food cooked in micaceous pottery. The pots are completely safe to cook in, and unlike much pueblo pottery, can be utilitarian.

Picuris potters had to research and discover other sources for their clay. They were successful in securing new sources, but like some of their techniques, the site is kept a secret. Unlike Taos potters, Anthony and the Picuris potters use a micaceous slip that adds a bronze luster to the surface. The shapes of his pots are influenced by traditional Picuris pottery, but also Maria Martinez and ancient Egyptian and Greek forms.

Anthony sold his first pots to Leo Trujillo at Chimayo Trading Post in Española. Leo has a good collection of his work and continues to sell his pots and extol their virtues. Anthony is thankful for this encouragement over the years. His work is also available at Robert Nichols in Santa Fe and sometimes at the Millicent Rogers Museum in Taos. He also sells work from his home. When you visit, you might find Anthony cooking in one of his pots. He claims that food cooked in them is superior to food cooked any other way.

SELECTED PICURIS ARTISTS/CRAFTSPEOPLE

Frances Martinez, P.O. Box 383, Peñasco, NM 87553—Pottery.

Robert Dale Tsosie, P.O. Box 88, San Jose, NM 87565, 505-421-2986—Navajo/Picuris Pueblo, stone sculpture.

TAOS

D.H. Lawrence, Frank Waters, Mabel Dodge Luhan, Nicolai Fechin, Ernest Blumenshein, Leon Gaspard, Georgia O'Keefe, Ansel Adams, Maynard Dixon, John Nichols, and many other cultural luminaries have been drawn to this beautiful community for many reasons: the light, the turbulent afternoon cloud displays, the culture of Taos Pueblo, the beautiful adobe architecture, and the friendship of the artistic community. The culture of Taos far outweighs its small population—it might have more

Small gathering, location unknown. Photograph courtesy of Rowena Martinez, El Rincon, Taos, New Mexico

culture per person than any city we know. Collectors the world over have searched for the work of Taos artists.

When visiting Taos, be sure to see some of the early artists' homes to get a sense of the way they lived. Taos is a unique, beautiful, and magical place. It is not laid out to show off all its facets. You must seek them out.

79. El Rincon
114 Kit Carson, Taos, NM 87571
505-758-9188
Daily 10:00–6:00
Owner: Rowena Martinez
♦ M, V, AE, C, S, HA (two steps, will assist)
El Rincon means "inside corner,"

and it applies to the layout of this building. This is Taos' oldest trading post. Originally opened in 1908 at Pueblo del Sur, just off the plaza, it moved to this location in 1922. In that year, Ralph Meyer, the owner, married Rowena. She still watches over the store and has maintained a small museum of items collected by Ralph Meyer, along with memorabilia pertaining to the post.

For anyone who enjoys history or Taos' literary and artistic traditions, El Rincon is a must-stop. The large room off the post was painted with mineral pigment by Tony and Mabel Dodge Luhan. Nina, Rowena's daughter, recalls riding on the shoulders of Frank Waters as he danced with beautiful young ladies. The ballroom was featured in Waters' book, *The Man Who Killed the Deer,* as were Ralph and Rowena. Mabel Dodge Luhan shares a grave with Ralph. Nina said there was considerable discussion about the appropriateness of this, but the issue was put to rest when Frank Waters commented, "I don't think anyone would mind moving over to make room for Mabel."

Today, El Rincon remains undaunted by time. The shop is tightly packed with old and new items. Ask to see the rugs. Like many old establishments, El Rincon requires time and careful observation to see everything. Old Taos pottery sits on

Rowena Martinez, owner of El Rincon, Taos, as a young woman, circa 1922.

a dark shelf above the door. Santos hide against the ancient vigas. Trays of jewelry sit stacked behind the counter. Be sure to express your particular interests. From the eighty-year-old kachina dolls sitting next to old photos, to Kit Carson's pants, this business embodies a unique essence of the West.

Bk, **J,** K, P, **R, Antiques**

80. Françoise

103 H East Plaza, Taos, NM 87571
505-758-9255
Daily: Summer: 9:00–6:00,
Winter: 10:00–6:00
Owner: Françoise Drayer

Tucked beneath the portal on the east side of the plaza is this jewel of a store. When you walk in the door, the jewelry resembles an enormous lake of silver. It is a marvelous collection of contemporary and antique jewelry of Navajo, Zuni, Hopi, Taos, and Santo Domingo origin. Françoise says that if you don't find that perfect piece (it is hard to believe you wouldn't), she will help you design one and have it made for you.

There are rattles, peyote wands, stone axes, tablitas, dance kilts, blankets, hides, baskets, and an expanded selection of small pottery pieces. The pottery is diverse but represents some of the finest potters from San Ildefonso, Santa Clara, Zuni, Acoma, Nambe, San Juan, Jemez, Zia, Santo Domingo, Taos, Hopi, and the Navajo Nation. If you have particular interests, mention them to Françoise.

B, F, **J, P,** Dance Paraphernalia

81. Broken Arrow

P. O. Box 1601, 222 N. Plaza, Taos, NM 87571
505-758-4304, 800-952-9787
Daily Summer: 9:00–8:00,
Winter: 10:00–6:00
Owners: Jess, Joel, and Julie Payne
♦ M, V, AE, D, C, S, HA, I

Broken Arrow showcases many of the Southwest's finest Native American artists. The Payne family has worked hard to secure work from varied

Françoise Drayer runs Françoise, and her son, Steven, runs Pueblo and Plains, Taos, New Mexico

sources and to develop a beautiful display space.

We were impressed with their kachina dolls that included the work of Cecil Calnimptewa, Jr., Neil David, Sr., Marlin Pinto, Jon Cordero, Wilmer Kaye, Lauren Honyouti, Tim Talawepi, Glenn Fred; sandpainters Eugene "Baatsoslanii" Joe, and the Ben family. Their old pawn and contemporary silver and gold jewelry is created by Navajo, Hopi, Zuni, Santo Domingo, and other pueblo artists. They have pottery by Lucy McKelvey, the Nampeyo family, Sylvia Naha,

Dorothy Torivio, Steve Lucas, Diane Tabo, Gloria Kahe, Thomas Natseway, Karen Forrest Naranjo, the Lewis family, Ray Tafoya, and others.

The Paynes have developed a business around "name" artists. They sell work as an investment but also carry more affordable items as well.

B, Bk, **J**, **K**, P, Pt, R, S, Sp

82. Old Taos

108 Teresina Lane, Taos, NM 87571
505-758-7353
W–Sun 10:00–5:00 (hours vary)
Owner: Steve Eich
◆ C, S, HA (one small step)
  One-half block off the northwest

corner of the plaza is this little treasure chest. It is a tightly packed store where even the ceiling has not escaped serving as a display area. Steve opened in 1988, but the building is obviously one of Taos' older structures. Discover a rustic, hand-carved, tramp art ashtray stand, a large eccentric sculpture, or antique pueblo pottery. Steve has a good eye and a divining rod for finding the obscure but sublime. He can be hard to catch, but it's well worth the effort.

B, Bk, J, M, P, **Antiques**

83. Pueblos and Plains

110 Paseo del Pueblo Norte, Taos, NM 87571
505-758-0211
Daily: 10:00–6:00
Owner: Steven Drayer
◆ M, V, AE, C, S, HA
  Steven Drayer sells only things he is interested in. He sells pottery from every pueblo, particularly Santa Clara and Hopi; Navajo pottery, quality Hopi kachina dolls, new (Taos, Zuni, Hopi, Navajo) and old Indian jewelry, Santo Domingo Pueblo jewelry, Apache and Hopi baskets, and Southwest paintings from the more recognized artists.

B, J, K, P, Pt

84. Blue Rain Gallery

115 McCarthy Plaza, Taos, NM 87571
505-751-0066, 1-800-414-4893

M–Sat: 10:00–6:00
Owners: Leroy and Tammy Garcia,
Director: Gary Luhan

♦ M, V, D, AE, C, S, HA

Blue Rain represents many artists:
Painting by Anderson Kee (Navajo),
Carla Romero (Hispanic), and Pretty
Land Eagle (Taos Pueblo); pottery
by Linda Cain, Autumn Borts, Hisi
Nampeyo, and Dextra Nampeyo; Hopi
kachina dolls by Stetson Honyuptewa;
sculpture by Tim Washburn; jewelry
by Charlie Johns; and others. This
gallery also carries works by non-
Native American artists that represent
Native cultures in their work.
J, K, P, Pt, S

85. Tony Abeyta Gallery
#3 St. Francis Plaza, Rancho de Taos,
NM 87557
505-751-9671
Daily: 10:00-5:00
Owner: Tony Abeyta,
Manager: Leroy Garcia

♦ M, V, AE

This talented artist, known for his
vibrant colors and sensuous textures,
opened the gallery in this picturesque
plaza in 1996. The gallery sells his cal-
ligraphy, monotypes, oil and acrylic
paintings, and mixed media pieces.
By appointment, you may visit his studio. He is also represented by Peggy
Lannings, Sedona; Quintana's, Portland
Oregon, and Four Corners Gallery,
Toronto.

TAOS PUEBLO
GOVERNOR'S OFFICE: P.O. Box
1846, Taos, NM 87571, entrance off
NM 68 on the north side of the town
of Taos
505-758-9593, FAX 505-758-4604
Summer: 8:00-5:30, Winter: 8:30-4:30
hours may vary

♦ ENTRANCE FEE

♦ Permits for photography, video,
sketching, and painting at the gate,
not permitted at ceremonies

♦ Do not climb ladders or trespass in
areas marked off limits

♦ TAOS PUEBLO POWWOW:
second weekend in July.

♦ FEAST DAY: September 30

♦ LANGUAGE: Tiwa

Taos has always been a favorite destination for visitors to the Southwest.
We suggest that you arrive as close to
the 8:00 AM opening time as possible.
In the late morning and early afternoon, the pueblo can lose some of its
magic under the trammel of large
crowds. You might be greeted by a
number of friendly dogs that run and
play in the plaza. Don't be alarmed;
we always found them harmless. If
you arrive early, don't drive in or wander around until you have registered.
The pueblo strictly enforces rules
about visitation. Many families live at

Taos, and it is important to remember
that you are a visitor.

It is easy to understand the fasci-
nation this pueble has held for artists,
wanderers, and romantics. On cool
mornings the smell of burning piñon
and the sight of morning light on the
five-story adobes is enough to steal
your heart. If one image epitomizes
the Southwest, it might be ladders
casting a shadow on the adobe walls
at Taos.

The micaceous pottery from Taos
is well known. The artists here also
create jewelry, flutes, sculptures,
prints, and sewing and leather goods.
The shops are tucked into the adobe
structures in a natural manner that
harmonizes with the overall environ-
ment. One shop on the north side
allows tours of a home. Someone will
certainly be selling bread, still warm
from a horno. Be sure to try it.

The people of Taos Pueblo believe
that their mission is to carry their culture for future generations. They also
believe that they contain the history of
all races. Because of this, they have
made their beautiful pueblo open to
the many visitors that come each day,
and they endure the problems associated with such crowds. Maybe on
your visit you will feel the stirrings of
some ancient ancestral knowledge
deep within yourself.

86. **Morning Talk Indian Shop**

P.O. Box 2328, Taos Pueblo, NM
87571
505-758-1429
Daily: Summer: 9:00–5:00,
Winter: 9:00–4.:30
Owner: Jimmy Morningtalk
♦ M, V, C, S, HA (two small steps
and threshold between rooms)

When we visited, Jimmy Morningtalk was in the middle of an ambitious
expansion which will allow a larger
inventory. He carries Taos-made jewelry and guarantees all the work. The
pottery includes small to ambitious
work from Taos, Santa Clara, and San
Ildefonso, along with blankets and
beaded plains cradleboards.
C, I, **J**, M, P, R, Sp, Cradleboards

87. **Tony Reyna Indian Shops**

P.O. Box 1892, Taos, NM 87571, Taos
Pueblo Road and Taos Pueblo Plaza
Daily 9:00–5:00
505-758-3835
Owner: Tony Reyna
♦ HA (with some difficulty)

Tony Reyna Indian Shops are the
oldest Indian-owned shops in Taos. He
opened in 1950 at the pueblo road location and in 1982 at the pueblo. Besides
some of the finest examples of Margaret
Tafoya pottery, you will find work by
Harrison Begay, Robert Chee, Beatin

Morning Talk Indian Shop, Taos Pueblo.
Hand-tinted photograph

Yazz, J.D. Roybal, Neal David, Sr., Helen Hardin, and Maria Martinez, and books by Howard Rainer. For those with a limited budget, there are John Rainer, Jr., flutes and beautiful Taos micaceous pottery. The pottery by Domenguita Naranjo of San Juan Pueblo is particularly noteworthy. Tony is part of Taos' history. The space inside is small, but full of wonders. The pueblo road location has the greatest treasures. Tony suggests that collectors ask about their areas of interest.
Bk, F, J, **P**, Pt, S, Sv

88. Wahleah's Gift Shop

South side of Taos Pueblo; 3848 Inca St. NE, Albuquerque, NM 87111, 505-294-8056
Daily: Summer: 8:30–5:00,
Winter: 9:00–4:00
Owner: Wahleah
♦ M, V, T, S, HA (first room only and back door to t-shirt room)

Wahleah's is one of the largest shops at Taos Pueblo. Rooms meander through the building like a train. Wahleah's stepfather rebuilt the building with beautiful skylights. It is the work of an artist. Butane lanterns hang from the vigas for the unusual dark day. This was one of the pueblo's first shops. Originally, Wahleah's great-grandmother sold work from her home. Her grandmother Lucinda Bernal and mother Pauline Lujan followed by opening the shop.

Robert Mirabel is a multi-talented Taos artist. His flutes may be seen at the Smithsonian National Museum in Washington D.C., the Albuquerque Museum, and Quast Gallery in Taos.

The dramatic natural light is a memorable feature. Every corner discloses wonders. At times the pottery represents all nineteen pueblos. The storytellers and Hubert Lujan's pottery from Taos Pueblo is a pleasant surprise. Wahleah carries a wide range of inventory from Acoma Christmas ornaments to small alabaster and river rock sculptures by Taos Pueblo artists Ned and Lewis Archuletta. Also from Taos Pueblo are concha belts by Wanda Valdez and drums, bows, and dance staffs by James Concha. The clothing selection is impressive and the t-shirts are of the highest quality.

When we spoke with Wahleah, we admired how articulate, organized, friendly, and elegant she was. This store reflects these qualities. After entering the pueblo, it is the first shop on the right side of the river.
F, I, J, K, **P**, R, S, Sv, **Clothing**

SELECTED TAOS AREA ARTISTS/CRAFTSPEOPLE

Rowena Gibson, P.O. Box 1297, Española, NM 87532—Pottery.

R.C. Gorman, 210 Ledoux St., Taos, NM 87571, 505-758-3250—Navajo paintings and prints.

Robert Mirabal, Yellow Aspen Cloud Productions, P.O. Box 641, Taos, NM 87571, 505-751-1143—Handmade flutes, musical cassettes, author.

Bernice Suazo-Naranjo, P.O. Box 516, Mora, NM 87732—Pottery.

Naveek, P.O. Box 3034, Taos, NM 87571, 505-758-0749—Contemporary jewelry with traditional influence, semi-precious stones, 18k gold, silver, and turquoise.

Sharon "Dry Flower" Reyna, P.O. Box 3031, Taos, NM 87571—Sculpture.

David Gary Suazo, P.O. Box 965, Taos NM 87571—Prints.

Information Resources

♦ ♦ ♦

ARIZONA

Amerind Foundation

P.O. Box 400, Dragoon, AZ 85609,
64 miles east of Tucson on I-10,
Dragoon exit 318, southeast 1 mile,
left 3/4 mile
520-586-3666
Daily 10:00–4:00, M and T, closed in
summer
Admission fee, museum store
Private museum with prehistoric
and historic Indian artifacts, art gallery.

Canyon de Chelly Monument and Museum

P.O. Box 588, Chinle, AZ 86503
520-674-5500
Museum open daily 8:00–5:00,
Canyon Rim Drive always open
Cliff dwellings and museum with
archaeological finds from the Four
Corners area. Paved scenic rim roads
or valley floor with 4WD vehicle,
horseback or on foot with authorized

Navajo guide. The only "no guide"
exception is White House Ruin Trail.

Casa Grande O'odham Tash Indian Festival

P.O. Box 11165, Casa Grande, AZ
85230-1165
520-836-2125, -4723
Tohono O'odham arts and crafts
are sold during the O'odham Tash
Indian Celebration at Casa Grande,
held the second week of February.
Call for information.

Gila River Arts and Crafts Museum

P.O. Box 457, Sacaton, AZ 85247
520-315-3411
Gift shop selling arts and crafts
from over thirty tribes in the
Southwest, California, and Mexico,
including Tohono O'odham and Pima
baskets and Maricopa pottery.

Grand Canyon National Park

Grand Canyon, AZ 86023, South
Rim—South Entrance: 58 miles from
I-40, Williams, AZ, 80 miles from
Flagstaff via Hwy 180; or East
Entrance: Desert View, 30 miles from
Cameron, AZ, US 89. North Rim—
215 driving miles from South Rim
(closed in winter)
520-638-7888
Visitor Center open 8:00–5:00 with
extended summer hours
Entrance fee.

Hatathli Museum and Gallery

Third and fourth floors of Hatathli
Center at Navajo Community
College, Tsaile Campus, 23 miles east
of Canyon de Chelly
520-724-3311, x6653
M–F 8:30–4:30
Donation.

Navajo managed; exhibits about prehistoric and modern Indians, sandpainting collection and multicultural exhibitions. Local Navajo arts and crafts are available for sale.

The Heard Museum of Anthropology and Primitive Art

22 E. Monte Vista Rd.,
Phoenix, AZ 85004
602-252-8840
M–Sat 9:30–5:00, Sun 12:00–5:00,
(Wed 5:00–8:00 free)
Admission fee, museum shop

Exhibitions built around artifacts of the Indians of the Americas. Of Particular interest are the Fred Harvey Fine Art Collection; the Barry Goldwater collection of Hopi kachina dolls; the C.G. Wallace collection of Navajo and Zuni jewelry; twentieth-century prints, paintings, and sculptures; and the Read Mullan collection of textiles.

The Heard Museum has many important events and exhibitions including the Annual Guild Indian Fair and Market (March, call 602-251-0261).

Museum of Northern Arizona

3101 N. Fort Valley Rd.,
Flagstaff, AZ 86001,
Hwy 180 to the Grand Canyon
520-774-5211
Daily 9:00–5:00

The museum has collections in archaeology, ethnology, geology, biology, and fine arts. There are approximately eight changing exhibitions annually, including the Native American Artists Heritage Exhibition during the summer representing Zuni, Hopi, and Navajo artists. Work may be purchased from this show and from the artists directly during the three scheduled courtyard events. Demonstrations of crafts and dances are held throughout the summer.

Navajo National Monument

HC 71, Box 3, Tonalea, AZ 86044, 56 miles northeast of Tuba City on US 160, then 9 miles northwest on AZ 564 at Black Mesa Jct
520-672-2366
Daily 8:00–5:00, closed major holidays
Gift shop

Anasazi cliff dwellings; many trails require park guide and reservations. Five-hour hiking tour leaves 10 AM, tickets at 8:00 AM to first 25 people. One-mile self-guided tour.

Pueblo Grande Museum

4619 E. Washington St., Phoenix, AZ, 6 miles east off US 60-80-89
602-495-0900
M–Sat 9:00–4:45, Sun 1:00–4:45
December Indian Market is noted for kachina dolls.

COLORADO

Anasazi Heritage Center

27501 Hwy 184, Dolores, CO 81323
970-259-2449, 882-4811
Museum and research facility.
Daily 9:00–5:00.

Hovenweep National Monument

McElmo Rt., Cortez, CO 81321
40 miles west of Cortez off Rt. 666
970-749-0510 (8:00–5:00)
970-529-4461—dispatch.

Mesa Verde National Park

P.O. Box 8, Colorado 81330, off US 160 between Cortez and Mancos
Summer 8:00–6:30, remainder of the year 8:00–5:00
303-529-4475
Admission fee, gift shop.

NEW MEXICO

Aztec Ruins National Monument

P.O. Box 640, Aztec, NM 87410, along US 550
505-334-6174
Summer 8:00–6:00, until 5:00 remainder of the year
Admission fee, bookstore

A reconstructed Anasazi village.

Chaco Culture National Historical Park

Star Rt. 4, Box 6500, Bloomfield, NM 87413, 60 miles south of Bloomfield in northwest NM
505-786-7014
Year-round except Christmas, dawn to dusk, visitor center 8:00–5:00, until 6:00 Memorial Day to Labor Day
Admission fee
Major Anasazi site.

ALBUQUERQUE

The Albuquerque Museum of Art, History and Science

2000 Mountain Rd. NW, Albuquerque, NM, near Old Town Plaza
505-242-4600
T–Sun 9:00–5:00.

Maxwell Museum of Anthropology

University of New Mexico
Anthropology building at Redondo Blvd. NE, by Martin Luther King Blvd.
Albuquerque, NM 87131-1201
505-277-4405
T–F 9:00–4:00, Sat 10:00–4:00, Sun noon–4:00, closed Mon and major holidays
Donation, gift shop
Exhibits of archaeology; historic and living anthropology of the Southwest; Permanent and traveling exhibitions.

SANTA FE

Institute of American Indian Arts Museum

108 Cathedral Place, Santa Fe, NM 87501
505-988-6281
M–Sat 10:00–5:00, Sun noon–5:00
Admission fee, gift shop
Houses the national collection of contemporary Indian art.

Museum of Fine Arts

P.O. Box 2087, 107 W. Palace Ave., Santa Fe, NM 87504
505-827-4468, -6463
Daily 10:00–5:00 except major holidays, Fri open until 8:00
Closed Mon (gift shop open)
Admission fee, gift shop.

Museum of Indian Arts and Culture

708 Camino Lejo, Santa Fe, NM
Gift shop: P.O. Box 2065, Santa Fe, NM 87504
505-827-4468, -6463; gift shop 505-982-5057
Daily 10:00–5:00 except major holidays, closed Mon (gift shop open)
Admission fee, gift shop
Prehistoric, historic, and contemporary Indian arts.

Museum of International Folk Art

706 Camino Lejo, Santa Fe, NM
P.O. Box 2087, Santa Fe, NM 87504
505-827-6350, -6463;
gift shop 505-982-5186
Daily 10:00–5:00 except major holidays, closed Mon (gift shop open)
Admission fee, gift shop.

Palace of the Governors

914 Palace Ave., Santa Fe, NM 87501
505-827-6476, -6463
Daily 10:00–5:00 except major holidays, closed Mon (gift shop open)
Admission fee, gift shop
Native American artists sell work under the portal.

School of American Research, Indian Arts and Research Center

P.O. Box 2188, 660 Garcia St., Santa Fe, NM 87504
505-982-3584, -2188
Year-round docent guided tours Fri 2:00
Admission fee
Over 9,000 southwest Indian art objects, reservations required, collection of historic southwestern Indian art.

Wheelwright Museum of the American Indian

P.O. Box 5153, 704 Camino Lejo, Santa Fe, NM 87502
505-982-4636
M–Sat 10:00–5:00, Sun 1:00–5:00
Donation, gift shop.

TAOS

Ernest L. Blumenschein Home
222 Ledoux St., Taos, NM, south of
Taos Plaza
P.O. Drawer CCC, Taos, NM 87571
505-758-0505, -0330
Daily 9:00–5:00, closed major holidays
Admission fee, bookstore.

Fechin Institute
227 Paseo del Pueblo Norte, 2 blocks
north of Taos Plaza on N. Pueblo Rd.
505-758-1710
Memorial Day weekend–Oct 2,
T–Sun 1:00–5:30 and by appt.
Admission fee.

Millicent Rogers Museum
P.O. Box A, Taos, NM 87571, 1/4
mile north of Taos off NM 522. Turn
left on Museum Rd. before blinking
light, follow signs
505-758-2462
Daily 10:00–5:00
Admission fee, gift shop
    Collection of Native American
and Hispanic art.

Van Vechten Lineberry
Taos Art Museum
P.O. Box 1848, 501 N. Pueblo Rd.,
Taos, NM 87571, 1/2 block north of
Kachina Lodge
505-758-2690
T–F 11:00–4:00, Sat & Sun 1:30–4:00,

Closed Mon and Major holidays
Gift shop
    Paintings by all nineteen members
of the Taos Society of Artists.

UTAH

**Edge of the Cedars Museum and
Indian Ruins**
660 W. 400 N., Blanding, UT 84511
801-678-2238
Daily: Summer: 9:00–6:00,
Winter 9:00–5:00
Admission fee.

Monument Valley Navajo Tribal Park
P.O. Box 360289, Monument Valley,
UT 84536, 24 miles north of Kayenta
on US 163, then 3 miles east, follow
signs
810-727-3353
Daily: May–Sept 7:00–8:00,
8:00–5:00 remainder of the year
Admission fee, gift shop
    Dramatic geological formations,
cliff dwellings, petroglyphs; self-
guided and guided tours.

SELECTED OUT-OF-AREA BUSINESSES

ARIZONA

Bahti Indian Arts
4300 N. Campbell
Tucson, AZ 85718
520-577-0290

**Canyon Country Originals
Internet Trading Post**
Tucson, AZ 85750
520-721-8757, FAX 520-733-0411
Web site: http://www.canyonart.com

Gallery 10, Inc.
34505 North Scottsdale Rd., #33
Scottsdale, AZ 85262
602-945-3385

Indian Territory
5639 N. Swan Rd.
Tucson, AZ 85718
520-577-7961

**Jacob Lake Inn Gift Shop
Jacob Lake Inn**
Jacob Lake, AZ 86022,
north rim of the Grand Canyon
520-643-7232
Web site:
http://www.jacoblake.com/index.html

John C. Hill
6962 East 1st. Ave., Ste 104
Scottsdale, AZ 85251
602-946-2910

Leona King Gallery
7171 E. main
Scottsdale, AZ 85251
602-945-1209, 800-227-2589

Medicine Man Gallery
7000 E. Tanque Verde Rd.
Tucson, AZ 85715
520-722-7798, 800-4BAYETA

Morning Star Traders Inc.
2020 E. Speedway
Tucson, AZ 85719
520-881-2112

Sewell's Indian Arts
7087 E. 5th Ave.
Scottsdale, AZ 85251
602-945-0962

COLORADO

The Southwestern Gallery
Woodlawn Plaza
1212 W. Littleton Blvd.
Littleton, CO 80120
303-795-7338

UTAH

Johnston's Primitive Arts
N. Hwy 89, P.O. Box 93
Kanab, UT 84741
801-644-2655

Lema Trading Company
P.O. Box 474, 860 S. Main
Moab, UT 84532
801-259-5942

Southwest Indian Traders
P.O. Box 1494, 550 Main St.
Park City, UT 84060
801-645-9177

SELECTED OUT-OF-AREA ARTISTS/CRAFTS-PEOPLE

Leona F. Antone, HC 03, Box 1037, Ajo, AZ 85321, 520-295-3774—Tohono O'odham miniature horsehair baskets.

Norma Antone, P.O. Box 10105, Casa Grande, AZ 85230—Tohono O'odham miniature horsehair baskets.

Nanaba "Midge" Aragon, 25408 Illinois Ave., Sun Lakes, AZ 85248, 602-895-6672—Traditional and Traditional-inspired weavings.

Mary Duwyenie, 3723 E. Taylor St., Phoenix, AZ 85008-6316—Weaving and pottery.

Alex Maldonado, 5536 E. San Angelo, Guadalupe, AZ 85283, 602-839-3028—Pascua/Yaqui flute maker

Barbara Teller Ornelas, 4802 East Copper, Tucson, AZ 85712, 520-327-3852—Weaving.

Emerson H. Quannie, P.O. Box 882, Mesa, AZ 85211—Hopi overlay and contemporary gold and silver, semi and precious stones.

Kevin Quannie, 1431 E. Ardmore, Phoenix, AZ 85040, 602-268-5402—Kachina dolls, contemporary and bronze sculpture, oil painting, pastels, contemporary gold and silver jewelry.

Marilou Schultz, 844 E. 8th Place, Mesa, AZ 85203, 602-834-3791—Weavings, specializes in Burntwater and Moki rugs, takes special requests.

Manfred Susunkewa, 6914 W. McKinley St., Phoenix, AZ 85043, 602-936-5244—Traditional-style kachina dolls.

Urshel Taylor, 2901 W. Sahuaro Divide, Tucson, AZ 85742, 602-297-4456, 800-487-0180—Ute/Pima painter/sculptor.

Glossary

◆ ◆ ◆

BASKETS

Coiled Basket: One of the most difficult to make, coiled baskets have bundles of fibers as a foundation, wrapped with another material, bent into a spiral and stitched. They can be found in many colors. Hopis use a galleta grass foundation and a yucca leaf wrapping. Most Navajo, Jicarilla Apache, and Paiute basketmakers use a rod foundation of slender sticks such as willow or sumac, wrapping the coils with flexible sumac splints.

Havasupai Basket: Coiled baskets made by the Havasupai people of the Grand Canyon region.

Jicarilla Apache Basket: Traditional coiled basket of sumac and willow, decorated with bold geometric abstractions, made by the Jicarilla Apache of New Mexico. They also make jar-shaped baskets that are pitch lined to hold water.

Navajo Wedding Basket: Used in Navajo ceremonies and traditionally made by Southern Paiutes and Utes, the Navajo wedding basket is a coiled basket of sumac and willow, with a broken dark red band surrounded by broken bands of black triangular shapes. Innovative forms of these baskets are now being made by Navajos of the northwestern Navajo Nation and the Southern San Juan Paiutes. These baskets are also called ceremonial baskets.

San Juan Paiute Basket: The San Juan Paiutes are located in an area between Tuba City and Page, Arizona, and Navajo Mountain, Utah. They make finely coiled baskets of sumac and willow and are known for variations on the wedding basket, and their own innovative designs which use a diversity of motifs including butterflies, bees, other animals, and abstractions.

Tohono O'odham Basket: The Tohono O'odham people are located south of Casa Grande, Arizona, and were previously known as Papago. They create coiled baskets with willow and devil's claw and miniature horse hair baskets. They also create split stitch baskets with white yucca stitches and green beargrass coils.

Western Apache Basket: Conical-shaped burden baskets with fringe and bands of buckskin made by the

Western Apache. Also available are water jar–shaped coiled baskets with and without a pitch coating.

Yucca Basket: Yucca baskets, used as sifters or trays, are found plain or twill-plaited. Warp and weft are woven under and over in even geometric, checkerboard, or twill patterns.

TEXTILES

Aniline Dyes: Commercial synthetic dyes that can achieve brilliant colors.

Chimayo Rug: A Hispanic weaving style begun by Gabriel Ortega in the eighteenth century in Chimayo, New Mexico. Today Chimayo weavings are made into a variety of products such as rugs and jackets.

Handspun Wool: Used by Navajo rug weavers, spun with a drop spindle from raw wool, thus making an uneven strand.

Manta: A cloth woven by Navajo and Pueblo Indians as a blanket and often worn around the shoulders or as a dress.

Pendleton: A company in Oregon that makes brightly colored, soft, woolen blankets and wool products.

Tapestry: The finest woven rug containing ninety or more threads per inch. It is the most time consuming of weavings and the most expensive.

Vegetal Dyes: Dyes made from plants and used in rugs or baskets. Using vegetal dyes takes more time because the materials such as bark and roots must be collected.

Zapotec Rugs: Rugs imported from Oaxaca, Mexico, and made by the Zapotec Indians, usually cruder in technique and inexpensive.

JEWELRY

Appliqué: Decoration created by applying metal to the exterior of a metal form. This can vary from simple forms to detailed figures.

Beadwork: Glass beads, available in different sizes, are sewn onto a base, usually of leather. Forms may be realistic often using modeling with light and dark tones, or they may be abstract. Beadwork is the recognized decorative work of the Utes and Western, Mescalero, and Jicarilla Apaches.

Bola: A string tie worn around the neck created from a single concha or jewelry element backed with a slide

combined with a length of braided leather or other material with metal tips.

Cluster, Needlepoint, Petit point: Jewelry using an assemblage of stone such as turquoise, coral, or other material. Cluster uses the largest stones; needlepoint uses stones shaped like rice grains; petit point, the smallest, may use rounded stones. Look for symmetry and uniform stones.

Concha: Silver plaques that may be flat, domed, or stamped and worn on a belt. This form of personal adornment was influenced by Spanish Colonial ironwork and Plains Indian silver belts.

Dead Pawn: Jewelry that was pawned and not redeemed. Some unscrupulous dealers put fake pawn tickets on items. Dead pawn is not necessarily old.

Depression Jewelry: During the Depression, Santo Domingo Pueblo made necklaces out of black plastic batteries, combs, or other plastic material as a substitute for heishe. Made often with a thunderbird motif, these are very collectible items.

Fabrication: Describes the building of a piece of jewelry, using solder with other techniques to join pieces of metal together.

Fetish: Originally fetishes were found stones that resembled animals and were considered to contain the embodiment of the animal's spirit. Today fetishes are commercially carved from a variety of stone and other materials and usually represent animals.

Hallmark: The signature of an artist stamped on the back of a piece of jewelry. This may be initials or the artist's logo. Some weavers hallmark their rugs.

Heishe: Santo Domingo word for "shells" usually drilled and made into beads and strung as necklaces.

Imitation Turquoise: Reconstituted from dust, plastic, and dyes, most often found in machine-made jewelry.

Inlay Channel: Channels of metal are used to hold stones in place in a pattern. Stones are bonded into the channels. The metal and stone are polished simultaneously to create a smooth surface. Look for even grinding with no stray marks.

Jacla: Navajo "earstrings," long earrings often hung at the bottom of a necklace by traditional Navajo.

Ketoh: A leather strap decorated with silver and worn at the wrist as a bow guard, preventing injury from the snap of a bowstring. Today worn by Navajo and Pueblo men as personal adornment.

Knifewing: A Zuni deity with out-stretched arms, a common jewelry motif in the thirties.

Liquid Silver: Handmade tubes made from sheet silver and cut into small segments. These silver tubes are strung together to form moving rivers of silver.

Lost Wax Casting: A design made in wax and cast in metal. A poorly cast piece has bubbles in small detailed areas. A less time-intensive jewelry process than fabrication.

Mosaic: Similar to channel inlay without the use of metal channels to hold the stones. Edges of stones or pieces of shell seem to touch one another, with a clear or colored epoxy base gluing them down to a metal or shell base.

Naja: This shape is now often found as the centerpiece of squash-blossom necklaces. Originally a crescent shape of ancient Roman design, this is an Old World amulet design used on horse bridles to ward off the evil eye. The Navajos had contact with and were influenced by the jewelry of various Plains Indians such as the Comanches who used this design around 1830–50.

Overlay: Jewelry created by sawing a design from one sheet of metal and soldering it to another. Low areas are oxidized and sometimes textured. Originally Hopi, overlay resulted from a project initiated by the Museum of Northern Arizona in Flagstaff in 1938. The project promoted a search for a Hopi style of silverwork different from other Indian groups.

Persian Turquoise: A turquoise not native to the Southwest. It was introduced by Lorenzo Hubbell in 1890s.

Pueblo Crosses: Double crosses that resemble dragonflies in Native American cultures, with Spanish and Mexican origins.

Reconstituted Turquoise: Created by using turquoise in a granulated, dust, or small chip form in an acrylic or resin base.

Sandcast: Jewelry made from a mold carved from a heat resistant material such as stone, and cast in metal. Navajo design tends to be abstract and curvilinear. There are examples of tufa (volcanic rock) cast work, which maintains more of the porous surface quality of volcanic rock. Quality work has no file marks, deep cracks, bubbles, or evident silver solder.

Silver Beads: Formed from soldering two hollow domed discs together. Plain or decorated.

Squash blossom: This Spanish decorative motif is centuries old. A squash-blossom necklace has silver pomegranate-shaped beads, influenced by Spanish/Mexican trouser and jacket ornaments.

Stabilized Turquoise Turquoise hardened with a liquid resin or plastic, but its color has not been altered.

Stampwork: Repeated marks or patterns struck with hammer and dies to create designs on the surface of the metal. Jewelry created with stampwork tools was influenced by Mexican leather working. Quality stampwork is even and has a clear mark.

Treated Turquoise: Turquoise that has been treated with resins or a foreign substance to enhance the color or hardness of the stone or to darken the matrix. Treatment with resin allows softer grades and more of the stone to be used. Turquoise that is treated is usually less expensive than untreated.

Turquoise: A stone that varies in color from pale green to deep blue. The first setting of turquoise used by the Navajos is said to be about 1880, with general use of turquoise after 1900.

POTTERY

Appliqué: Decoration created by applying clay to the exterior of a form. This can vary from simple forms to detailed figures.

Beeweed: A wild plant whose juices are used by Pueblo potters to create rich dark blacks.

Casas Grandes Pottery: A style of pottery named for the region of Mexico where it is produced.

Firecloud: Dark discolorations on pottery caused by fuel resting on the clay during traditional firing. Some potters welcome these into the pot's overall design.

Melon Bowls: Ribbed pottery done by Pueblo artists, in the shape of melons, often with ribbed ridges.

Micaceous Pottery: Traditionally done by the pueblos of Taos, Nambe, Picuris, and San Juan. Micaceous clay contain flecks of mica that reflect light, making a pot appear silvery or golden.

Mud Toys: Unfired clay folk art toys made in the shape of people and animals that are brightly painted. Very fragile. Traditionally created for Navajo children.

Pitch Pots: In traditional Navajo pottery, a final coating of amber-colored piñon pine pitch seals and waterproofs the surface. Pitch is also sometimes used to seal and waterproof baskets.

Polychrome: Use of three or more colors.

Scraffito: A technique of scratching a design into the surface of a clay form.

Sherds: Broken clay pottery pieces often ground up to strengthen clay.

Slipcast: Pottery produced by pouring liquid clay into molds, sometimes called greenware.

Storyteller: A figurative form of pottery begun at Cochiti Pueblo in the late fifties depicting an adult covered with a swarm of children to which she tells a story. Today, this form and variations are popular across the Southwest.

Temper: Ground pot sherds, sand, or volcanic rock mixed with clay to strengthen it and make it workable.

Wedding Vase: A two-spouted pot form.

GENERAL

Anasazi: A Navajo word for "the Old Ones." Anasazi refers to a pueblo-building culture of the Four Corners area, whose cities were abandoned in the thirteenth century. Chaco Canyon, Hovenweep, Mesa Verde, and Canyon de Chelly are among the best-known sites.

Brush Arbor: An open structure created in the summer to provide shade and allow breezes to pass. Common in the rural Navajo Nation and created from branches, wooden poles, and other simple materials.

Bullpen: The original floor plan of most trading posts using high counters to form a U shape. The trader's goods were on shelves behind the counters allowing the customer to see the inventory but preventing self-service.

Checkerboard Region: Located outside the Navajo Nation, alternating tracts of land owned by the Navajo Nation, private interests, railroad, and the federal government.

Cradleboards: Occasionally used by Native Americans to carry infants. As an art form these may be covered with leather, bead, or quill work.

Diné: Navajo word which translates as "the People." The Navajo refer to themselves as such.

Dinétah: The Navajo homelands.

Dleesh: White clay used to paint the body for ceremonies.

Dye Chart: Displays the colors, plants, plants that made them, and dyed wool. Often accompanied by a small incomplete weaving.

Ex-voto: A religious folk art painting used as a request for divine intervention or created to acknowledge a miracle.

Folk Art: Originally referring to work from strong ethnic and community origins. In recent years, the work of self-taught artists creating idiosyncratic and personal images, or variations of traditional forms.

Hogan: A traditional six- or eight-sided Navajo dwelling made of logs, stone, or other material and covered with mud. Doors usually face east and a chimney is in the center of the roof.

Horno: A beehive-shaped oven used for baking bread.

Kachina: Supernatural being of the Hopi and Zuni.

Kachina Dolls: Representations of the physical form of Hopi kachinas, made from cottonwood roots, carved and painted. Traditionally they were given to children to teach them about the pantheon of Hopi kachinas.

Kiva: A chamber used by the Pueblo peoples for ceremonial gatherings.

Koshare: A Pueblo clown figure that provides moral and ethical instruction and helps facilitate dances. Usually seen in white and black paint, dark eyes, loin cloth, and simple head gear.

Navajo Dolls: Stylized human figures, representing Navajo ceremonial super-natural figures such as *Yei'ii* and *Yei'ii bichai*. Today associated primarily with the tourist trade, these dolls can depict figures that are composite or unique to the artist's imagination (sometimes imitative, but not to be confused with kachina dolls made by the Hopis). Navajo dolls also exist as historical artifacts and for ceremonial use.

Penitente: A religious group of the mountains of northern New Mexico that once practiced self-flagellation as part of Holy Week celebration.

Petroglyph: A prehistoric carving or drawing on a rock surface.

Pictograph: A prehistoric painting on rock.

Powwow: A gathering of Native Americans, sometimes for dances or socializing.

Retablo: Most commonly refers to a holy image on a painted panel, usually of wood.

Ristra: Chiles strung together and hung.

Sandpainting: Paintings created with colored sand used in Navajo ceremonies. Commercial sandpaintings are glued to a board to become permanent.

Santero: Maker of religious objects.

Santo: Spanish term for saint.

Scratchboard: A drawing technique in which special paper is coated with india ink, and white lines are scratched into the coating.

Skinwalker: Usually a taboo subject for artwork or discussion, this menacing Navajo witch is said to be able to transform itself from human to animal.

Tablita: A flat, wooden, decorated headdress worn by Pueblo women in various dances.

Viga: Exposed wooden beams found in many pueblo-style adobe homes that create the structure for the ceiling.

Yei'ii: Supernatural beings, the Holy People of the Navajo.

Yei'ii bichai: The human personifications of the Navajo Holy People. *Yei'ii bichai* dancers participate in a nine-day healing ceremony.

Yucca: A spike-leafed southwestern plant used in basketry and as paint brushes by Pueblo potters.

Further Readings and References

◆   ◆   ◆

Most of the information obtained in this book comes from personal interviews and on-site information gathered between 1992 and 1995.

The following texts were used in preparation of this book. Also included are books suggested by those we interviewed.

GENERAL

Bahti, Mark. *A Consumer's Guide to Southwestern Indian Arts & Crafts.* Tucson: Bahti Indian Arts, 1975.

Bulow, Ernie. *Navajo Taboos.* Gallup: Buffalo Medicine Books, 1991.

Eaton, Linda B, *Native American Art of the Southwest.* Lincolnwood, Illinois: Publications International, 1993.

Faunce, Hilda. *Desert Wife.* Lincoln: University of Nebraska Press, 1981.

Gillmor, Frances, and Louisa Wade Wetherill. *Traders to the Navajos.* Albuquerque: University of New Mexico Press, 1953.

Harjo, Joy, and Steven Strom. *Secrets from the Center of the World.* Tucson: University of Arizona Press, 1989.

Hillerman, Tony. *The Joe Leaphorn Mysteries.* New York: Random House, 1989.

Hillerman, Tony, ed. *The Spell of New Mexico.* Albuquerque: University of New Mexico Press, 1976.

Jacka, Jerry, and Lois Essary Jacka. *Beyond Tradition: Contemporary Indian Art and Its Evolution.* Flagstaff: Northland Publishing, 1988.

———. *Enduring Traditions: Art of the Navajo.* Flagstaff: Northland Publishing, 1994.

Kluckhohn, Clyde, W. W. Hill, and Lucy Wales Kluckhohn. *Navajo Material Culture.* Cambridge, Massachusetts: Belknap Press, 1971.

Lindig, Wolfgang, and Helga Teiwes. *Navajo: Tradition and Change in the Southwest.* New York: Facts on File, 1991.

Lummis, Charles F. *Mesa, Cañon, and Pueblo.* New York: The Century Company, 1925.

Manley, Ray. *Ray Manley's Collecting Southwestern Indian Arts and Crafts.* Tucson: Ray Manley Publishing, 1979.

Mays, Buddy. *Indian Villages of the Southwest.* San Francisco: Chronicle Books, 1985.

Newcomb, Franc Johnson. *Navajo Neighbors.* Norman: University of Oklahoma Press, 1966.

Page, Susanne, and Jake Page. *Hopi.* New York: Harry N. Abrams, 1986.

Trimble, Stephen. *The People: Indians of the American Southwest.* Santa Fe: School of American Research Press, 1993.

Waters, Frank. *Masked Gods.* Athens: Swallow Press/Ohio University Press, 1984.

Williams, Terry Tempest. *Coyote's Canyon.* Salt Lake City: Peregrine Smith, 1989.

———. *Pieces of White Shell: A Journey to Navajoland.* New York: Charles Scribner's Sons, 1983, 1984.

BASKETS

Mauldin, Barbara. *Traditions In Transition: Contemporary Basket Weaving of the Southwestern Indians.* Santa Fe: Museum of New Mexico Press, 1987.

Tanner, Clara Lee. *Indian Baskets of the Southwest.* Tucson: University of Arizona Press, 1983.

Whiteford, Andrew Hunter. *Southwestern Indian Baskets: Their History and Their Makers.* Santa Fe: School of American Research Press, 1988.

FETISHES

Branson, Oscar T. *Fetishes and Carvings of the Southwest.* Tucson: Treasure Chest, 1976.

Cushing, Frank Hamilton. *Zuni Fetishes.* Las Vegas: KC Publications, 1988.

Finkelstein, Harold. *Zuñi Fetish Carvings.* Decatur, Georgia: South West Connection, 1994.

FOLK ART

Rosenak, Chuck, and Jan Rosenak. *The Museum of American Folk Art Encyclopedia of Twentieth Century Folk Art and Artists.* New York: Abbeville Press, 1991.
————. *The People Speak: Navajo Folk Art.* Flagstaff: Northland Publishing, 1994.

WEAVING AND TEXTILES

Berlant, Anthony, and Mary Hunt Kahlenberg. *Walk In Beauty: The Navajo and Their Blankets.* Salt Lake City: Peregrine Smith Books, 1991.
Dedera, Don. *Navajo Rugs: How to Find, Evaluate, Buy and Care for Them.* Flagstaff: Northland Press, 1975.
Harmsen, Bill. *Patterns and Sources of Navajo Weavings.* Denver: Harmsen Publishing Company, 1990.
Hedlund, Ann Lane. *Reflections of the Weaver's World.* Denver: Denver Art Museum, 1992.
James, H.L. *Rugs and Posts.* West Chester, Pennsylvania: Schiffer Publishing, 1988.
Kent, Kate Peck. *Navajo Weaving: Three Centuries of Change.* Santa Fe: School of American Research Press, 1985.

JEWELRY

Adair, John. *The Navajo and Pueblo Silversmiths.* Norman: University of Oklahoma Press, 1944, 1989.
Bird, Allison. *Heart of the Dragonfly.* Albuquerque: Avanyu Publishing, 1992.
Branson, Oscar T. *Turquoise: The Gem of the Centuries.* Tucson: Treasure Chest Publications, 1976.
Cirillo, Dexter. *Southwestern Indian Jewelry.* New York: Abbeville Press, 1992.
Jernigan, E.W. *White Metal Universe: Navajo Silver from the Fred Harvey Collection.* Phoenix: The Heard Museum, 1981.
Woodward, Arthur. *Navajo Silver: A Brief History of Navajo Silversmithing.* Flagstaff: Northland Press, 1971.
Wright, Barton. *Hallmarks of the Southwest.* West Chester, Pennsylvania: Schiffer Publishing, 1989.
Wright, Margaret Nickelson. *Hopi Silver: The History and Hallmarks of Hopi Silversmithing.* 4th ed. Flagstaff: Northland Publishing, 1992.

KACHINAS

Hopi Kachina Dolls. Flagstaff: Museum of Northern Arizona (Volume 63, Number 4), 1992.

Wright, Barton. *Clowns of the Hopi.* Flagstaff: Northland Publishing, 1994.

————. *Hopi Kachinas, The Complete Guide to Collecting Kachina Dolls.* Flagstaff: Northland Press, 1977.

————. *Kachinas: a Hopi artist's documentary.* Flagstaff: Northland Press and The Heard Museum, Phoenix, 1973.

————. *Kachinas of the Zuni.* Flagstaff: Northland Press, 1985.

SANDPAINTING

Joe, Eugene Baatsoslanii, and Mark Bahti. *Navajo Sandpainting Art.* Tucson: Treasure Chest Publications, 1978.

McCoy, Ronald. *Summoning the Gods: Sandpainting in the Native American Southwest.* Flagstaff: Museum of Northern Arizona, 1992.

Parezo, Nancy J. *Navajo Sandpainting: From Religious Act to Commercial Art.* Albuquerque: University of New Mexico Press, 1983.

Reichard, Gladys A. *Navajo Medicine Man Sandpaintings.* New York: Dover Publications, 1977

TRADING POSTS

Clark, Jackson H. *The Owl in Monument Canyon.* Salt Lake City: University of Utah Press, 1993.

Hegemann, Elizabeth Compton. *Navajo Trading Days.* Albuquerque: University of New Mexico Press, 1963.

Historic Trading Posts. Flagstaff: Museum of Northern Arizona (Volume 57, Number 3), 1986.

James, H.L. *Rugs and Posts.* West Chester, Pennsylvania: Schiffer Publishing, 1988.

McNitt, Frank. *The Indian Traders.* Norman: University of Oklahoma Press, 1962.

Moon, Samuel. *Tall Sheep: Harry Goulding: Monument Valley Trader.* Norman: University of Oklahoma Press, 1992.

Poling-Kempes, Lesley. *The Harvey Girls.* New York: Paragon House, 1991.

Richardson, Gladwell. *Navajo Trader.* Tucson: University of Arizona Press, 1991.

Roberts, Willow. *Stokes Carson: Twentieth-Century Trading on the Navajo Reservation.* Albuquerque: University of New Mexico Press, 1987.

Schmedding, Joseph. *Cowboy and Indian Trader.* Caldwell, Idaho: The Caxton Printers, Ltd., 1951.

Underhill, Ruth M. *The Navajos.* Norman: University of Oklahoma Press, 1956.

POTTERY

Blair, Lawrence. *Margaret Tafoya.* West Chester, Pennsylvania: Schiffer Publishing, 1986.

Cohen, Lee. *Art of Clay: Timeless Pottery of the Southwest.* Santa Fe: Clearlight, 1993.

Dillingham, Rick. *Acoma and Laguna Pottery.* Santa Fe: School of American Research Press, 1992.

———. *Fourteen Families in Pueblo Pottery.* Albuquerque: University of New Mexico Press, 1994.

Dittert, Alfred E., Jr., and Fred Plog. *Generations in Clay.* Flagstaff: Northland Publishing, 1980.

Gault, Ramona. *Artistry In Clay: A Buyer's Guide to Southwestern Indian Pottery.* Santa Fe: Southwestern Association on Indian Affairs, Inc., 1991.

Hartman, Russell P., and Jan Musial. *Navajo Pottery, Traditions and Innovations.* Flagstaff: Northland Publishing, 1989.

Navajo Pottery. Flagstaff: Museum of Northern Arizona (Volume 58, Number 2), 1987.

Toulouse, Betty. *Pueblo Pottery of the New Mexico Indians.* Santa Fe: Museum of New Mexico Press, 1987.

Trimble, Stephen. *Talking with the Clay.* Santa Fe: School of American Research Press, 1987.

Index

◆ ◆ ◆

Page numbers in *italics* refer to photographs.

List of Trading Posts, Galleries, etc., by State

Arizona

About the Authors

◆　◆　◆

BORN IN PENNSYLVANIA, Patrick Eddington spent Saturday afternoons as a child watching John Wayne, Roy Rogers, and other Western film stars. As he looked at the plateaus and redrock backdrops in those films, he found it hard to believe such a place really existed. A few years later his family moved to Utah, and he found himself standing in the matinee landscapes of Monument Valley and wanting to learn all he could about these Western lands. Soon he was drawn not just to the landscapes, but to the people who live here. He completed a B.F.A. and an M.Ed. at the University of Utah, finding that his respect for Native American creations grew as he studied art and graphic design. He is now a recognized collector of folk art.

Susan Makov was born on Long Island, New York, the daughter of two artists. She was educated at Syracuse University, State University of New York at Buffalo, and Brighton Polytechnic, England, but she found her most intense interests when she moved to Ogden, Utah, in 1977 to join the faculty at Weber State University. She embraced many aspects of living in the West, including shooting black powder muskets, going horseback riding, participating in Mountain Man Rendezvous, and studying Native American arts and crafts. Susan is a full professor of art, teaching photography, printmaking, and drawing, and she has over fifty exhibitions on her résumé.

Patrick and Susan now reside in Salt Lake City, Utah. Each has collaborated on limited edition broadsides with various authors, and they both write, teach, create art, and are continually preoccupied with photographing the Southwest. They created the *Trading Post Guidebook* in hopes of providing a resource they have often wished they had as they discovered the back roads and back rooms of the Southwest together.